W9-AVI-335

★ THE WEST POINT ATLAS OF WAR ★

THE CIVIL WAR

Compiled by The Department of Military Art and Engineering
The United States Military Academy

Chief Editor
Brigadier General Vincent J. Esposito, USA

Tess
Press

Copyright © 1995 Professor and Head, Department of History, United States Military Academy,
as Trustee for the (Vincent J. Esposito) Military Art Award Fund.

Published by Tess Press, an imprint of
Black Dog & Leventhal Publishers, Inc.
151 West 19th Street
New York, NY 10011

All rights reserved. No part of this book, either text or illustration, may be used
or reproduced in any form without the prior written permission from the publisher.

Cover and interior design: Lindsay Wolff

The content of this book was originally published in 1959 under the title *The West Point Atlas of American Wars,
Volume I (1689-1900)* and *Volume II (1900-1953)*. Since then, generations of West Point cadets have used the
atlases as an important part of their study of military history in preparation for their service as officers in
the United States Army. While the maps and corresponding text represented the finest military scholarship
available at that time, subsequent scholarship has in some cases altered historical interpretations. Readers of
this book—like West Point cadets—therefore should complement their study with more current works to
develop a complete picture of the history presented.

ISBN-10: 1-60376-020-2
ISBN-13: 978-1-60376-020-1

h g f e d c b a

Printed in China

CONTENTS

★

OVERVIEW

On 12 April 1861, Fort Sumter was fired upon, initiating the bloody conflict between the states that would last four years. The major civil war campaigns, except those of Banks and Farragut, are shown on the map and will be covered in detail in the maps that follow.

With the advent of war both sides hastily began preparations, although neither fully appreciated the tremendous problems involved. Some Confederates believed one sizable victory would be enough to deter the North, while many Northerners fully expected the 75,000 militia (initially called up to serve for three months) would be an ample number to deliver a knockout victory. Neither side was ready for war. The Union at least might have expected to be prepared, but instead it had only a small regular army of about 16,000, scattered mostly in small units through the western frontier.

There were two major theaters of war: Virginia and the Mississippi-Tennessee River area. In 1861, neither side had an overall strategy. Jefferson Davis, the Confederate president, never developed one, between being forced on the defensive early in the war and not fully understanding the significance of the western theater. In contrast, Abraham Lincoln quickly apprehended the North's advantage in manpower, resources, and naval strength. He also saw the importance of a naval blockade and of taking the offensive. Later, he appreciated the importance of the Mississippi Valley. But it was not until the emergence of Grant as commander in chief that a fully coordinated strategy was put into effect.

Both sides, particularly the Union, overrated the importance of the two capitals; hence the bloody campaigns in Virginia, which by themselves could not be decisive. Meanwhile, in the west, the foundation for Union victory was slowly being built by the battles along the great waterways. The campaign arrows trace the evolution of the Union strategy: first, a naval blockade of the Confederacy; second, the east–west cleavage of the Confederacy by subjugating the Mississippi River area; third, the drive across Georgia to split the previously severed eastern portion; and lastly, the closing of the pincers on Lee and Johnston by Grant and Sherman.

An understanding of the geography of the area and of the railroad systems helps explain the successes and failures during the war. Possessing naval superiority, the Union found it desirable to use the Ohio, Cumberland, Tennessee, Mississippi, and Potomac Rivers as axes of advance as well as supply routes. The many streams in Virginia were of great defensive value to Robert E. Lee. The great Appalachian chain of mountains restricted the Union approach to the Confederate heartland around Atlanta that, when it was taken in 1863, became the gateway to the South. The Shenandoah Valley, hemmed in by mountains, was the scene of Thomas J. "Stonewall" Jackson's brilliant exploits as well as a centerpiece of Lee's strategy. The railroads, though still in their infancy, made it possible for the armies to attain strategic mobility and to accomplish logistical feats hitherto unknown in military history.

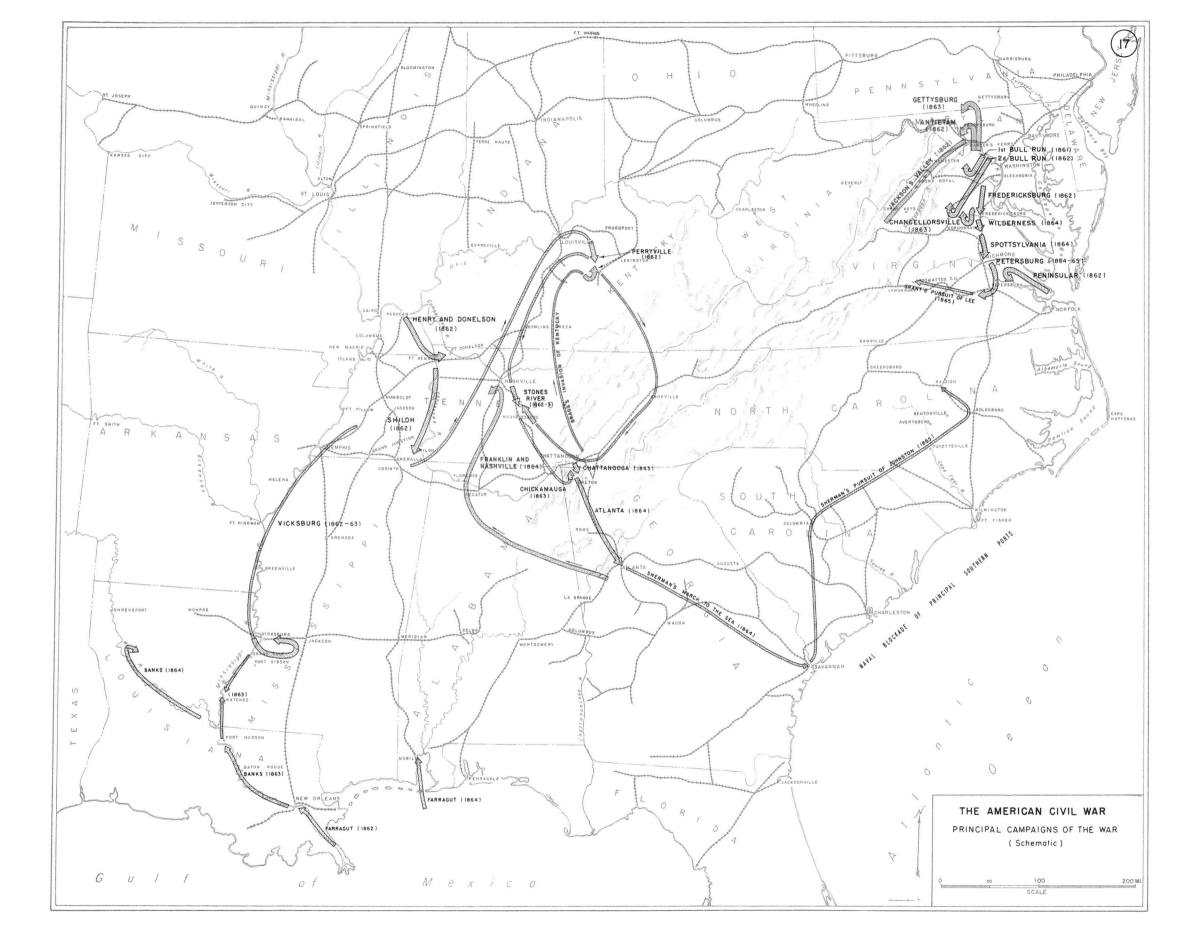

THE AMERICAN CIVIL WAR

PRINCIPAL CAMPAIGNS OF THE WAR

(Schematic)

FIRST BULL RUN CAMPAIGN: 1

Bull Run was the first major campaign of the war, and following a minor success in western Virginia on 11–12 July 1861, the Union commander, Maj. Gen. George B. McClellan, was riding high. The locations of the capitals made it certain that the first campaign would be in Maryland or Virginia. Pressured by public opinion in the North, Brig. Gen. McDowell, the Union commander of the northeastern division of Virginia, began his advance on Centreville to do battle with his counterpart, Brig. Gen. Pierre G. T. Beauregard. Both were considered in the first rank. Beauregard had Brig. Gen. Joseph E. Johnston, one of the prewar army's outstanding officers, Brig. Gen. Benjamin Huger and Brig. Gen. Theophilus H. Holmes, who, along with Col. John B. Magruder, were "old army." McDowell's second in command was Gen. Robert Patterson, a veteran of the War of 1812 and the Mexican War, and Maj. Gen. Benjamin F. Butler, a political appointee.

Beauregard's force was located at Manassas, an ideal position from which to guard against the expected southward advance of McDowell via either Fredericksburg or Culpeper. On 2 July, Patterson crossed the Potomac at Williamsport, and by the 15th, he was in the vicinity of Charlestown. On the eve of the first major confrontation, each side eyed the other in the Valley.

Just prior to his departure from Washington, McDowell organized his army into five divisions, which reduced the burden of control, compared with Beauregard, who was attempting to command seven brigades. His army left Alexandria on 17 July and arrived two and a half days later, tired and hungry after a march of 20 miles or so. (Only a month earlier, a small Union force had marched 46 miles over mountain roads and inflicted defeat on the Confederates at Romney in West Virginia, all in slightly less than 24 hours. In a few more months hardened soldiers of both sides would consider it normal to march 15 miles a day.)

An efficient intelligence system had forewarned Beauregard of McDowell's departure (throughout the war, security in Washington would be porous). On 18 July, Johnston received orders from President Davis to join Beauregard at Manassas. (This would be the first of several throughout the war in which the discretionary phrase "if practicable" was used: a classic escape hole for those issuing the orders.) Using then Col. J. E. B. Stuart's cavalry as a screen, he moved by foot to Piedmont and then by train to Manassas. His leading brigade, commanded by Thomas J. Jackson, was headed for combat and immortality.

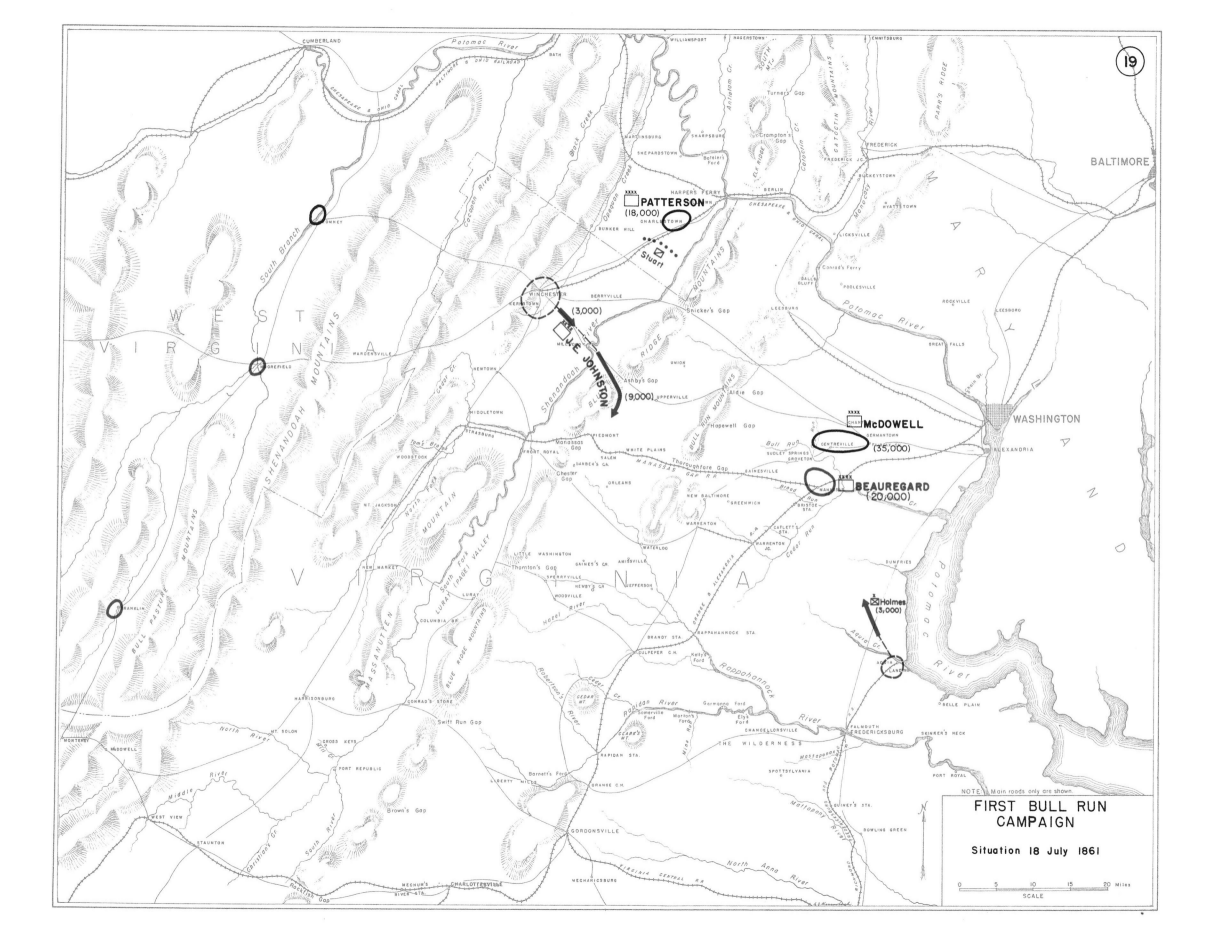

FIRST BULL RUN
CAMPAIGN

Situation 18 July 1861

FIRST BULL RUN CAMPAIGN: 2

Aglance at Beauregard's dispositions along Bull Run shows his troops spread over a distance of ten miles in a cordon defense. He had no centrally located reserve until Johnston's troops arrived. An abortive attack by Brig. Gen. Daniel Tyler lowered Union morale, particularly in Maj. Gen. Israel B. Richardson's brigade, and served to encourage the Confederate troops on the eve of their first major engagement.

Bull Run could be forded at several points but, because of its steep banks and the heavily wooded approaches, cut up by many small tributaries, it was a formidable obstacle, particularly to the east of Stony Bridge. The dominant heights were the Centreville ridge, Henry House Hill, Bald Hill, and the hill to the southeast of Manassas Junction.

Three days passed, during which time approximately 12,000 reinforcements had reached Beauregard, while McDowell failed to make use of his numerical advantage. He was a green commander in charge of green troops and, as so often happens in these circumstances, the commander devised an overcomplicated plan, primarily dependent on Patterson's preventing Johnston from reinforcing Beauregard.

It was in the execution that McDowell's plan went awry. As the Union army moved out early on 21 July 1861, fumbling and bumbling delayed the attack. Tyler's assault at Stone Bridge jumped off at daybreak, but with so little energy that Confederate Col. Nathan G. Evans soon spotted it for what it was—a feint.

Meanwhile, Beauregard had been joined by Johnston and was planning his own offensive toward Centreville by way of Blackburn and McLean's fords and, at 5:30 A.M., gave the orders for his right-flank brigades to move in that direction, although his frequent changes of order created confusion. While he was still attempting to get his attack underway, he became aware of the violent fighting that had broken out on his extreme left where Col. David Hunter's division had had crossed Bull Run at Sudley Springs at about 9:30 A.M. and run into Evans's blocking force. Evans valiantly contested the Union advance but eventually the Union commanders displayed some knowledge of tactics and began to outflank the Confederate line. Now manned by Capt. Hiram E. Bartow and Gen. Barnard Bee, the remnants of Evans's unit began to withdraw (at first orderly but then precipitously) back to Henry Hill House. McDowell now ordered Tyler's division to cross Bull Run in an assault on the Confederate left. Col. William T. Sherman led Tyler's attack. It was now about 11:30 A.M. Beauregard, hearing the pounding off to his left, therefore canceled the attack on Centreville and moved some of those units over toward Henry Hill House. During this chaotic period, Brig. Gen. Kirby Smith, one of Johnston's units from the Shenandoah Valley, arrived at Manassas Junction. Jackson was also approaching Henry Hill House.

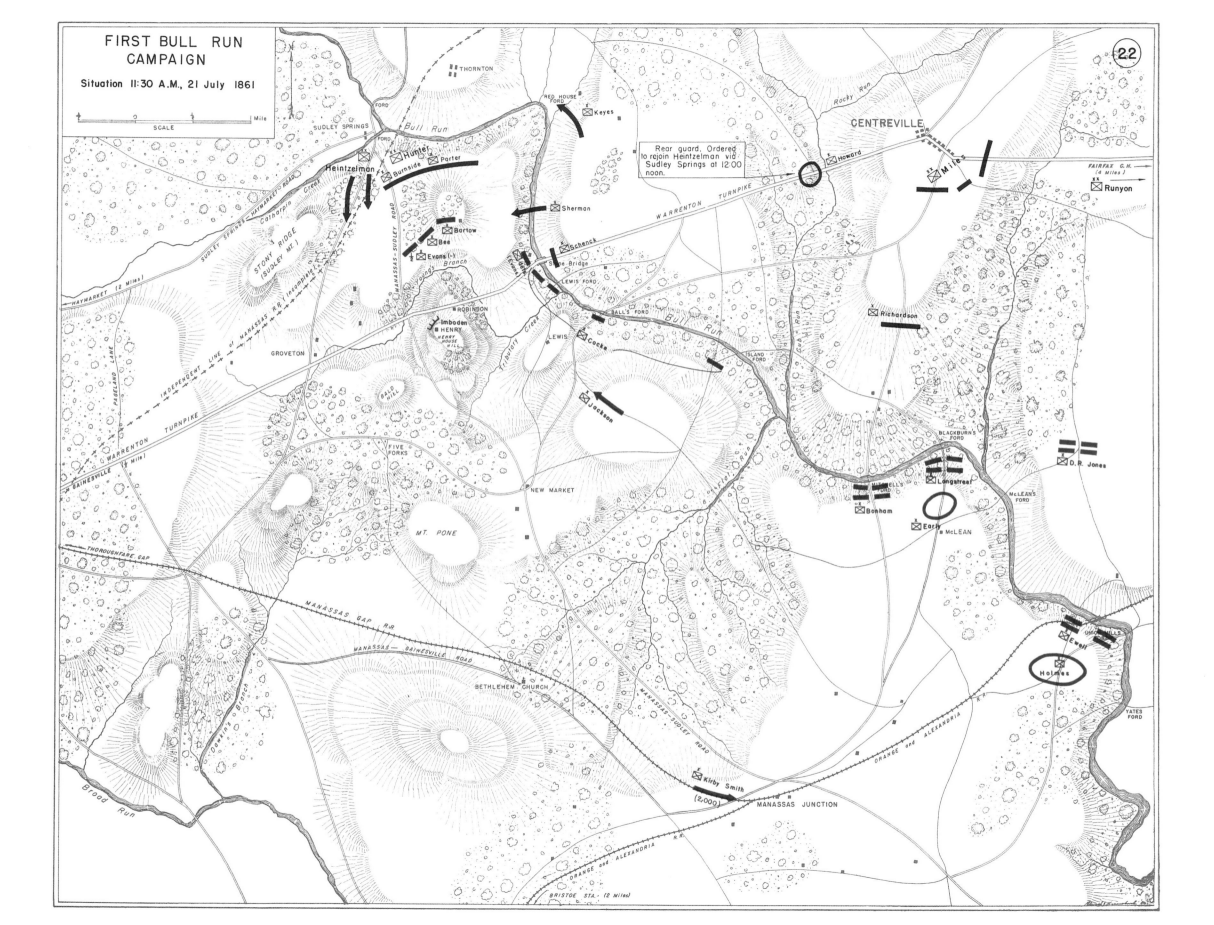

FIRST BULL RUN CAMPAIGN

Situation 11:30 A.M., 21 July 1861

SCALE

Mile

22

THORNTON

CENTREVILLE

Rocky Run

RED HOUSE FORD

⊠ Keyes

FORD

SUDLEY SPRINGS

FORD

Bull Run

Rear guard. Ordered to rejoin Heintzelman via Sudley Springs at 12:00 noon.

⊠ Howard

WARRENTON TURNPIKE

FAIRFAX C.H. (4 Miles)

⊠ Miles

xx Runyon

⊠ Hunter

⊠ Porter

Heintzelman

⊠ Burnside

HAYMARKET ROAD

Catharpin Creek

⊠ Sherman

STONY RIDGE (SUDLEY MT.)

⊠ Bartow

⊠ Bee

⊠ Schenck

⊠ Evans (-)

Young's Branch

Stone Bridge

LEWIS FORD

HAYMARKET (2 Miles)

SUDLEY SPRINGS

MANASSAS-SUDLEY RR. (Incomplete)

BALL'S FORD

Bull Run

⊠ Richardson

INDEPENDENT LINE of MANASSAS R.R.

Imboden HENRY

ROBINSON

HENRY HOUSE HILL

LEWIS

⊠ Cocke

ISLAND FORD

Cub Run

GROVETON

Tributary Creek

WARRENTON (5 Miles)

WARRENTON TURNPIKE

BALD HILL

⊠ Jackson

BLACKBURN'S FORD

GAINESVILLE (5 Miles)

PAGELAND LANE

FIVE FORKS

⊠ D.R. Jones

⊠ Longstreet

MITCHELL'S FORD

McLEAN'S FORD

NEW MARKET

⊠ Bonham

⊠ Early

McLEAN

MT. PONE

THOROUGHFARE GAP

MANASSAS GAP R.R.

⊠ Ewell

UNION MILLS

MANASSAS-GAINESVILLE ROAD

MANASSAS-SUDLEY ROAD

Holmes

BETHLEHEM CHURCH

ORANGE and ALEXANDRIA R.R.

YATES FORD

Bull Run

Dawkins Branch

Broad Run

⊠ Kirby Smith

(2,000)

MANASSAS JUNCTION

ORANGE and ALEXANDRIA R.R.

BRISTOE STA. (2 Miles)

FIRST BULL RUN CAMPAIGN: 3

The Confederate retreat to Henry Hill House had been something of a rout, and Beauregard and Johnston arrived there just as the survivors of the earlier fight to the north were rallying there. They attempted to hearten the troops on the hill, with some success; but it was primarily the reassuring sight of Jackson's brigade, "standing like a stone wall," that gave courage to the fleeing forces. Beauregard stayed at the scene of battle and by personal example continued to rally his troops. Meanwhile, Johnston, having arranged the command details with Beauregard, moved to the rear to coordinate and direct the movements of the Confederate units coming from Manassas Junction and the extreme right flank.

McDowell, on the other hand, allowed himself to be sucked into the minutiae of the battle, personally leading brigades and regiments. His bravery and battlefield leadership were commendable, but they were displayed at the expense of his duties as an army commander. Likewise Hunter, Maj. Gen. Samuel P. Heintzelman, Maj. Gen. Ambrose Burn-side, and Gen. William Buel Franklin became involved in leading regiments, so that their own commands suffered from lack of direction.

McDowell was determined to continue the assault and make his victory complete. Thus, at about 2:00 P.M., when the infantry he had in the immediate vicinity of Henry Hill House still outnumbered the Confederates there by approximately two to one, he launched his attack up the hill. The battle raged back and forth without either side gaining a substantial advantage. Then the batteries of Capt. James Ricketts and Capt. Charles Griffin began to swing the tide for the Union. But they were surprised by the 33rd Virginia (wearing blue uniforms), and the gunners and supporting infantry were shot down.

Now, Beauregard's reinforcements were beginning to arrive, while the exhausted Union infantry began to wilt. As the critical point in the battle neared, Beauregard owed much to Jackson, who had skillfully selected and vigorously defended the original position at Henry Hill House.

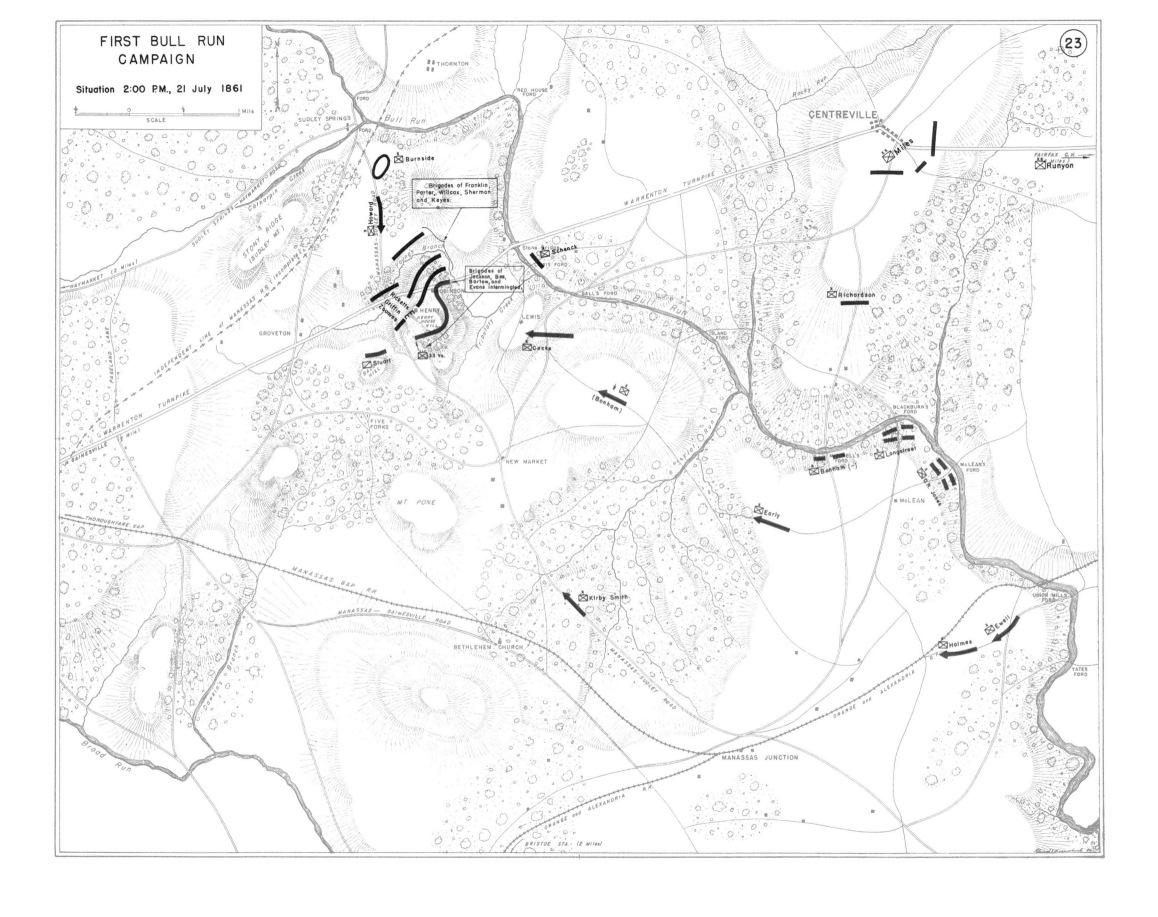

FIRST BULL RUN
CAMPAIGN

Situation 2:00 P.M., 21 July 1861

SCALE
Mile

23

THORNTON

RED HOUSE FORD

CENTREVILLE

SUDLEY SPRINGS
FORD

Bull Run

WARRENTON TURNPIKE

Miles

FAIRFAX C.H.
Miles
Runyon

Burnside

Brigades of Franklin, Porter, Willcox, Sherman and Keyes.

Howard

Stone Bridge
Schenck

LEWIS FORD

BALL'S FORD

Richardson

Brigades of Jackson, Bee, Bartow, and Evans intermingled.

ROBINSON

Ricketts
Griffin
Arnold

R HENRY

HENRY HOUSE HILL

LEWIS

ISLAND FORD

Cocke

33 Va.

Stuart
BALD HILL

(Bonham)

FIVE FORKS

BLACKBURN'S FORD

NEW MARKET

Longstreet

McLEAN'S FORD

MT. PONE

Bonham (-)

McLEAN
D. R. JONES

Early

MANASSAS GAP R.R.

UNION MILLS ROAD

MANASSAS - GAINESVILLE ROAD

Kirby Smith

Ewell

BETHLEHEM CHURCH

Holmes

YATES FORD

ORANGE and ALEXANDRIA R.R.

MANASSAS JUNCTION

ORANGE and ALEXANDRIA R.R.

BRISTOE STA. (2 Miles)

FIRST BULL RUN CAMPAIGN: 4

When Gen. Jubal Early and Gen. Edmund Kirby Smith arrived at the scene of the action about 4:00 P.M., the tide turned in Beauregard's favor. The pressure brought to bear on the Union right flank by these fresh units caused McDowell's forces to withdraw all the way back to Centreville, via Sudley Springs and Stone Bridge. At first they fell back in fairly good order although there were some signs of rout and panic in some units and little supervision from senior officers. Under McDowell's direction, Col. Dixon Stansbury Miles's division formed a rear guard, but it was impossible to rally the rest of the army short of Washington.

On the Confederate side there was an almost equal amount of confusion. Johnston ordered Bonham's and Longstreet's fresh troops on the Confederate right to cross at Blackburn's and Mitchell's fords and take up the pursuit. Once across, the two commanders lost precious time in squabbling. Then a burst of artillery fire from the Federal rear guard caused Brig. Gen. Milledge L. Bonham, who was in overall command, to call off the pursuit. Meanwhile, a false alarm that Federal troops were advancing on Manassas Junction from Union Mills Ford caused Beauregard to order a new concentration at the ford, further diverting men from the pursuit. The cavalry attempted to pursue at once, but they were too few in number to pose any serious threat to the fleeing Federals. Jackson felt that the pursuit should be renewed that night, but the Confederate infantry was exhausted by its long day of combat, and Johnson and Beauregard knew it would be impossible to continue the chase.

Thus, the first battle of the war—between two ill-prepared forces—ended in a dramatic Confederate victory. But since an effective pursuit was not initiated, the full fruits of victory eluded the victors. Union losses in killed, wounded, and captured totaled 2,896; Confederate, 1,982. Among the many commanders on the field, three had shown definite promise: Jackson, Sherman, and Evans.

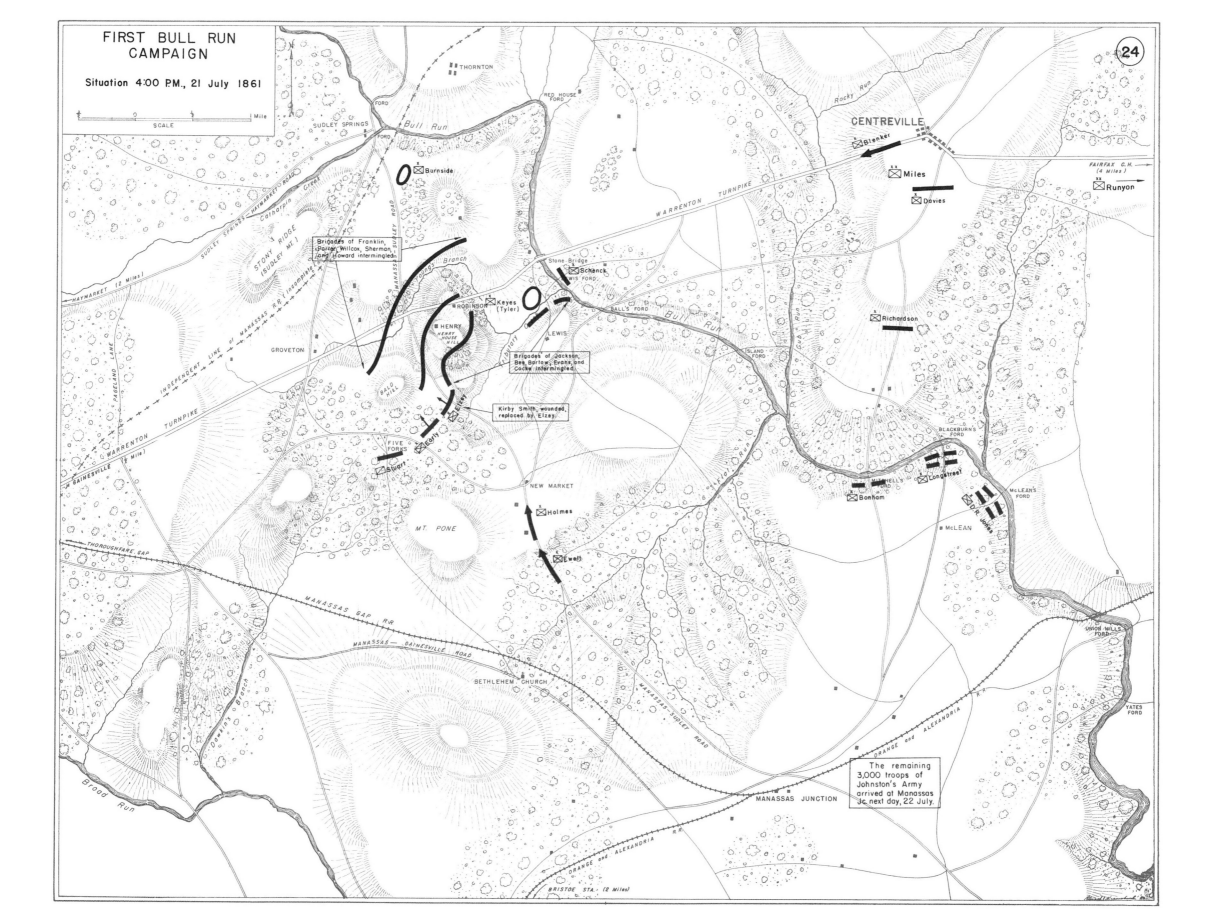

HENRY & DONELSON CAMPAIGN: 1

The map below shows the strengths and dispositions of the opposing forces in the west at the beginning of 1862. During the preceding six months there had been much minor activity and local political maneuvering in the border states as they faced the momentous question of secession. While Missouri held for the Union, in Kentucky there was disagreement between the pro-Confederate governor and pro-Union legislature; the standoff resulted in a kind of neutrality, but one that commanders of neither side respected. On 3 September 1861, Maj. Gen. Leonidas Polk occupied Columbus, and, two days later, Brig. Gen. Ulysses S. Grant seized Paducah.

The Union military command in the sprawling western theater was exercised through a series of departments that, on 9 November 1861, were organized—from west to east—as the department of Kansas under Hunter; Missouri under Maj. Gen. Henry W. Halleck; and Ohio under Brig. Gen. Don Carlos Buell. Now operations along the Mississippi and the lower reaches of the Tennessee and Cumberland would be solely under the command of Halleck. But if the Union's geographical division had been improved, its command structure had not. Buell and Brig. Gen. Winfield Scott Hancock were equals, and each received his orders directly from McClellan in Washington.

The Confederacy, however, had recognized the importance of unified direction, and in September 1861 had appointed Gen. Albert Sydney Johnston to command all forces from Arkansas to the Cumberland Gap. His immediate subordinates, Polk and Maj. Gen. William J. Hardee, were considered first-rate assistants.

Johnston's problems of defense were numerous. He had a numerically inferior force but had to defend an extremely broad front, although he also benefited from operating on internal lines with excellent railway connections.

The terrain of the area played an important part in the formulation of strategy. The Mississippi, Tennessee, and Cumberland rivers served as avenues of approach for military operations and, together with the Ohio, supplemented other means of logistical support. The Appalachian chain, culminating in the Cumberland Mountains, separated the eastern and western theaters. No east–west railroads crossed the mountains for the two hundred miles between Louisville and Chattanooga.

In January 1862, four different Union plans for offensive operations in the western theater were proposed by Buell, Halleck, Lincoln, and McClellan but none could be agreed on. Buell, under pressure to invade eastern Tennessee, made half-hearted gestures, one of which resulted in a victory at Mill Springs by Brig. Gen. George H. Thomas. Halleck and Grant had demonstrated up the Tennessee to divert Confederate attention from Buell's cherished plan to advance on Nashville, but Buell did not move. Finally, on 1 February 1862, Halleck, without arranging for Buell's cooperation, authorized Grant to move up the Tennessee River against Fort Henry.

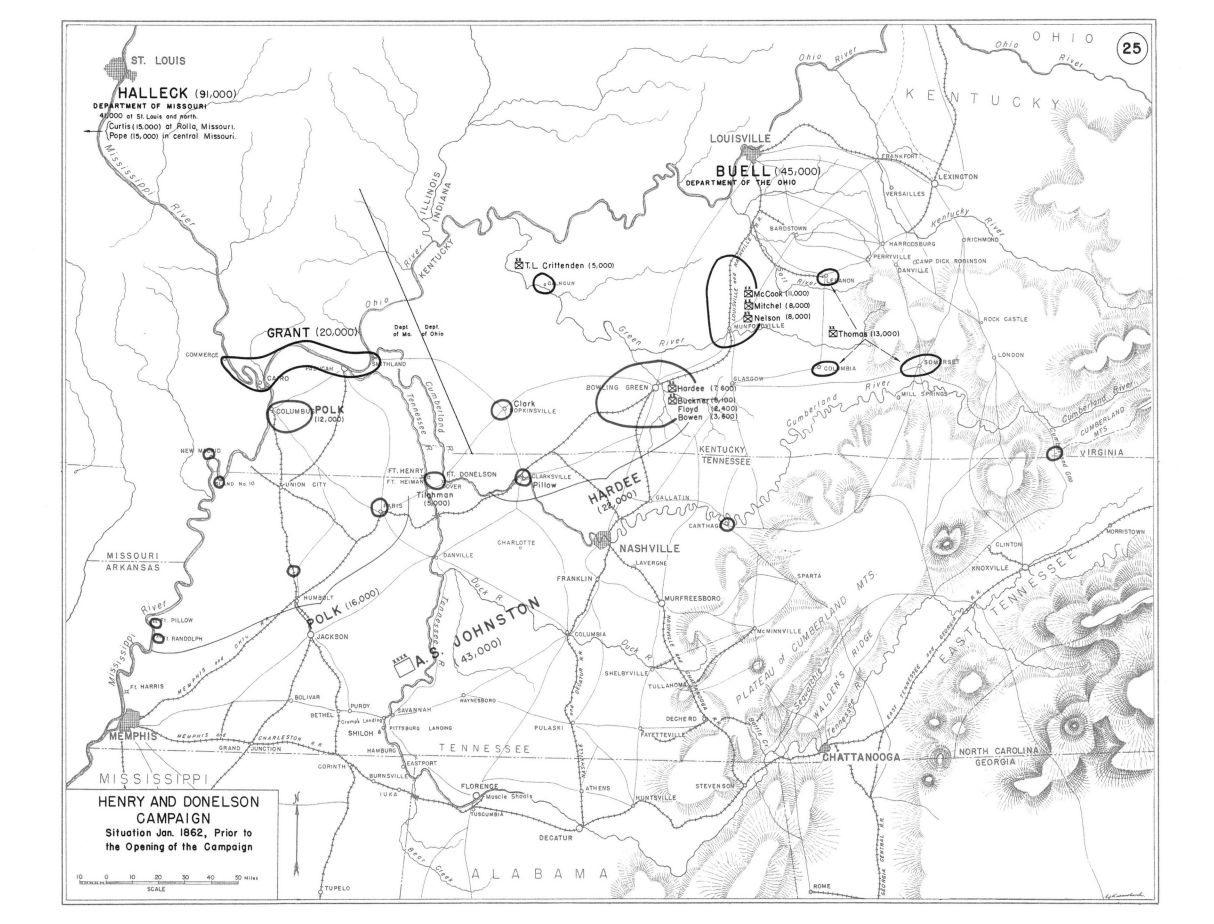

HENRY AND DONELSON CAMPAIGN

Situation Jan. 1862, Prior to the Opening of the Campaign

SCALE

10   0   10   20   30   40   50 Miles

HENRY & DONELSON CAMPAIGN: 2

Grant began the move up the Tennessee on 2–3 February 1862, shuttling his division because he lacked adequate transports. By 6 February, he was in position four miles from Fort Henry and ready to launch his attack. When he had originally conceived the idea of attacking the fort, he had expected Commodore Andrew H. Foote's fleet to be able to destroy it on its own. Grant thought he would be using his infantry merely to cut off the fleeing garrison. The fort's commander, Brig. Gen. Lloyd Tilghman, shared Grant's view that Fort Henry was an easy target for the Union gunboats (although situated on a commanding bend of the river and armed with seventeen cannon, it had been built too low for effective defense) and early on 6 February sent 2,500 of his men to Fort Donelson on the Cumberland River, which was about eleven miles away to the east and connected by two dirt roads that wound through a rugged terrain of hills, marshes, streams, and thick woods, lately made more difficult by heavy rains.

Grant's infantry and gunboats moved out at 11:00 A.M. on 6 February, and two hours later Fort Henry, now manned by only 70 soldiers and the hapless Tilghman, surrendered. But slowed by the rain-soaked terrain, Brig. Gen. John A. McClernand could not block the escape of the majority of the garrison.

Grant now seized the opportunity to increase Johnston's difficulties and to drive his strategic penetration deeper by dispatching gunboats upstream to destroy the Memphis & Ohio Railway bridge over the Tennessee, thus severing Johnston's major means of communication between the wings of his army.

Grant's seizure of Fort Henry posed a real problem for Johnston: should he draw his forces back all along the line or resist Grant's penetration by counterattacking? Fortunately for the Union, he tried to do both. Thus he sent 12,000 reinforcements under Floyd to Fort Donelson and at the same time withdrew his right wing from Bowling Green to Nashville.

In the meantime, Grant was impatient to advance on Fort Donelson, but the weather was so bad that his troops could not be supplied. Also, he had to wait for naval support to move into position on the Cumberland. On 12 February, he began to move and, by the evening of the 12th, his troops commanded a ridge overlooking Floyd's entrenched defenders. Foote tried the same tactics that had been successful at Fort Henry, but Donelson's defenses were much more effective and inflicted so much damage that the Union gunboats were forced to retire.

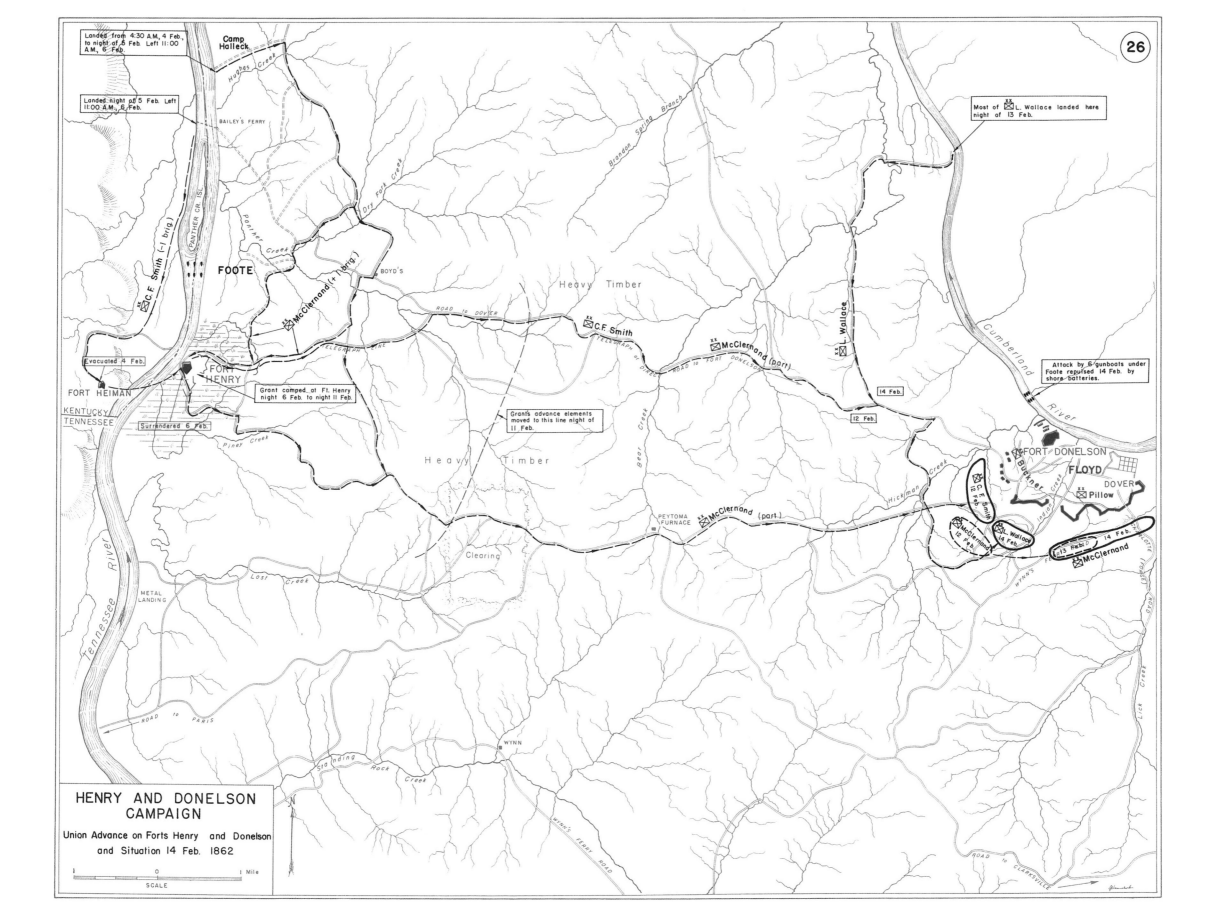

Landed from 4:30 A.M., 4 Feb. to night of 5 Feb. Left 11:00 A.M., 6 Feb.

Camp Halleck

Landed night of 5 Feb. Left 11:00 A.M., 6 Feb.

Hughes Creek

BAILEY'S FERRY

Most of ⊠ L. Wallace landed here night of 13 Feb.

PANTHER CR. ISL.

Panther Creek

Dry Fork Creek

Brandon Spring Branch

Cumberland River

FOOTE

⊠ C.F. Smith (-1 brig.)

⊠ McClernand (+1 brig.)

BOYD'S

Heavy Timber

ROAD to DOVER

⊠ C.F. Smith

TELEGRAPH LINE

⊠ McClernand (part)

⊠ L. Wallace

14 Feb.

Attack by 6 gunboats under Foote repulsed 14 Feb. by shore batteries.

Evacuated 4 Feb.

FORT HEIMAN

FORT HENRY

Grant camped at Ft. Henry night 6 Feb. to 11 Feb.

TELEGRAPH OR DIRECT ROAD to FORT DONELSON

12 Feb.

River

KENTUCKY
TENNESSEE

Surrendered 6 Feb.

Piney Creek

Grant's advance elements moved to this line night of 11 Feb.

Beer Creek

Heavy Timber

Hickman Creek

FORT DONELSON

⊠ Buckner

FLOYD

⊠ C.F. Smith 12 Feb.

DOVER

⊠ Pillow

Tennessee River

METAL LANDING

Lost Creek

PEYTOMA FURNACE

⊠ McClernand (part)

Clearing

⊠ McClernand 12 Feb.

⊠ L. Wallace 14 Feb.

Indian Creek

WYNN'S FERRY ROAD

⊠ 13 Feb. ⊠ McClernand 14 Feb.

ROAD to PARIS

WYNN

Standing Rock Creek

N

WYNN'S FERRY ROAD

Lick Creek

ROAD to CLARKSVILLE

HENRY AND DONELSON CAMPAIGN

Union Advance on Forts Henry and Donelson and Situation 14 Feb. 1862

1   0   1 Mile

SCALE

Fort Donelson was far stronger than Fort Henry. Its longer side measured about 500 yards but, more important, it was on a commanding height. There were two main batteries on the river side, one just above the river level and the other one hundred feet higher. It was the lower batteries that inflicted the damage on Foote's flotilla. The crenellated line in red on the map below show the Confederate entrenchments that followed the line of a ridge and were backed up by artillery. Here Floyd placed most of his troops, with Brig. Gen. Simon Buckner commanding the right and Brig. Gen. Gideon J. Pillow the left. Had there been any kind of vigorous attack on Grant's columns as they struggled through the broken terrain and before Union reinforcements arrived, it could well have led to some anguish on Grant's part; but there was not and the Confederates went to ground. On the 15th, McClernand extended his force in a wide arc that closed up the Confederate left, sealing Floyd's garrison.

Grant was concerned about his men having to endure a long siege. The weather was brutal (12°F on the morning of the 14th) and they were hungry, many without adequate clothing. But the Confederates were also suffering; morale was low and there was no leader of Grant's stature to take command of the situation. Floyd decided to make a breakout and try to get to Nashville.

About dawn on 15 February, Pillow led off the attack. The plan was to attack through the Union right. After several hours of hard fighting Pillow, aided by Col. Nathan Bedford Forrest's cavalry, broke through McClernand's line and forced it southward. An escape route had been opened and McClernand's right flank exposed; but at the critical moment Floyd lost his nerve and, after several conferences with Pillow and Buckner, ordered his men back to their entrenchments. Grant, seizing the moment, requested Commodore Foote to make a show of force and then ordered Brig. Gen. C. F. Smith to attack to his front. Finally, about 3:00 P.M., Grant rode over to the right of his line and directed McClernand (now joined by Brig. Gen. Lew Wallace) to retake the lost positions. It was cool; it was decisive.

Smith succeeded in seizing the outer line of entrenchments but was driven back by the returning Confederates; by nightfall of 15 February, the garrison was again locked down. To the irresolute Floyd it seemed an opportune time to call for another council of war, which decided on surrender. Floyd and Pillow both made their escapes by boat on the night of the 15th, leaving the luckless Buckner and all but a fraction of the beleaguered garrison of 11,500 to go into the bag. Early on 16 February, Grant received Buckner's note asking for terms. Grant's now famous reply, "No terms except unconditional and immediate surrender," produced the desired result.

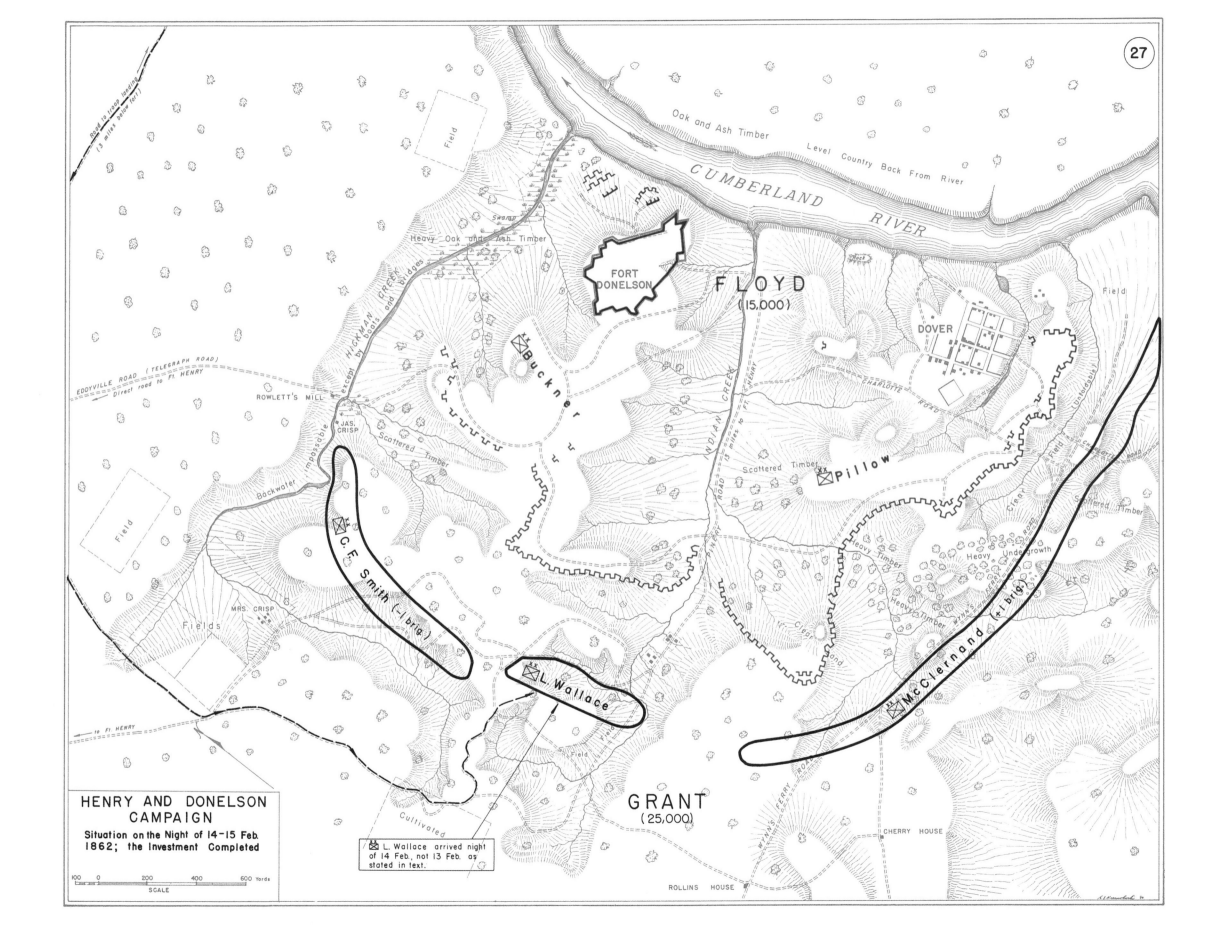

27

Road to troop landing
(3 miles below fort)

CUMBERLAND RIVER

Oak and Ash Timber

Level Country Back From River

Swamp

Heavy Oak and Ash Timber

FORT DONELSON

FLOYD (15,000)

DOVER

Buckner

EDDYVILLE ROAD (TELEGRAPH ROAD)
Direct road to Ft. HENRY

ROWLETT'S MILL

JAS. CRISP

Scattered Timber

CHARLOTTE ROAD

Pillow

INDIAN CREEK

Scattered Timber

Field

Backwater

C. F. Smith (-1 brg.)

FERRY ROAD 13 miles to Ft. HENRY

Heavy Timber

Heavy Undergrowth

MRS. CRISP

Fields

Heavy Timber

Clear Land

McClernand (+1 brg.)

Scattered Timber

L. Wallace

to Ft. HENRY

Field

Cultivated

GRANT (25,000)

WYNN'S FERRY ROAD

CHERRY HOUSE

HENRY AND DONELSON CAMPAIGN

Situation on the Night of 14-15 Feb. 1862; the Investment Completed

L. Wallace arrived night of 14 Feb., not 13 Feb. as stated in text.

100 0   200   400   600 Yards
SCALE

ROLLINS HOUSE

HENRY & DONELSON CAMPAIGN: 4

If one compares the relative positions of the opposing forces when it began (map 7) with those at the end (map below), it becomes clear that the Henry and Donelson campaign had important strategic results. Johnston's forward defense was now broken; lateral communications between his right and left wings had been severed by the cutting of the Memphis and Ohio Railroad by Grant (now a major general). Johnston's earlier opportunity to destroy Grant's smaller force had evaporated as Union reinforcements poured in. In addition, Union gunboats controlled the Tennessee as far south as Florence—an important demonstration of the importance of the navy in Union strategy in the western theater.

At the beginning of the campaign Buell had been concentrated in the Munfordville area. McClellan (now in overall command in Washington) advocated an advance into eastern Tennessee. Halleck, on the other hand, had pressed for Buell to advance into the Clarksville-Nashville area to cover Grant's exposed east flank. Buell had begun an advance south and, on 16 February (the day Fort Donelson surrendered), he had occupied Bowling Green. He had then followed the retreating Confederates at a respectable distance, while sending one division around by water to move on Nashville. It was this unit that secured Nashville when the remainder of Buell's army arrived on 24 February.

After the capture of Henry and Donelson, Grant occupied Clarksville at Halleck's insistence (he wanted Buell to catch up), although Grant was eager to push on. Halleck was concerned that the Confederates might launch an offensive from the Columbus area, based on reports that Beauregard had arrived in the theater with reinforcements and was to join Polk in a powerful drive northward. Indeed, Beauregard had arrived, but alone in a kind of exile. He had been unable to work with Gen. Joseph E. Johnston in the east and had a difficult relationship with Jefferson Davis, so he had been transferred to the western theater, assuming overall command between the Mississippi and Tennessee Rivers. Johnston was relegated to command of the small force at Murfreesboro.

So, on 27 February 1862, Halleck's forces were concentrated in two locations under Pope and Grant, and Buell was at Nashville. The Confederates were much more widely dispersed, but Gen. A. S. Johnston, at Beauregard's urging, had evolved a plan for concentrating in the vicinity of Corinth in preparation for taking the offensive. On the Union side, two plans to retain the initiative were being discussed. The one decided on would lead to the bloody fields of Shiloh.

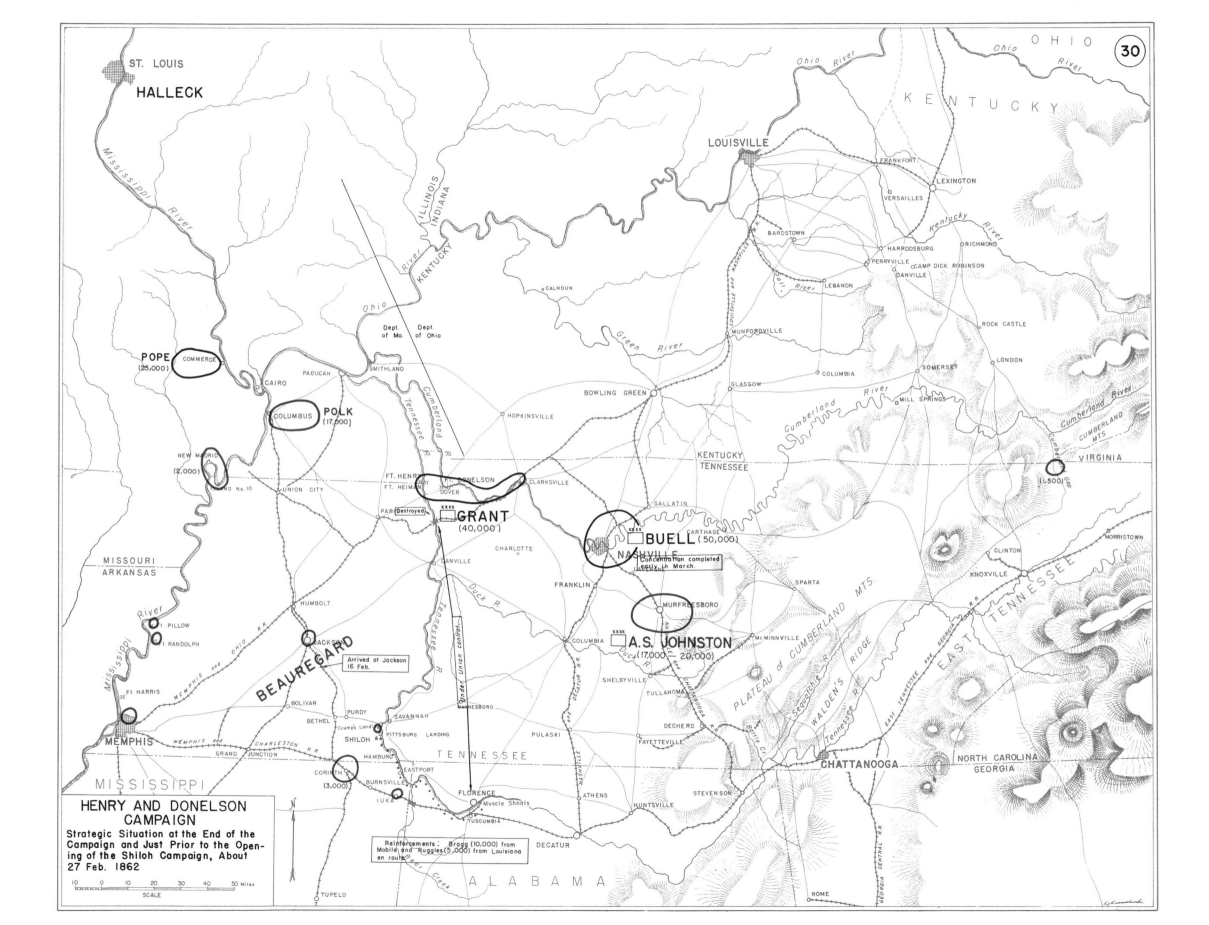

HENRY AND DONELSON
CAMPAIGN

Strategic Situation at the End of the
Campaign and Just Prior to the Opening of the Shiloh Campaign, About
27 Feb. 1862

10 0 10 20 30 40 50 Miles
SCALE

SHILOH CAMPAIGN: 1

General Johnston spent eight days at Murfreesboro before beginning his movement to Corinth to link up with Beauregard. And so the Confederate forces united to create an army of 40,000 that Johnston would lead into battle against Grant at Shiloh.

On the Union side the preparations for the coming campaign were complacent. Halleck was elated by Grant's successes but exasperated because McClellan maintained Buell on an equal status with his own. He bombarded Washington with requests for more troops and a unified command (with himself as unifying commander). On 11 March 1862, Lincoln gave Halleck overall command of the Knoxville-Missouri River area, and Halleck immediately ordered Buell to join Smith, encamped at Pittsburg Landing

By the evening of 5 April, the day before the battle of Shiloh, Grant's army of six divisions spread out in clumps from Pittsburg Landing while his headquarters was at Savannah, nine miles downstream—a strange dislocation of command that would have a serious impact in the first two hours of the battle.

At Pittsburg Landing, Grant's army was encamped wherever units could find suitable clearings. No plans had been made for the defense of the position, and Grant seems to have had only vague thoughts about fortifying it. The most conspicuous oversight, though, was the lack of security. Only a sketchy line of infantry outposts covered the camp, and there was no effort at distant patrolling or reconnaissance. Meanwhile, Johnston's army was concentrated a mere two miles in front of Sherman and Gen. Benjamin Mayberry Prentiss, and was preparing to attack the next morning.

The area in which the Union army was encamped was triangular and bordered by water courses. Except for a few clear spaces the ground was covered with forest and undergrowth, much of it impassible for cavalry. The highest terrain was a ridge running east to west, two hundred feet above the Tennessee River. Tillman Creek divided the ridge into two plateaus, with a swampy area along Owl Creek.

It was not until 4:00 P.M. on 5 April 1862, that Johnston could get his tired and hungry troops deployed for battle. Beauregard was sure that Grant had been forewarned of the impending attack, but Sherman to the south and Grant, himself, were both unsuspecting. On the night of 5 April, Grant reported to his superior, Halleck: "I have scarcely the faintest idea of an attack . . . being made on us . . ."

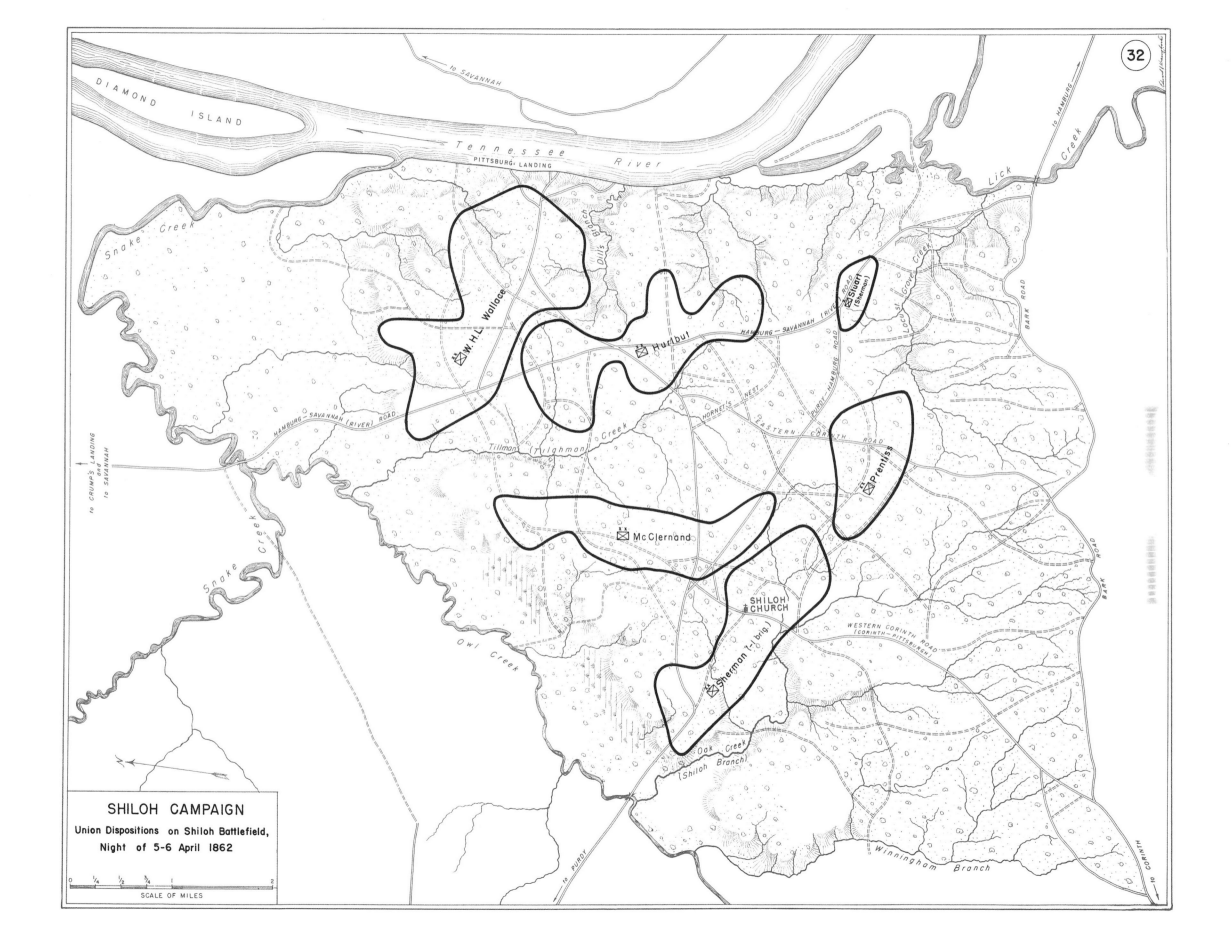

32

DIAMOND ISLAND

Tennessee River

to SAVANNAH

to HAMBURG

Lick Creek

PITTSBURG LANDING

Snake Creek

Dill's Branch

Snake Creek

to CRUMP'S LANDING and to SAVANNAH

HAMBURG–SAVANNAH (RIVER) ROAD

W.H.L. Wallace

Hurlbut

HAMBURG–SAVANNAH (RIVER) ROAD

Stuart (Sherman)

Locust Grove Creek

BARK ROAD

Tillman (Tilghman) Creek

HORNET'S NEST

EASTERN CORINTH ROAD

PURDY–HAMBURG ROAD

Prentiss

McClernand

SHILOH CHURCH

WESTERN CORINTH ROAD (CORINTH–PITTSBURG)

BARK ROAD

Owl Creek

Sherman (-1 brig.)

Oak Creek (Shiloh Branch)

to PURDY

Winningham Branch

to CORINTH

SHILOH CAMPAIGN

Union Dispositions on Shiloh Battlefield,
Night of 5-6 April 1862

0 ¼ ½ ¾ 1 2
SCALE OF MILES

SHILOH CAMPAIGN: 2

About 6:00 A.M. on 6 April, Johnston's army moved forward, hoping to envelop the Union left. The attack, however, soon degenerated into a general frontal assault; a confused melee that was difficult to control. The Union left under Sherman began to buckle, but was propped up by McClernand. Prentiss, supported by Brig. Gen. Stephen A. Hurlbut, fought stubbornly but, by 9:00 A.M., was forced to withdraw to the Hornet's Nest.

Grant now labored with all his energy to restore the situation. Brig. Gen. William Nelson was to move up to a point opposite Pittsburg Landing and Lew Wallace was to set out a skirmish line. Grant then directed two regiments to secure Snake Creek Bridge, an escape route if it was needed.

When Prentiss was forced back, it exposed McClernand's left flank, but the line held. At 10:30 A.M., Sherman was pushed back and this exposed McClernand's right flank, forcing him to withdraw. And so it went on. On the Confederate side, the troops were exhausted and had taken heavy casualties; some had dropped out to feast on abandoned Union supplies. Their success was precarious and, having committed all his reserves, Johnston was at the mercy of Union reinforcements, which were a few miles from the battlefield.

Shortly after noon, Sherman's exhausted force, finding its flanks turned, was forced to pull back. Gen. Braxton Bragg and Gen. John Breckinridge also managed to crumble the Union left. At the Hornet's Nest, Wallace and Prentiss had successfully held their ground for five hours, withstanding as many as twelve assaults, including at least one led personally by Johnston. But Johnston was to pay the price; he was killed at about 2:30 P.M. Shortly after 4:00 P.M. Sherman and McClernand withdrew to prepared positions covering the Hamburg-Savannah road. Here, exhausted and decimated, they would make their final stand. Wallace and Prentiss were surrounded; they tried to cut their way out and Wallace was killed; Prentiss pulled back his flanks into a defensive cordon but at 5:30 P.M. was forced to surrender his 2,200 men. He had won valuable time for Grant.

After Prentiss's surrender, Bragg was eager to assault Pittsburg Landing but he lacked the manpower to do so. Beauregard had issued orders to suspend the attack along the length of the line, but Jackson's Alabamans, who had run out of ammunition, nevertheless went in with bayonets through heavy artillery fire, and were repulsed. Both armies, exhausted and rain-drenched, settled in for the night.

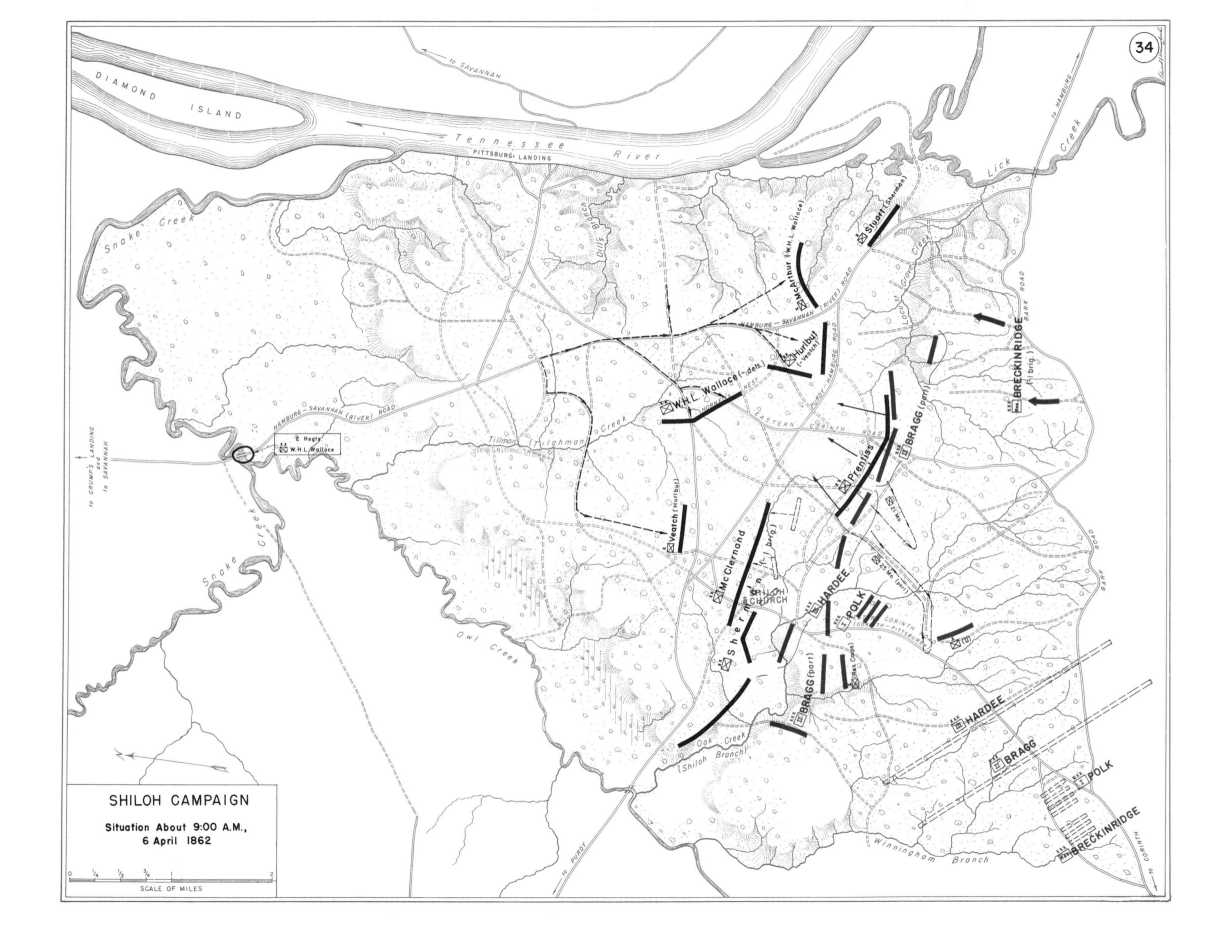

34

DIAMOND ISLAND

to SAVANNAH

Tennessee River

PITTSBURG LANDING

Snake Creek

Lick Creek

to HAMBURG

Stuart (Sherman)

McArthur (W.H.L. Wallace)

(RIVER) ROAD

Locust Grove Creek

HAMBURG - SAVANNAH

BARK ROAD

BRECKINRIDGE (1 brig.)

Hurlbut (-Veatch)

W.H.L. Wallace (-dets.)

HORNETS' NEST

PURDY - HAMBURG ROAD

EASTERN CORINTH ROAD

BRAGG (part)

Tillman (Tilghman) Creek

to CRUMP'S LANDING and to SAVANNAH

HAMBURG - SAVANNAH (RIVER) ROAD

2 Regts
W.H.L. Wallace

Prentiss

21 Mo.

Veatch (Hurlbut)

25 Mo. (part)

McClernand (-1 brig.)

Sherman (-1 brig.)

SHILOH CHURCH

HARDEE

POLK (CORINTH - PITTSBURG)

(Res. Corps)

BRAGG (part)

Owl Creek

Oak Creek (Shiloh Branch)

BRAGG

HARDEE

to PURDY

Shiloh Branch

BRAGG

POLK

to CORINTH

Winningham Branch

BRECKINRIDGE

SHILOH CAMPAIGN

Situation About 9:00 A.M.,
6 April 1862

0   1/4   1/2   3/4   1   2

SCALE OF MILES

SHILOH CAMPAIGN: 3

The Union forces went onto the attack at daybreak on 7 April, but as Grant and Buell had both decided independently to go on the offensive, coordination could only be effected at the division level. Nelson began the action at about 5:00 A.M., with an advance along the Hamburg-Savannah Road and halted briefly to allow Brig. Gen. Thomas L. Crittenden and Brig. Gen. Alexander M. Crook (the major part of whose division had arrived at dawn) to join the line. Together they moved again at around 9:00 A.M., by which time Confederate resistance had begun to stiffen. And Buell's army found itself in a real fight.

On the other flank, Sherman, who had been alerted during the night, began his advance shortly after Nelson's and soon encountered sharp artillery fire that caused him to halt and wait for Buell to resume his advance. Grant's other division commanders received their attack orders by 8:00 A.M. and moved forward on either side of Sherman. By 10:00 A.M., Union forces were attacking all along the line, and the weight of their attack, reinforced by 25,000 fresh troops, was too much for Beauregard to contain. He was gradually forced back in fighting that was as intense of that of the previous day. Shortly after noon, Brig. Gen. Thomas J. Wood's division of Buell's army joined the fray.

By noon, Beauregard had apparently decided that he must retreat, but he did not issue the necessary orders until 2:30 P.M. By 4:00 P.M. the Confederates, now reduced to about 20,000 effectives, had retreated behind Breckinridge's covering force of about 2,000 men and were en route to Corinth. They had fought valiantly and stubbornly, as a look at the casualties of Brig. Gen. Patrick R. Cleburne's brigade of Hardee's corps illustrates. They had entered the battle of 6 April with 2,750 men and resumed the fight the next day with 900. By the end of the battle, only 58 were left standing. Similar appalling losses were suffered by some of Grant's units.

Once the Union army reached the line of its original camps, it seemed to lose all steam and no pursuit was attempted until the 8th; and when it was handled roughly by Forrest's cavalry, no further attempts were made. Like Bull Run, Shiloh had been a clash of still-raw armies and the toll was heavy. The Union losses in killed, wounded, and missing were 13,700; the Confederates, 10,700.

With the Mississippi now open almost to Memphis, the Union future in the western theater appeared bright. Halleck had a large, battle-seasoned force within twenty miles of Corinth, while Beauregard had little strength to oppose a determined drive to the south, but somehow, as we shall see, Halleck failed to capitalize on his advantage.

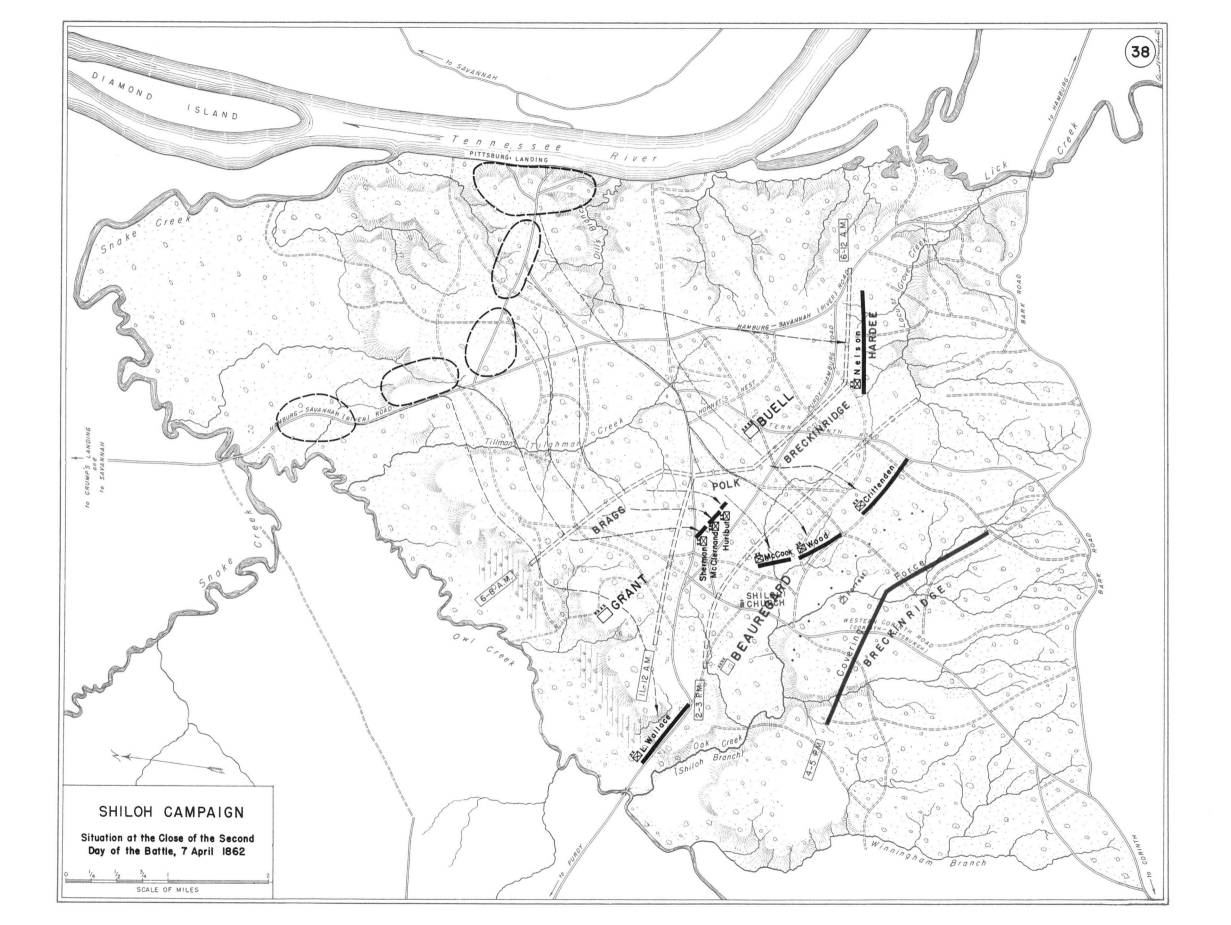

38

DIAMOND ISLAND

to SAVANNAH

Tennessee River

to Hamburg

Lick Creek

PITTSBURG LANDING

Snake Creek

Blundi's Branch

Locust Grove Creek

BARK ROAD

6-12 A.M.

HAMBURG — SAVANNAH (RIVER) ROAD

HAMBURG — SAVANNAH (RIVER) ROAD

Tillman (Tilghman) Creek

HORNET'S NEST

HARDEE

Nelson

BUELL

BRECKINRIDGE

POLK

Crittenden

to CRUMP'S LANDING and to SAVANNAH

BRAGG

Sherman
McClernand
Hurlbut

McCook
Wood

SHILOH CHURCH

GRANT

6-8 A.M.

BEAUREGARD

WESTERN CORINTH ROAD (CORINTH — PITTSBURGH)

Force

BRECKINRIDGE

Covering Force

BARK ROAD

Snake Creek

Owl Creek

11-12 A.M.

2-3 P.M.

L. Wallace

Oak Creek

Shiloh Branch

4-5 P.M.

to PURDY

Winningham Branch

to CORINTH

SHILOH CAMPAIGN

Situation at the Close of the Second
Day of the Battle, 7 April 1862

0   1/4   1/2   3/4   1   2

SCALE OF MILES

PENINSULAR CAMPAIGN: 1

The day after the battle of Bull Run (21 July 1861), Maj. Gen. McClellan was summoned to Washington and given command of what would become the Army of the Potomac. His job was to defend Washington and rebuild an army much shaken by its defeat. In November he was appointed head of all land forces. McClellan, always the perfectionist, had spent an inordinate amount of time in organizational detail while Gen. J. E. Johnston's army held Centreville only thirty miles away and Confederate batteries had effectively closed down the Potomac below Washington. McClellan seemed unable to develop a workable overall strategy for the prosecution of the war, and, after abandoning several plans, decided to threaten the Confederate capital at Richmond by moving up the Peninsula from Fort Monroe at its tip. On 17 March 1862, McClellan's army began to embark for Fort Monroe, and Lincoln assumed the role of overall commander in order to free McClellan to concentrate entirely on his invasion.

When McClellan joined his 50,000 men at Fort Monroe on 2 April, he thought first of a naval envelopment of Yorktown, but the Union navy did not have the forces to overcome Confederate gunboats on the York and James rivers (something he should and could have learned before he started). He therefore decided to move up the Peninsula but, again, his preparation was poor and obstacles he should have known about came as a surprise, not least Magruder's line of fortifications that spanned the whole lower Peninsula. Magruder's force was numerically much inferior to McClellan's but McClellan, who had been fooled

by some clever maneuvering on Magruder's part into thinking a much stronger force barred his way, turned back and decided to lay siege to Yorktown, thus conceding the initiative to the Confederates. However, Johnston, who had come down from Centreville and commanded the Confederates on the Peninsula, preempted McClellan, and on the night of 3 May, began a withdrawal toward Richmond. The Union forces, under Brig. Gen. Edwin V. Sumner, took up the pursuit and found the Confederate rear guard under Lt. Gen. James Longstreet near Williamsburg. After a hotly contested action of attack and counterattack, Longstreet managed to successfully extricate his force. Rather than riding with his advance guard, McClellan all the while remained in Yorktown, which eventually fell, and a slow Union advance up the Peninsula began. Fifteen days later they were astride the Chickahominy River. A Union naval attempt to get up the James was thwarted on 15 May, when their attempt to reduce the Confederate forts at Drewry's Bluff, only seven miles from Richmond, was repulsed.

Johnston prepared his defenses at Richmond and, in the Shenandoah Valley, Jackson was doing a magnificent job tying up the Union forces under McDowell that otherwise could have come south to support McClellan. In typical fashion McClellan, with 105,000 men, was convinced that Johnston with 60,000 outnumbered him two to one, and so he sat before Richmond and again surrendered the initiative. Meanwhile, the foul weather conditions were beginning to have a serious impact on the Union army.

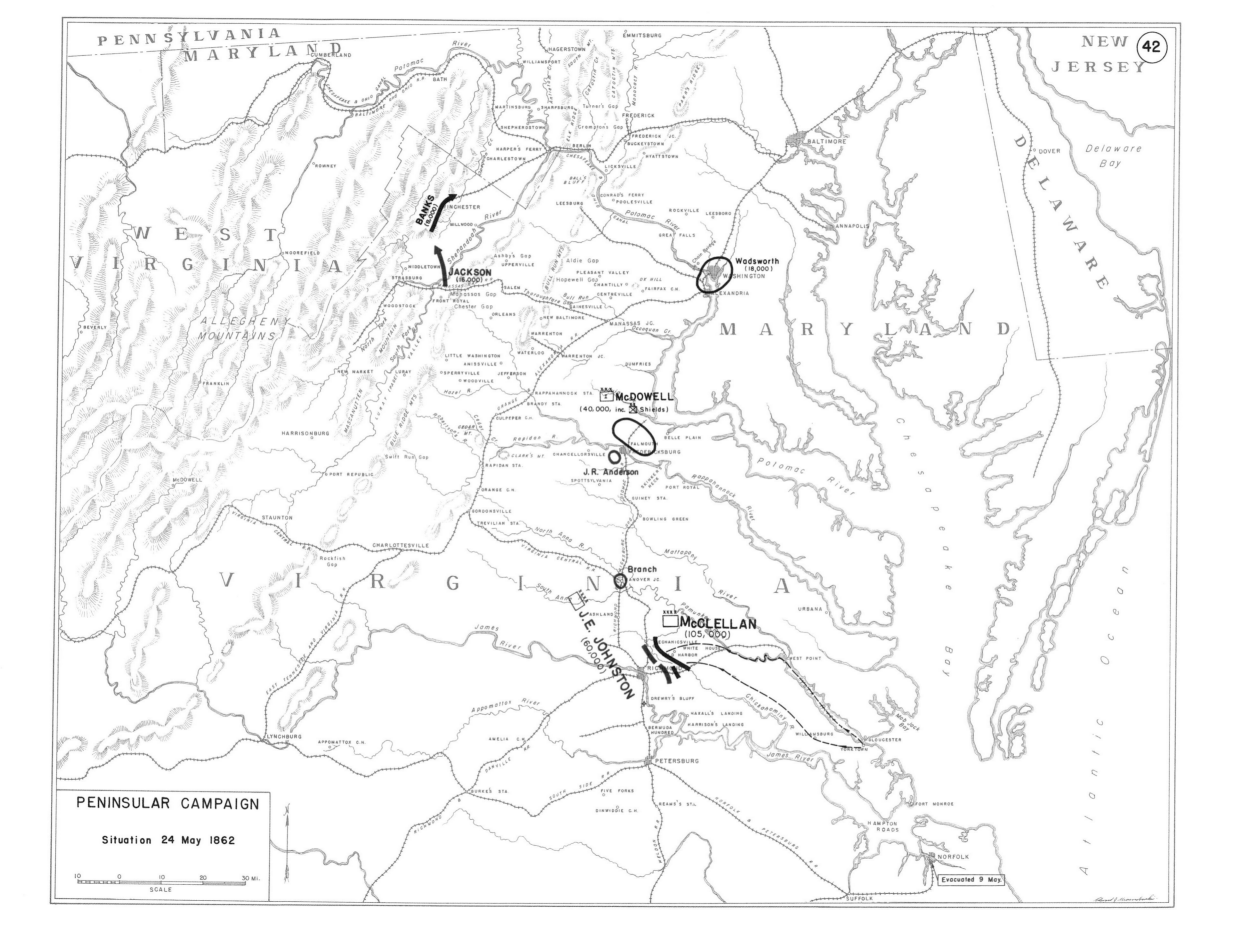

PENNSYLVANIA

MARYLAND

WEST VIRGINIA

VIRGINIA

MARYLAND

NEW JERSEY

DELAWARE

Delaware Bay

Chesapeake Bay

Atlantic Ocean

BANKS (8,000)

JACKSON (18,000)

Wadsworth (18,000)
WASHINGTON

McDOWELL
(40,000, inc. Shields)

J. R. Anderson

Branch

J. E. JOHNSTON
(60,000)

McCLELLAN
(105,000)

PENINSULAR CAMPAIGN

Situation 24 May 1862

10   0   10   20   30 MI.
SCALE

Evacuated 9 May.

42

PENINSULAR CAMPAIGN: 2

When McClellan finally arrived at the Chickahominy, he directed the III and IV Corps to seize bridgeheads on the south side of the river, with the intention of moving the entire army across when McDowell arrived from the Valley. In the meantime, McClellan kept most of the army on the north side from 20 until 31 May, leaving II and IV Corps isolated and as tempting as a tethered scapegoat.

Johnston had originally intended to attack McClellan's main force directly across the river on 29 May, but on hearing of McDowell's imminent arrival he decided to attack Maj. Gen. Erasmus Keyes' exposed corps on 31 May. His attack plan was well thought out: Maj. Gen. Ambrose P. Hill and Magruder were to contain the Union forces north of the river while Longstreet would hit Keyes from three directions. However, like much in war, the execution bore little resemblance to the plan. Longstreet took a wrong road and moved south, where he confused and delayed the advance of Gen. Daniel Harvey Hill (not to be confused with A. P. Hill) and Huger to the extent that no attack could be launched until 1:00 p.m., and even then Hill attacked alone and was contained by the Federal forces. It was only when he was reinforced by Longstreet that he could drive Keyes and Gen. Philip Kearny back. The looming rout of IV Corps was prevented by a flank attack on Whiting by Brig. Gen. John Sedgwick's division of II Corps, which Sumner sent over the river on his own initiative. Darkness ended the battle of Fair Oaks (also known as Seven Pines), which had been fought in violent weather and seas of mud. The Confederates not only bungled

an opportunity but also lost their commander, Johnston, who was wounded. Maj. Gen. Gustavus Wilson Smith took command and ordered Longstreet to attack the next day; but it was feebly executed and came to nothing. On 1 June 1862, Robert E. Lee arrived to take overall command.

After Fair Oaks, McClellan gradually shifted his forces to the south side of the Chickahominy but for several weeks showed no enthusiasm for the offensive. Again, he was convinced that Lee's numerical strength was greater than his own and so convinced himself that offensive action was unwise.

The Confederates, on the other hand, did not lack for vigorous leadership. While his men strengthened the fortifications of Richmond, Lee planned his offensive strategy, and to gain useful intelligence dispatched J. E. B. Stuart to gain information about the Union right flank. Stuart converted the reconnaissance into a full-scale raid that involved riding around the whole Union army; and although he confirmed the vulnerability of the Union right, he probably also alerted McClellan for, on 18 June, he began loading transports with the intention of moving his base to the James River. Lee now decided to hit the Union north flank. Jackson was recalled and arrived at Ashland Station on 25 June. The risks were great but the reward worth it. Lee could not sustain a battle of attrition. He needed a decisive and swift victory.

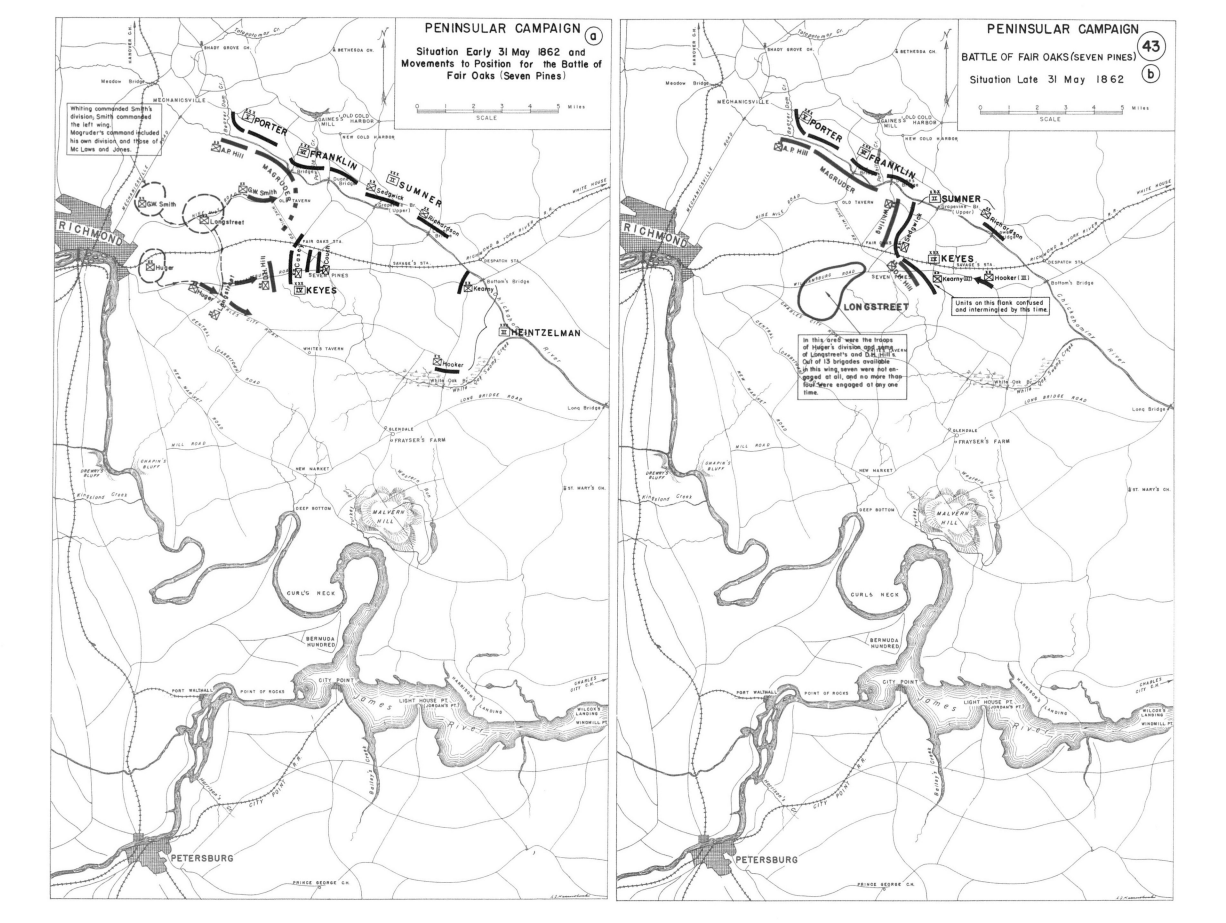

PENINSULAR CAMPAIGN (a)

Situation Early 31 May 1862 and
Movements to Position for the Battle of
Fair Oaks (Seven Pines)

PENINSULAR CAMPAIGN 43

BATTLE OF FAIR OAKS (SEVEN PINES)

Situation Late 31 May 1862 (b)

Whiting commanded Smith's
division; Smith commanded
the left wing.
Magruder's command included
his own division and those of
Mc Laws and Jones.

In this area were the troops
of Huger's division and some
of Longstreet's and D.H. Hill's.
Out of 13 brigades available
in this wing, seven were not engaged at all, and no more than
four were engaged at any one
time.

Units on this flank confused
and intermingled by this time.

Lee's dispositions for the battle of Mechanicsville present a good illustration of the basic military precepts of concentration of mass and economy of force. To the north (Union right flank) he assembled 65,500 troops to oppose Brig. Gen. Fitz-John Porter's 30,000; only 25,000 were left in front of Richmond to contain the remainder of the Union army (60,000). His plan called for Jackson to attack Porter's north flank early on 26 June, at which time A. P. Hill was to advance from Meadow Bridge, clear the Union pickets from Mechanicsville, and then move to Beaver Creek Dam, behind which lay the Union entrenchments. D. H. Hill and Longstreet were then to pass through Mechanicsville, while Huger and Magruder would distract the Union forces to their front. It was a fine plan.

But just as at Fair Oaks, things went wrong. Jackson was late and went into bivouac; A. P. Hill, despairing of Jackson's arrival, advanced at 3:00 P.M. without orders and without adequate support other than one of D. H. Hill's brigades, attacked anyway, and was bloodily repulsed. Only Magruder and Huger had any success. Energetically maneuvering and firing as though they had 50,000 men, they convinced McClellan (though not Maj. Gen. Joseph Hooker and Kearny) that a Union assault there could not succeed. Jackson had, for reasons not apparent, completely derailed Lee's plans. This was the first of several occasions over the next seven days when Jackson would fail to display initiative, resource-

fulness, or dependability—the very qualities that had, and would, raise him to the very highest ranks of military leaders.

Porter could rightly claim the victory on the 26th, but McClellan, utterly convinced, as always, that he was the underdog, ordered Porter to withdraw behind Powhite Creek and to get his artillery safely south of the Chickahominy, which he duly began to do at dawn on the 27th. But Lee was not about to let Porter off the hook. By 2:00 P.M. A. P. Hill was attacking vigorously and Jackson had worked his way around Porter's right, but again the latter was slow, took the wrong road, and had to backtrack. It was not until 4:30 that he launched his attack (assisted by Longstreet) and broke Porter's line at dusk; but Porter was well supported by his excellent artillery as well as two brigades from Sumner's corps, and he managed to get across the Chickahominy about 4:00 A.M., destroying the bridges behind him.

Gaines's Mill, as the battle became known, was a victory for Lee, but not the decisive one for which he had planned. Jackson's slowness had been a major factor, but Lee was not without fault, for he had failed to effectively coordinate the actions of his divisions. On the Union side, Porter had fought splendidly and almost unassisted for two days, while McClellan had held the remainder of the army out of harm's way.

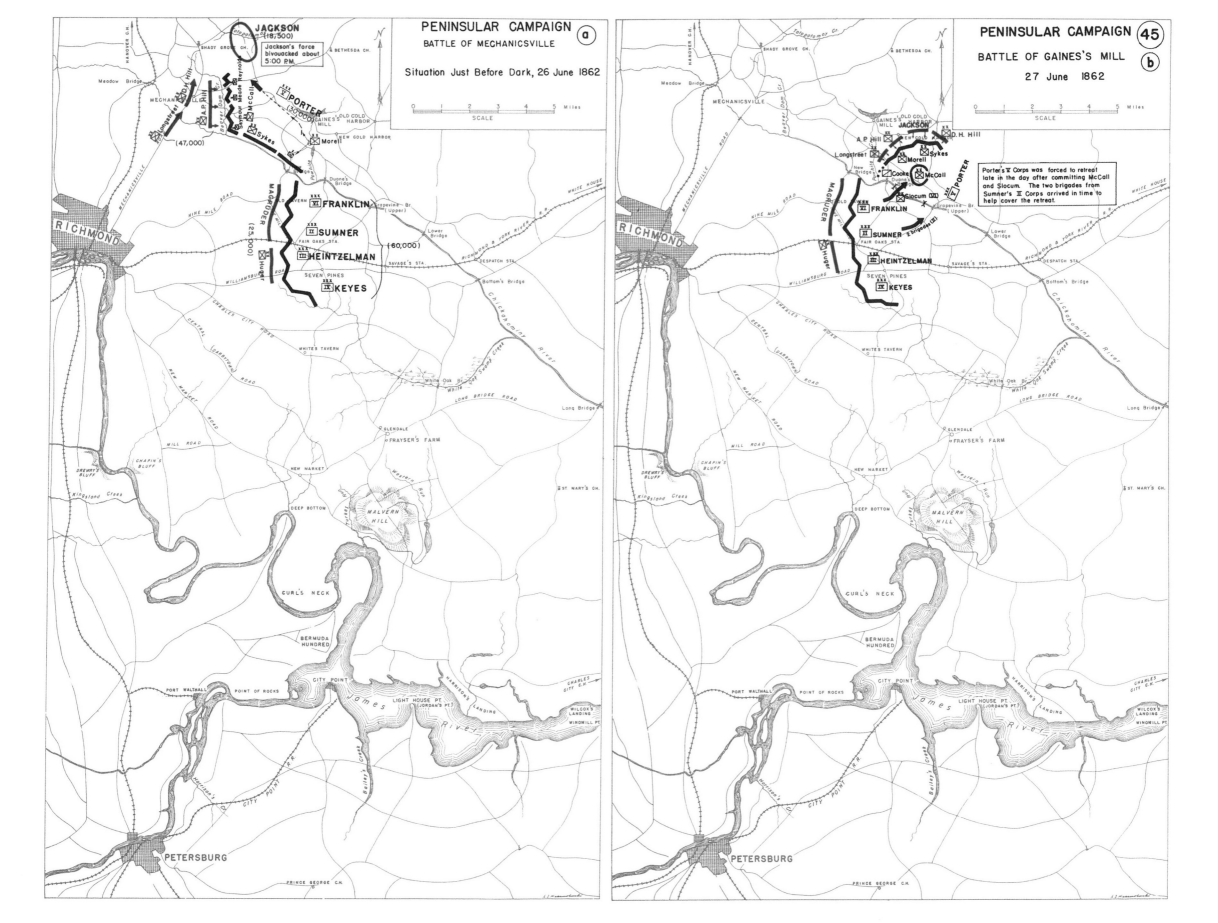

PENINSULAR CAMPAIGN

BATTLE OF MECHANICSVILLE

Situation Just Before Dark, 26 June 1862

JACKSON (18,500)

Jackson's force bivouacked about 5:00 PM.

PORTER (30,000)

(47,000)

MAGRUDER (25,000)

FRANKLIN

SUMNER

HEINTZELMAN

(60,000)

KEYES

RICHMOND

PETERSBURG

PENINSULAR CAMPAIGN 45

BATTLE OF GAINES'S MILL

27 June 1862

Porter's V Corps was forced to retreat late in the day after committing McCall and Slocum. The two brigades from Sumner's II Corps arrived in time to help cover the retreat.

JACKSON

A.P. Hill

D.H. Hill

Longstreet

Morell

Sykes

Cooke

McCall

Slocum

PORTER

MAGRUDER

FRANKLIN

SUMNER

2 brigades

HEINTZELMAN

KEYES

RICHMOND

PETERSBURG

PENINSULAR CAMPAIGN: 4

McClellan was now thoroughly unnerved and ordered the army to retreat to the James on the twenty-seventh, presumably because he wanted the reassurance of evacuation; but the truth was only one of his five corps had been committed to battle, and they had acquitted themselves well. If he had decided to stand and fight, Lee may well have found himself in a very difficult position, with major Union forces to his front and rear, because the corps of McDowell, Maj. Gen. Nathaniel Prentiss Banks, and Fremont had been formed into a new army under Maj. Gen. John Pope who was under orders to move south to aid McClellan. All of which McClellan knew, but somehow he could not shake off the excessive caution, the defeatism, that gripped him during the Gaines's Mill battle.

Lee spent the 28th trying to get some good intelligence on McClellan's intentions. Stuart's cavalry, his best source of information, had been sent east and south to reconnoiter, but again Stuart could not resist the temptation to raid, and put himself out of the picture for three vital days. Lee came to the conclusion that McClellan had gone south, and he ordered A. P. Hill to move and strike the Union columns in flank, and Jackson to press their

rear. Meanwhile, the Union II, III, and VI Corps had withdrawn to Savage's Station while waiting to pass through the narrow defiles of White Oak Swamp. Magruder ran into them and was checked and was slow to organize his attack because he was waiting on Jackson, who again was late, having spent the entire day of the 29th rebuilding a bridge. Inevitably, Magruder's assaults were beaten off, and the rearmost Union corps managed to extricate themselves from a dangerous position, due principally to Jackson's procrastination.

Two incidents are indicative of the lack of higher direction in the Union army. While Sumner was engaged at Savage's Station, Heintzelman decided that his corps was no longer needed and, entirely on his own initiative, withdrew to the south, as did Brig. Gen. Henry Slocum. During the night following its engagement at Savage's Station, the Union rear guard withdrew southward and, by noon of 30 June, McClellan's trains, reserve artillery, and rear guard had cleared White Oak Swamp Creek. However, because of poor reconnaissance, the supply and artillery trains had not made use of all available roads and a bottleneck developed at Glendale.

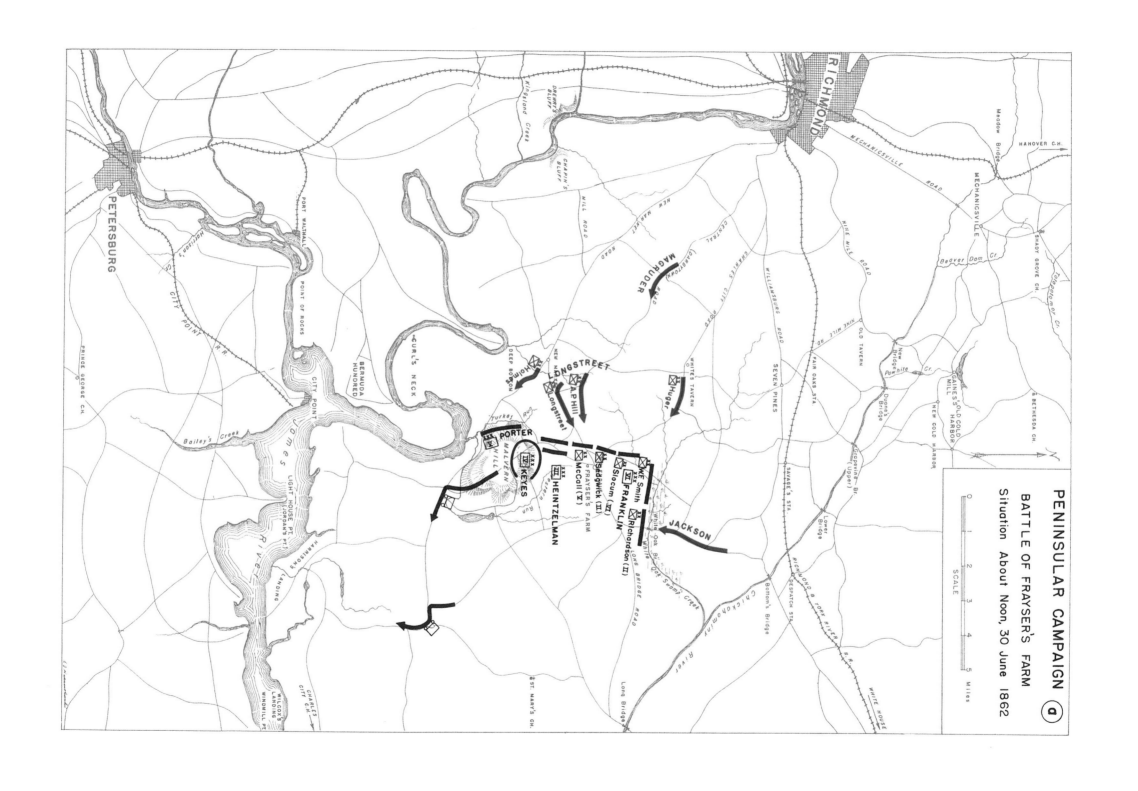

PENINSULAR CAMPAIGN

BATTLE OF FRAYSER'S FARM

Situation About Noon, 30 June 1862

Due to the bottleneck at Glendale, the Union troops had to take up defensive positions. Meanwhile, Lee's divisions, less Holmes, were converging on the Union position. Holmes, recently arrived from south of the James, was ordered to seize Malvern Hill, or at least to harass the Union baggage and artillery that were moving across it. Lee expected to deploy his divisions in one concentrated effort to destroy the Union army, but such was not to be the case. Huger's timidity, Magruder's vacillation, and Jackson's lethargy, plus poor staff work, combined to frustrate his intentions. Huger, slowed by obstructions placed by Union troops along the Charles City Road, made no attempt to move by other roads and failed to participate in the battle. Marauder was undecided whether to support Holmes or Longstreet. As a result, only A. P. Hill and Longstreet attacked in the battle of Fraser's Farm (and Longstreet did not assault with a concentrated force, but by brigade). They succeeded in forcing back Brig. Gen. George A. McCall's division, but Union reinforcements soon sealed off the penetration. Fighting lasted into the night, without any advantage to the Confederates. That night the last of three Union corps moved unmolested into the position on Malvern Hill that had been selected and occupied by Porter.

Lee was to have one more opportunity to destroy McClellan's army, but this time the prevailing circumstances were not to be as favorable as they had been on previous occasions. The Confederate troops had been attacking and marching for five days and had lost heavily in the process, while the Union position on Malvern Hill was the most formidable they had yet encountered.

Instead of outflanking the position, Lee attacked it directly, expecting his artillery to enfilade McClellan and clear the way for an infantry assault. But the Union artillery proved to be superior and took a heavy toll of the Confederate guns. Lee then canceled the attack; but late in the afternoon he had observed what he took to be a Union withdrawal and ordered an assault. This was badly mismanaged and ended up as a piecemeal assault; first by D. H. Hill, then by Jackson, and finally by Huger. A. P. Hill and Longstreet never entered the fray. The Union forces, under Porter (McClellan was at Harrison's Landing on the James River), had little difficulty repulsing the assaults, and on the following day withdrew to the Landing. Lee, having seen off McClellan, decided he had done enough and moved his army back to Richmond.

In the campaign, Lee had preserved Richmond and had put his opponent to flight, but the Union army, although somewhat demoralized, remained strong. Under a more energetic and confident commander it could have advanced on Richmond, but instead it remained ignominiously hunkered down at Harrison's Landing until August, when it was recalled to Washington.

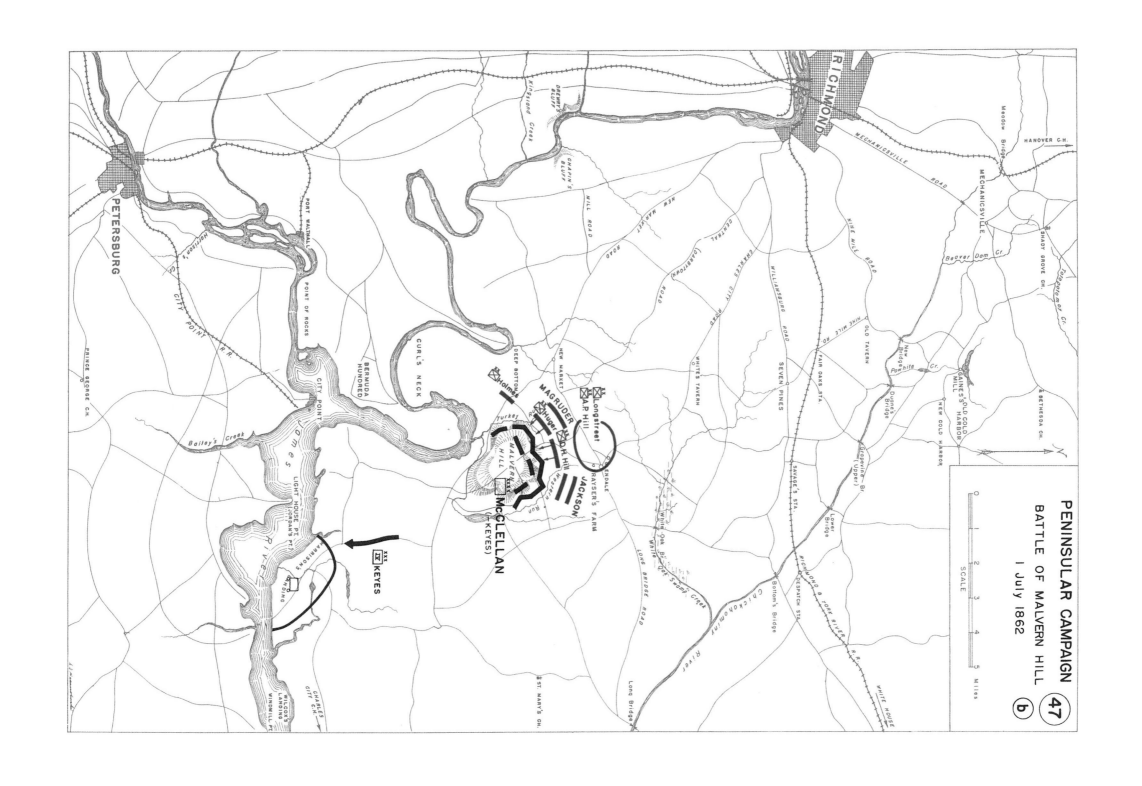

PENINSULAR CAMPAIGN
BATTLE OF MALVERN HILL
1 July 1862

47 b

SCALE
0 1 2 3 4 5 Miles

RICHMOND

PETERSBURG

McCLELLAN
(-KEYES)

MAGRUDER

A.P. Hill

Longstreet

D.H. Hill

JACKSON

Holmes

Huger

KEYES

JACKSON'S VALLEY CAMPAIGN: 1

The Valley is the area in between the Allegheny and the Blue Ridge Mountains, running northeast from Staunton to Harper's Ferry. It is drained by the Shenandoah River, which is formed by the North and South Forks, which flow either side of Massanutten Mountain, a barrier equally as formidable as the Blue Ridge Mountains. The road network in the Valley was good, the best being the Valley Turnpike, which ran from Staunton through Harrisonburg and along the North Fork to Winchester. The mountains could be crossed only at easily defensible passes, and railroads cut through only two of them. During the war, the Valley was valuable to the South both as an abundant granary and as a direct invasion route to Maryland and Pennsylvania. To the Union, the Valley had little military value except in a negative sense: to deny it to the Confederacy.

In November 1861, "Stonewall" Jackson, then a major general, had been sent to Winchester to command Confederate troops in the Shenandoah Valley. He was soon reunited with the Stonewall Brigade that he had led at Bull Run and, in December 1861, was joined by Brig. Gen. William W. Loring and 6,000 troops. His brief was to watch Banks and be prepared to return to Manassas if McClellan should advance on the town.

Banks crossed the Potomac in late February 1862, forcing Jackson to evacuate Winchester and move to Strasburg. Banks began his movement south from Winchester on 17 March but the Union cavalry scouts misinformed him that Jackson had left the Valley and

so Banks withdrew toward Washington. This was something Jackson had to prevent, so he moved north from Woodstock and arrived at the Union positions at Kernstown around 1:00 P.M. on 23 March, where he tried to envelop the Union right wing by way of Sandy Ridge. However, Col. Erastus B. Tyler's and Col. Nathan Kimball's brigades combined to drive the Confederates from the field, although there was no effective pursuit. Jackson fumed over his defeat but had achieved his goal. Banks returned to the Valley.

Fearing that Jackson might move down the Luray Valley and attack his communications at Front Royal, Banks decided to frustrate such a possibility by moving south to the New Market crossroads, which he occupied, along with Harrisonburg, on 26 April. Jackson had extended from Conrad's Store to Swift Run Gap. There, he took up a classic flanking position where, if Banks moved south of Harrisonburg, Jackson could cut him off. On 30 April, Jackson ordered Col. Turner Ashby to feint toward Harrisonburg and Gen. Richard S. Ewell to occupy Swift Run Gap. Jackson then took a circuitous route to West View, where he attached Brig. Gen. Edward Johnson's division and continued on to McDowell, which he reached on 7 May.

When Jackson heard that Banks was at Harrisonburg, he was compelled to move against him and persuaded Lee that a real opportunity existed in the Valley. Thus, the stage was set for the decisive phase of the Valley campaign, which was to have far-reaching effects.

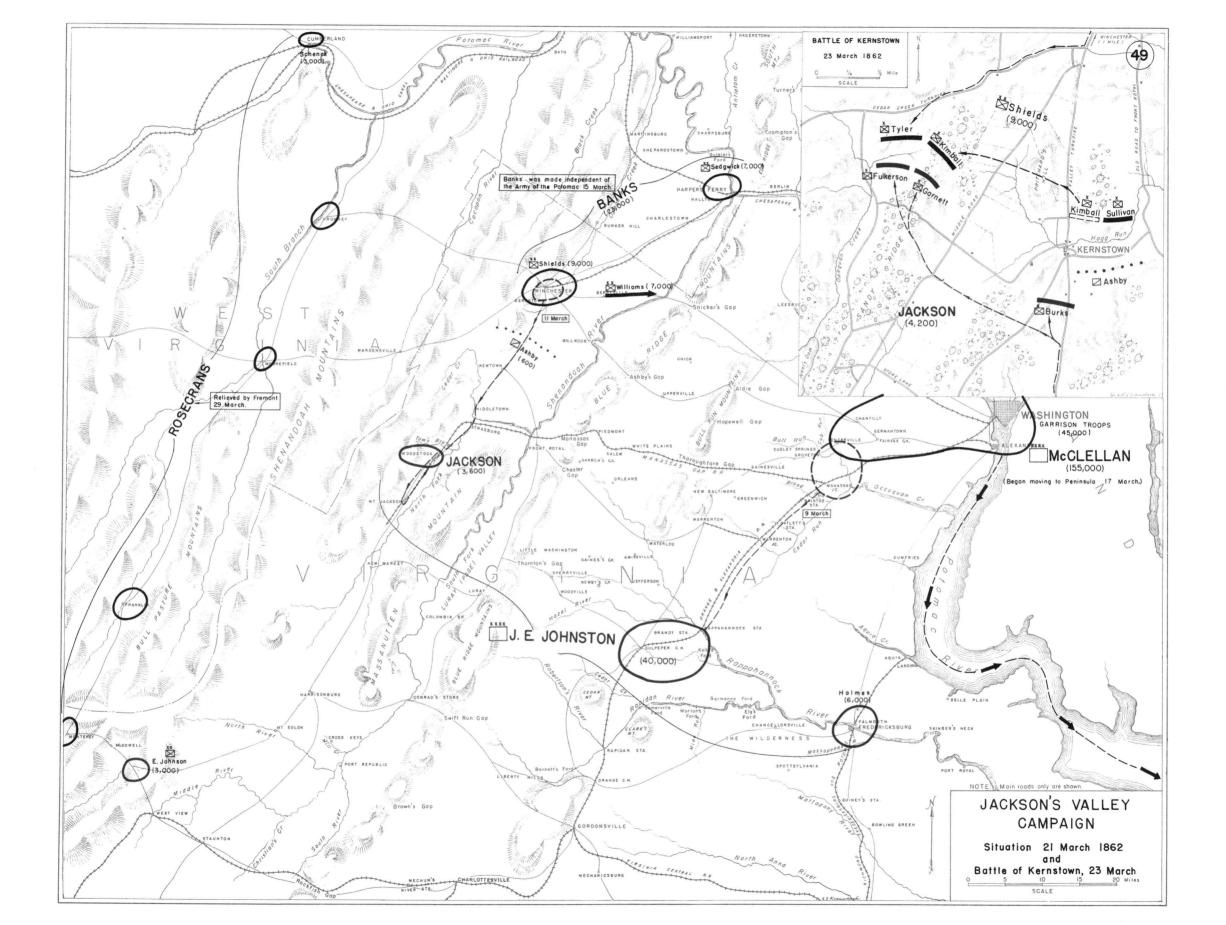

49

BATTLE OF KERNSTOWN
23 March 1862

SCALE
0   ¼   ½ Mile

Shields (9,000)

Tyler

Kimball

Fulkerson

Garnett

Kimball   Sullivan

KERNSTOWN

Ashby

JACKSON
(4,200)

Burks

CUMBERLAND

Schenck
(3,000)

Potomac River

WILLIAMSPORT   HAGERSTOWN

BATH

MARTINSBURG   SHARPSBURG   Turners Gap

SHEPARDSTOWN   Crampton's Gap

Sedgwick (7,000)

Banks was made independent of
the Army of the Potomac 15 March.

HARPERS FERRY   BERLIN

BANKS
(29,000)

CHARLESTOWN

BUNKER HILL

Shields (9,000)

WINCHESTER   Williams (7,000)

11 March   Snicker's Gap

Ashby
(600)

BLUE   RIDGE   MOUNTAINS

Ashby's Gap

UNION

Upperville   Aldie Gap

WEST

VIRGINIA

ROSECRANS

MOOREFIELD

WARDENSVILLE   NEWTOWN

Relieved by Fremont
29 March.

MIDDLETOWN

STRASBURG   PIEDMONT

Hopewell Gap

Tom's Brook   MANASSAS GAP

WOODSTOCK   JACKSON
(3,600)

FRONT ROYAL   WHITE PLAINS   Thoroughfare Gap

O'BARCH'S CH.   SALEM

Chester Gap   ORLEANS

NEW BALTIMORE   GREENWICH

MT. JACKSON   WARRENTON

WATERLOO

LITTLE WASHINGTON   GAINES'S CR.   AMISSVILLE

NEW MARKET   Thornton's Gap   SPERRYVILLE   NEWBY'S CR.   JEFFERSON

WOODVILLE

V   I   R   G   I   N   I   A

FRANKL

BULL PASTURE

LURAY   Columbia Br.

HARRISONBURG   CONRAD'S STORE

J. E. JOHNSTON

BRANDY STA.   RAPPAHANNOCK STA.

CULPEPER C.H.

(40,000)

CEDAR MT.

MONTEREY

McDOWELL

E. Johnson
(3,000)

CROSS KEYS

PORT REPUBLIC

Brown's Gap

GORDONSVILLE

WEST VIEW

STAUNTON

Rockfish Gap

MECHUN'S RIVER STA.   CHARLOTTESVILLE

CHANTILLY

GERMANTOWN

CENTREVILLE   FAIRFAX C.H.

Bull Run   SUDLEY SPRINGS   GROVETO

MANASSAS JC.

BRISTOE STA.

9 March

WARRENTON JC.   Cedar Run

CATLETT'S STA.

DUNFRIES

WASHINGTON
GARRISON TROOPS
(45,000)

ALEXANDRIA

McCLELLAN
(155,000)
(Began moving to Peninsula 17 March.)

Potomac River

AQUIA CR.

AQUIA LANDING

BELLE PLAIN

Holmes
(6,000)

FREDERICKSBURG   SKINKER'S NECK

RAPIDAN RIVER   Germanna Ford   Ely's Ford

CHANCELLORSVILLE   THE WILDERNESS

Mortons Ford   PORT ROYAL

SPOTTSYLVANIA

RAPIDAN STA.

Barnett's Ford   GUINEY'S STA.

LIBERTY MILLS

ORANGE C.H.

MECHANICSBURG   VIRGINIA CENTRAL R.R.   North Anna River

BOWLING GREEN

NOTE Main roads only are shown.

JACKSON'S VALLEY
CAMPAIGN

Situation 21 March 1862
and
Battle of Kernstown, 23 March

0   5   10   15   20 Miles

SCALE

JACKSON'S VALLEY CAMPAIGN: 2

Ashby's cavalry had screened Jackson's movements so effectively since he left Franklin on 12 May, neither Fremont nor Banks was sure of his location . . . Early on 21 May, Jackson's immediate command, reinforced by Brig. Gen. Richard Taylor's brigade of Ewell's division, started north. To the bewilderment of his subordinate commanders, Jackson turned east at New Market and, passing through Luray, absorbed Ewell's command. The unified force now turned north down the Luray Valley. He was heading to wipe out Col. John R. Kenly's command at Front Royal (which he did swiftly on 23 May) and then to move quickly on Harper's Ferry, thus forcing Banks to leave his fortified position at Strasburg and fight in the open. Early on the 24th, Banks began his withdrawal, passed through Middletown, and managed to escape to Winchester where, unwisely, he elected to make a stand. The Confederates enveloped his right, whereupon Banks retired across the Potomac.

Back in Washington, Lincoln saw a chance to catch Jackson at Strasburg. McDowell was ordered to Front Royal and Fremont to move on Harrisonburg but, by the night of 31 May, Jackson had slipped away south.

In the late afternoon of 1 June 1862, Jackson's rear guard, the weary Stonewall Brigade, passed south through Strasburg, followed by Ewell, who had slipped away from Fremont. When McDowell and Fremont closed in on Strasburg, the bird had flown. By the night of the 7th, Jackson had occupied Cross Keys and Port Republic and controlled the bridge between. That same day, Gen. James Shields moved toward Port Republic, his forces strung out along the road. Jackson could have moved east through Brown's Gap for safety but the separation of the Federal forces offered too tempting an opportunity. With the Port Republic bridge and fords in his possession, Jackson could readily concentrate against either Fremont or Shields. He first thought of attacking Fremont, but Fremont, nearer Harrisonburg than Cross Keys, could not be drawn into a battle.

Early on the 8th, a raid on Port Republic by Shields's cavalry surprised and almost captured the Confederate baggage trains and, indeed, Jackson himself. Chastened, Jackson now turned his attention to Shields and, on the night of the 8th, decided to attack, leaving a blocking force under Brig. Gen. Isaac R. Trimble to hold off Fremont. Early on 9 June, the attack was launched against the two brigades of Shields's division that had reached the field. The assault was sent in piecemeal against strong Union positions and was repulsed by vigorous counterattacks and excellent artillery support. Brig. Gen. Charles Sydney Winder's Stonewall Brigade took particularly heavy casualties and was in danger of being routed until it was shored up by reinforcements from Ewell. Finally, Taylor's envelopment on the south forced the Union brigades to withdraw, and Jackson pursued them almost to the Swift Run Gap road, where Shields's two rear brigades stopped him. Concluding that it was now impracticable to attack Fremont, Jackson concentrated all of his forces at Brown's Gap, where they remained until ordered back to the vicinity of Richmond on 17 June.

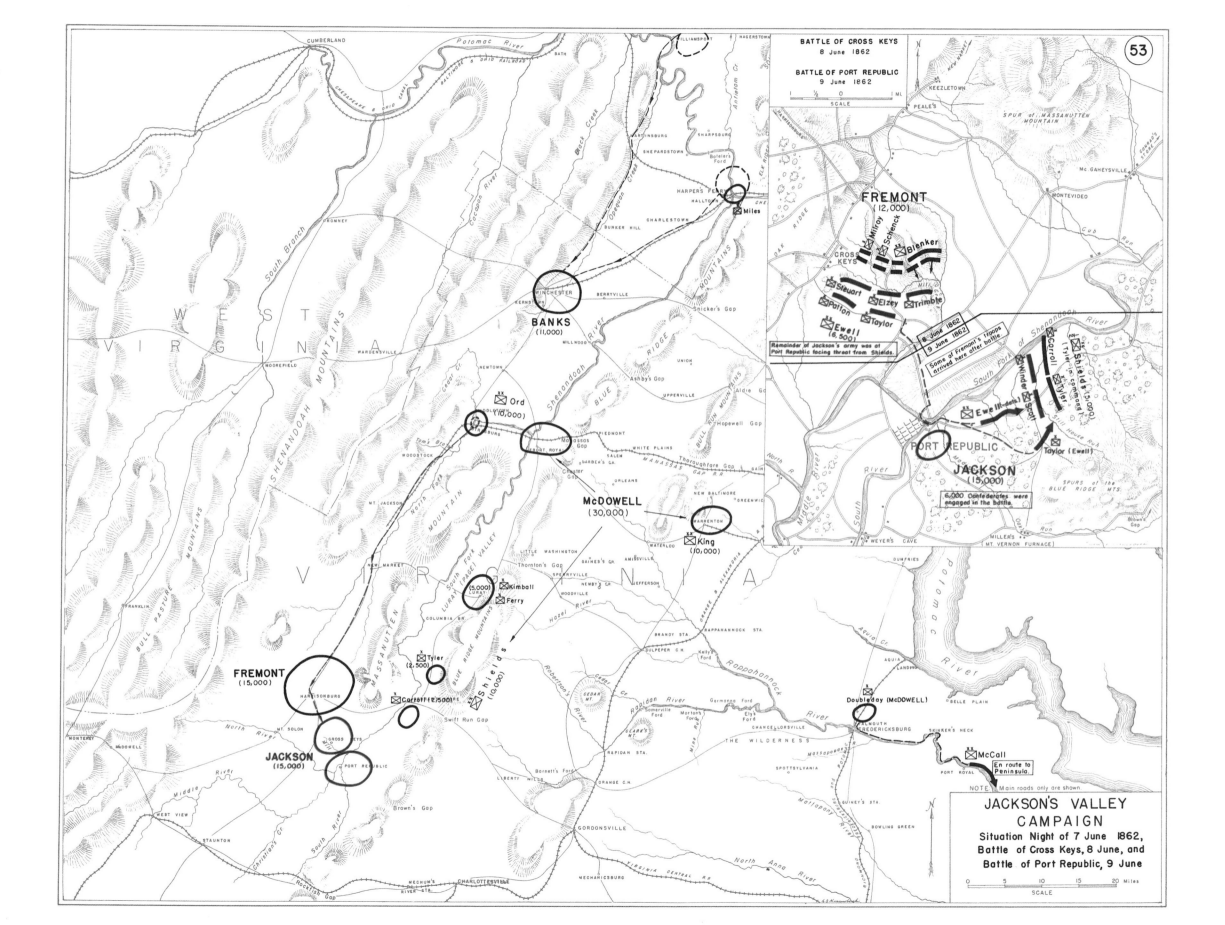

BATTLE OF CROSS KEYS
8 June 1862

BATTLE OF PORT REPUBLIC
9 June 1862

SCALE

FREMONT
(12,000)

Milroy
Schenck
Blenker

CROSS
KEYS

Stewart
Elzey
Trimble

Patton
Taylor

Ewell
(6,500)

8 June 1862
9 June 1862

Remainder of Jackson's army was at
Port Republic facing threat from Shields.

Some of Fremont's Troops
arrived here after battle.

Shields's (15,000)
(Tyler in command.)

Carroll
Winder Scott
Tyler
Ewell

PORT REPUBLIC

JACKSON
(15,000)

Taylor (Ewell)

6,000 Confederates were
engaged in the battle.

Miles

WINCHESTER

BANKS
(11,000)

Ord
(10,000)

McDOWELL
(30,000)

Warrenton

King
(10,000)

(5,000)
Luray

Kimball
Ferry

Tyler
(2,500)

FREMONT
(15,000)
Harrisonburg

Shields
(10,000)

Carroll (2,500)

Doubleday (McDOWELL)

JACKSON
(15,000)

CROSS
KEYS

PORT REPUBLIC

McCall

En route to
Peninsula.

NOTE: Main roads only are shown.

JACKSON'S VALLEY
CAMPAIGN

Situation Night of 7 June 1862,
Battle of Cross Keys, 8 June, and
Battle of Port Republic, 9 June

SCALE

SECOND BULL RUN CAMPAIGN: 1

The Union failures in the Valley campaign, caused by the impossibility of coordinating the different Union commands from Washington, convinced Lincoln that a new organization was needed. On 26 June 1862, he created the Army of Virginia that incorporated the forces of Banks, Fremont, McDowell, and several lesser forces. Its commander would be Pope, one of the more successful generals of the western theater, although junior to all of his corps commanders. Pope was given three objectives: to protect Washington; to ensure the safety of the Shenandoah Valley; and, by operating toward Gordonsville (which was a Confederate railroad hub and therefore vital to Lee), to draw Confederate troops away from Richmond, thus aiding McClellan's operations in the Peninsula.

On 11 July, Lincoln once more returned the direction of all military operations back to the military, and Halleck became general in chief. Pope was directed to remain in Washington until Halleck could assume his new duties. Pope ordered his corps to concentrate east of the Blue Ridge Mountains and left one division to protect Falmouth, which had been established by McDowell before he had moved south. It was probably a wider dispersal of his forces than Pope would have wished.

Halleck, with Lincoln's approval, decided to move the Army of the Potomac—McClellan's army—to Aquia Creek, just north of Falmouth, which at first glance seems open to criticism. Although McClellan seemed to be in a position to threaten Petersburg, the gateway to Richmond, Halleck knew that McClellan was not the man for the job. (It was the same old story; McClellan again wildly overestimated the strength of Lee's force that, in reality, was much smaller than his.)

During July and August 1862, Lee faced a dilemma as perplexing as that facing Halleck. He did not want to be in the Richmond area, but McClellan's presence there dictated he stay. But neither could he sit idly and watch Pope advance south and sever Confederate communication with the Valley and the west. Thus, when he learned on 12 July that Pope had advanced east of the Blue Ridge he immediately dispatched Jackson with two divisions to secure Gordonsville. Lee was always aggressive, and because he occupied a central position between Pope and McClellan, he looked for ways to strike them both. On 27 July, Lee decided to gamble on McClellan's characteristic docility and send A. P. Hill with 12,000 men to join Jackson to attack Pope who, on the 29th, left Washington to unite with McClellan when he came north. Influenced by Halleck's determination to hold the Aquia Landing, Pope moved to Cedar Mountain, from which he could launch cavalry raids against Gordonsville.

About noon on 9 August, Jackson arrived at Cedar Mountain. Banks was sent to delay him while Pope concentrated his forces to attack. In the fighting that followed, Winder was killed and his division badly mauled, and it was only the intervention of A. P. Hill's division that prevented a rout and enabled Jackson to mount a counterattack that drove Banks back across Cedar Creek. At the end of the day, Jackson's advance was stopped by Ricketts's division, which had been hurried forward by Pope.

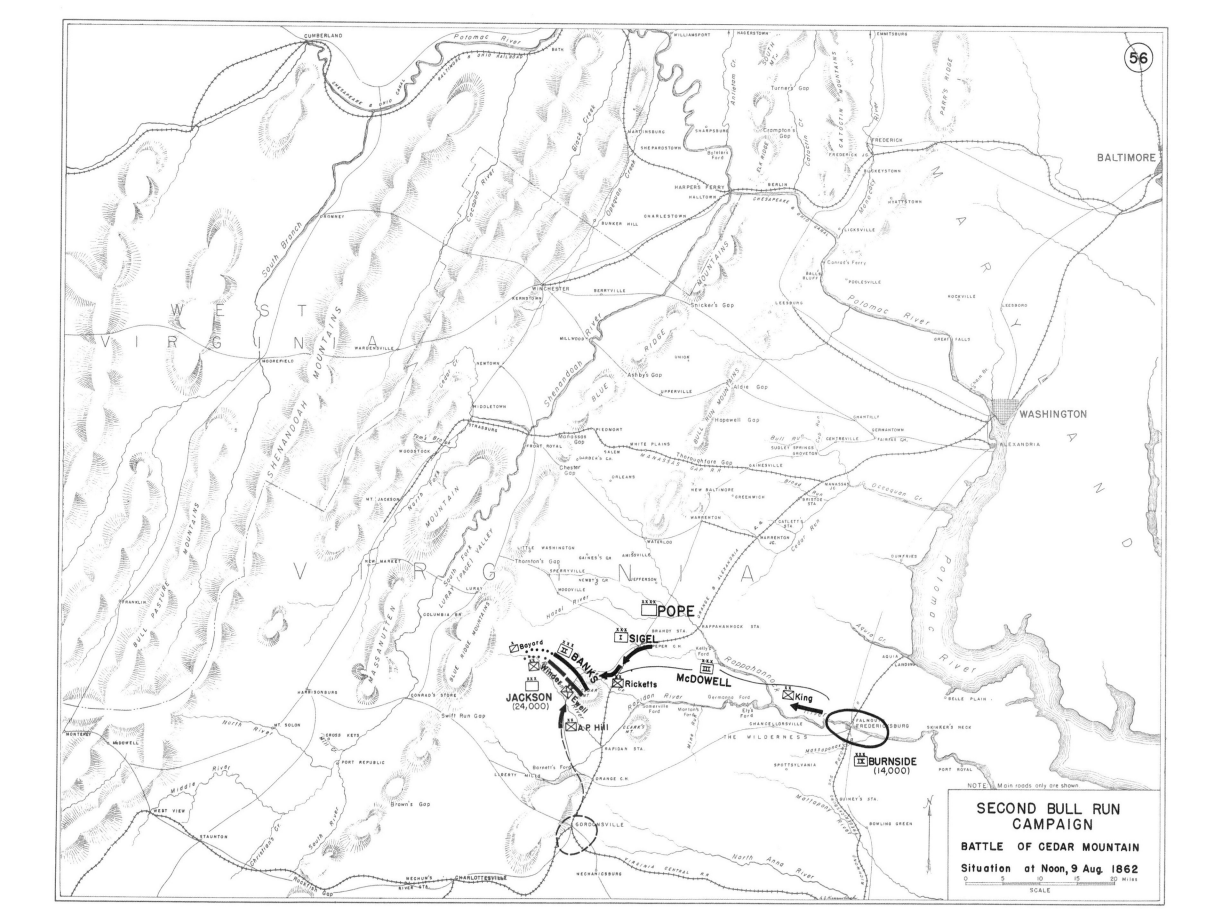

SECOND BULL RUN
CAMPAIGN

BATTLE OF CEDAR MOUNTAIN

Situation at Noon, 9 Aug. 1862

NOTE: Main roads only are shown.

SCALE
0   5   10   15   20 Miles

56

SECOND BULL RUN CAMPAIGN: 2

On 12 August, recognizing Pope's forces were no longer vulnerable to individual attack, Jackson pulled back to Gordonsville. Lee recognized that Jackson needed support and sent Longstreet on 13 August; and the next day, learning of McClellan's recall northward, started all but two brigades up toward Jackson. Lee's primary concern now was to defeat Pope before he could be reinforced by McClellan. Lee arrived at Gordonsville on 15 August and began planning his offensive against Pope. He massed his army behind Clark's Mountain with a view to moving to the Rapidan River, which he planned to cross on the 18th. However, his orders were intercepted by Union troops and Pope drew back northeast across the Rappahannock, pursued by Lee. By 24 August, the two armies faced each other across the river.

Lee, hopeful of cutting off and defeating Pope before he could be reinforced, discussed a new and audacious plan with Jackson. Jackson, with half of the army and Stuart's cavalry, was to move secretly up the Rappahannock, cross it, and then get astride Pope's lines of communication, forcing Pope to retreat. Early on 25 August, Jackson moved north and, by driving his men hard all day, reached Salem that night. At dawn the next day, his cavalry took the Thoroughfare Gap as a conduit for Jackson's army. Learning that the bulk of the Union supplies were at Manassas Junction, Jackson sent Stuart's cavalry and Trimble's brigade to seize it. This same night (26 August), Longstreet was at Orleans, en

route to join Jackson, and McClellan himself arrived in Alexandria. Meanwhile, Pope was aware of Jackson's movements and, on the 26th, sent troops to Waterloo to search out the Confederates, but that night the telegraph lines to Manassas went dead.

The morning of the 27th found Jackson concentrated at Manassas Junction, where his troops enjoyed themselves gorging on the Union stores, but he knew Pope was coming and so prepared a defensive position at Stony Ridge, near Sudley Springs, where he was joined by Ewell and A. P. Hill. Pope had been marching his forces to and fro in search of Jackson, while Jackson had been waiting for an opportunity to attack. At 5:30 P.M. on 28 August, he got his chance when King moved across his front. Ewell and Brig. Gen. William A. Taliaferro led the Confederate assault. The action was fierce but indecisive, with both sides taking heavy casualties. It was here that Brig. Gen. John Gibbon's brigade earned its title of "the Iron Brigade." On the Confederate side, Ewell was wounded and the Stonewall Brigade was reduced to about 400 men.

To the west, Longstreet had arrived at Thoroughfare Gap at 3:00 P.M. Finding his way blocked, he sent troops to force the gap at Hopewell to outflank Ricketts's division. McClellan insisted on keeping Franklin and Sumner at Alexandria despite Halleck's earlier instruction to send them to Pope because, true to form, he believed Jackson had 100,000 men, even though Pope had already told him that Jackson's true strength was 24,000.

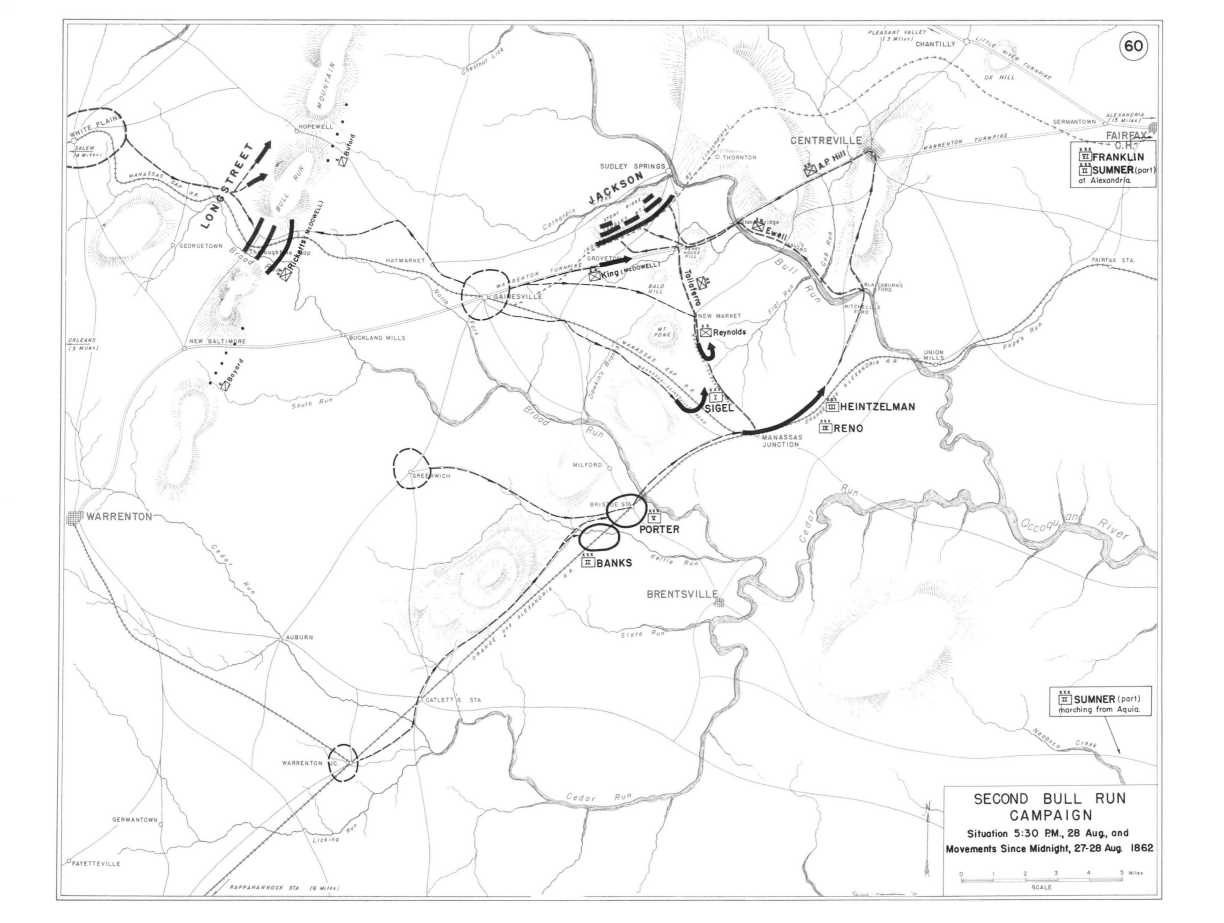

SECOND BULL RUN
CAMPAIGN

Situation 5:30 P.M., 28 Aug., and
Movements Since Midnight, 27-28 Aug. 1862

SECOND BULL RUN CAMPAIGN: 3

By dawn on 29 August, Heintzelman and Maj. Gen. Jesse L. Reno had reached Centreville; Gen. Franz Sigel and Maj. Gen. John F. Reynolds were at Warrenton Turnpike at Henry House Hill; Porter, Banks, and Ricketts were at Bristoe Station, while Brig. Gen. Rufus King was at Manassas Junction. Two cavalry brigades opposed Longstreet's advance.

Late on the night of the 28th, Pope had issued orders for the battle he expected to wage with Jackson the next day. Sigel and Reynolds were to attack at daybreak; Heintzelman and Reno to march to Sigel's support; Porter to move to Centreville, and McDowell to march east from the Gainesville area and join the attack. Pope visualized complete victory, but somehow he had left Longstreet out of the equation. Pope had the idea of attacking Jackson both from the east and west. Longstreet, he calculated, could not be at Gainesville before the 30th, whereas he had already passed through by 9:00 A.M. on the 29th.

McDowell and Porter were told of Longstreet's position by John Buford's cavalry scouts, and discussed which action to take. They could hear artillery fire to the north and see dust clouds to the west. Finally, McDowell, the senior of the two, decided to have Porter continue his march toward Gainesville while he moved his corps through New Market to aid Sigel. Meanwhile, the attack on Jackson from the east had been made as planned, Sigel and Reynolds having assaulted early in the morning and having been joined before noon by Reno and Heintzelman. But Pope's attacks were all frontal, piecemeal, and poorly coordinated, with no attempt to envelop Jackson's flank. Although the Confederate left came

close to breaking, all the Union attacks were beaten back. Longstreet remained inactive nearby, and despite Lee's repeated requests for him to attack Pope's south flank, he stayed in place. Had Lee been more forceful, the Confederates would probably have gained an important victory.

In the meantime, Porter had stopped at Dawkin's Branch, where he came into contact with Stuart's cavalry. Between 5:00 and 6:00 P.M. he received a message from Pope to attack the Confederate right but at the same time to stay in contact with Reynolds. Porter could not obey two contradictory orders but was, nevertheless, later court-martialed and dismissed from the service. It took twenty years for his name to be cleared.

By the morning of the 30th, Pope was convinced that Jackson was withdrawing, but Lee had others ideas. He wanted Longstreet to move around the Union left in an outflanking movement, and when Union attacks put Jackson's right wing under pressure it was Longstreet's enfilading artillery fire that relieved it. Both Lee and Longstreet now perceived the excellent opportunity to strike a decisive blow on Pope's southern flank. Lee ordered the attack and Longstreet set his five divisions in motion. Bald Hill was quickly seized and held, despite counterattacks by Sigel. Pope drew troops from his right to strengthen his left, and this gave an opportunity for Jackson to exploit his northern flank. The Union army was forced back to a position at Henry House (a mirror image of First Bull Run) but Lee could not dislodge them, and Pope made plans to withdraw to Centreville (a replay of First Bull Run).

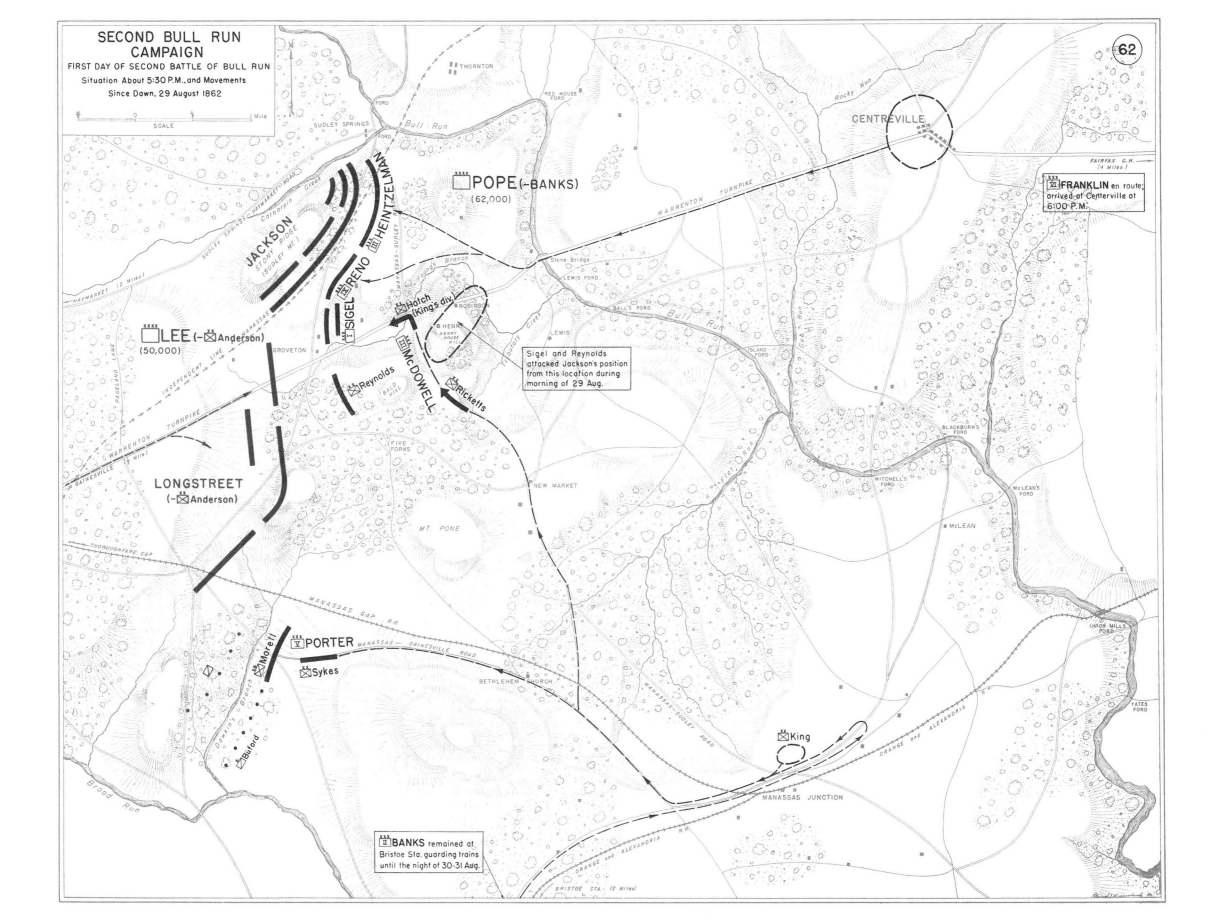

SECOND BULL RUN
CAMPAIGN

FIRST DAY OF SECOND BATTLE OF BULL RUN

Situation About 5:30 P.M., and Movements
Since Dawn, 29 August 1862

SCALE

62

THORNTON

RED HOUSE FORD

SUDLEY SPRINGS
FORD

Bull Run

CENTREVILLE

FAIRFAX C.H.
(4 Miles)

FRANKLIN en route;
arrived at Centreville at
6:00 P.M.

POPE (-BANKS)
(62,000)

WARRENTON   TURNPIKE

JACKSON
STONY RIDGE
(SUDLEY MT.)

Catharpin   Creek

SUDLEY SPRINGS-HAYMARKET ROAD

Stone Bridge

LEWIS FORD

BALL'S FORD

Bull Run

HEINTZELMAN

SIGEL   RENO

Hatch
(King's div.)

ROBINSON

HENRY
HENRY
HOUSE HILL

LEWIS

Young's Branch

MANASSAS-SUDLEY

ISLAND
FORD

LEE (-Anderson)
(50,000)

MANASSAS LINE

GROVETON

McDOWELL

Reynolds
BALD HILL

Ricketts

Catharpin Creek

Sigel and Reynolds
attacked Jackson's position
from this location during
morning of 29 Aug.

BLACKBURN'S
FORD

HAYMARKET (2 Miles)

INDEPENDENT LINE

PAGELAND LANE

WARRENTON   TURNPIKE

GAINESVILLE (1 Mile)

FIVE FORKS

NEW MARKET

MITCHELL'S
FORD

McLEAN'S
FORD

LONGSTREET
(-Anderson)

MT. PONE

McLEAN

THOROUGHFARE GAP

UNION MILLS
FORD

MANASSAS GAP R.R.

Morell   PORTER
Sykes

MANASSAS—GAINESVILLE ROAD

Dawkins Branch

BETHLEHEM CHURCH

MANASSAS-SUDLEY ROAD

YATES
FORD

Buford

King

ORANGE and ALEXANDRIA

Broad Run

MANASSAS JUNCTION

BANKS remained at
Bristoe Sta. guarding trains
until the night of 30-31 Aug.

ORANGE and ALEXANDRIA R.R.

BRISTOE STA. (2 Miles)

SECOND BULL RUN CAMPAIGN: 4

Pope issued his order for withdrawal to Centreville at 7:00 P.M. on 30 August, and the movement began after dark with McDowell's corps providing cover. Sigel's troops, the last to cross Bull Run, destroyed Stone Bridge. By midnight, the bulk of the Union army was in position at Centreville. Lee's men were too exhausted to make an aggressive pursuit.

Banks, who was at Bristoe Station, guarding the Union baggage trains, was ordered to rejoin the main army at Centreville, but since the railroad bridge over Bull Run at Union Mills had been demolished, he was instructed to destroy as much rolling stock as possible and those supplies he could not take with him and cross at Blackburn's Ford—all of which he managed to accomplish without serious interference from the Confederates.

Early on 31 August, Pope sent Halleck a message, saying that he had the gravest doubts that his army could withstand another Confederate attack. But Lee had no intention of trying to cross the swollen Bull Run and attack frontally. Instead, he sent Jackson to the north to get behind the Union position at Centreville. Longstreet remained in position one day to deceive Pope and then followed Jackson. Pope spirits improved when he correctly predicted Lee's intentions and he told Halleck he felt confident of coping with it. However, McClellan, at Alexandria, was in his usual nervous state and tried to get Halleck to authorize a general retreat to Washington. Halleck instead held Pope at Centreville.

Early on 1 September, Pope (who was again entertaining doubts about his ability to hold) ordered Sumner to go on a reconnoiter north of Centreville. At noon he sent McDow-ell to occupy Germantown and two brigades of IX Corps under Maj. Gen. Isaac I. Stevens to Chantilly to block Jackson. Stevens was later joined by Gen. Philip Kearny's division. That same morning, Jackson had started from Pleasant Valley toward Fairfax Court House, but his troops were hungry and almost exhausted from nearly seven days of marching and fighting. By the middle of the afternoon, they had advanced only three miles, and then they encountered Stevens's troops. The battle of Chantilly followed, and continued until dark. The Confederates attacked several times but, though outnumbering the defenders, were repulsed. Both Stevens and Kearny were killed. That night, Longstreet arrived to relieve Jackson's troops and the Union force retired to Germantown and Fairfax Court House. In the morning, Pope again wired Halleck, recommending withdrawal, and was given permission to move into the fortifications of Washington.

So ended the second Bull Run campaign. Lee, bold to the extreme, had outmaneuvered his opponents and won a notable victory. The Union, plagued with divided command problems and Pope's misconceptions at critical times, found its army practically besieged in Washington and the country threatened with invasion. Lee's victory, however, had not been without cost—he had suffered about 9,197 casualties while inflicting some 16,054 on his opponents.

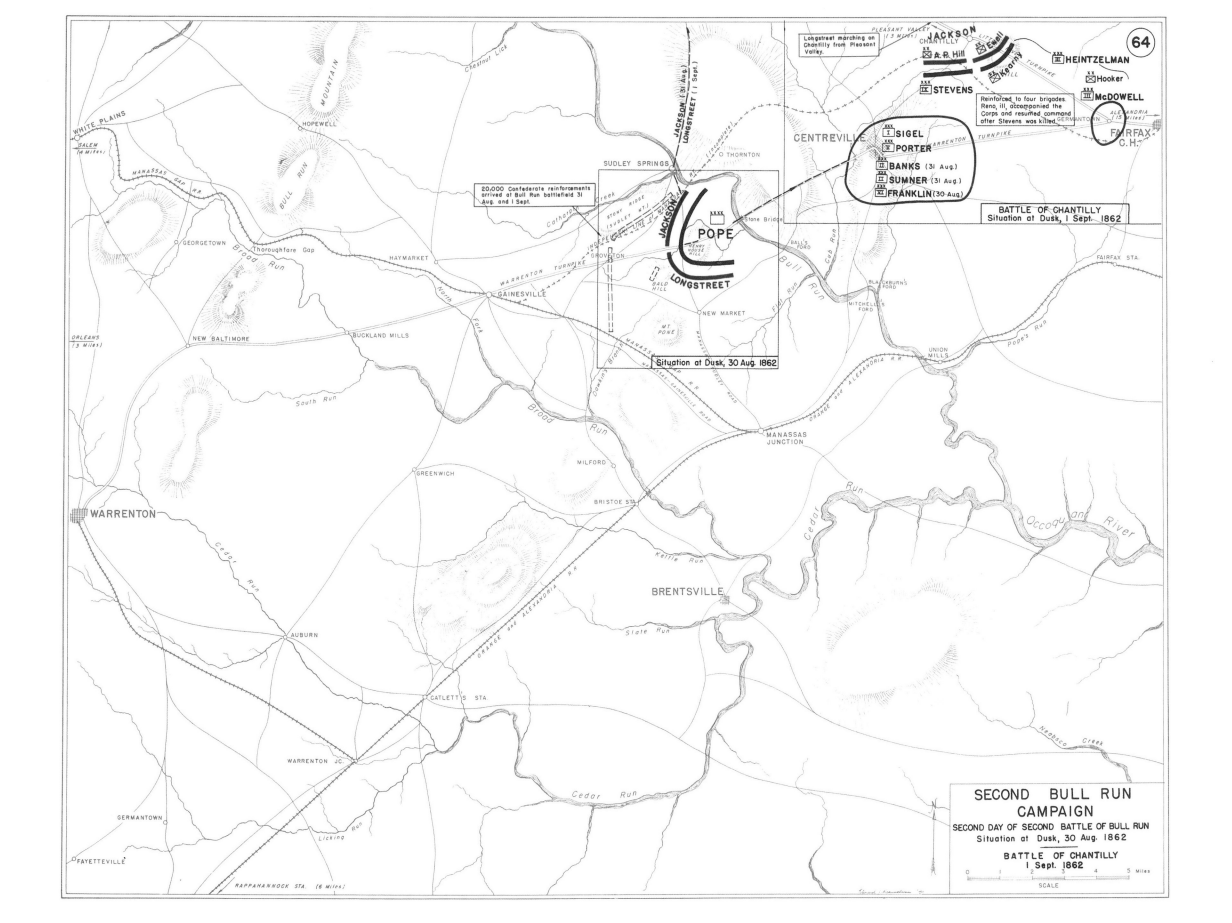

64

Longstreet marching on
Chantilly from Pleasant
Valley.

PLEASANT VALLEY
(3 Miles)
JACKSON
CHANTILLY
Ewell
A.P. Hill
Kearny
HEINTZELMAN
Hooker
STEVENS
McDOWELL
ALEXANDRIA
(15 Miles)

Reinforced to four brigades.
Reno, ill, accompanied the
Corps and resumed command
after Stevens was killed.

CENTREVILLE
FAIRFAX
C.H.

ALEXANDRIA
(15 Miles)

WARRENTON TURNPIKE

SIGEL
PORTER
BANKS (31 Aug.)
SUMNER (31 Aug.)
FRANKLIN (30 Aug.)

BATTLE OF CHANTILLY
Situation at Dusk, 1 Sept. 1862

SUDLEY SPRINGS

20,000 Confederate reinforcements
arrived at Bull Run battlefield 31
Aug. and 1 Sept.

Catharpin Creek
STONY RIDGE
(SUDLEY MT.)
JACKSON
POPE
HENRY
HOUSE
HILL
Stone Bridge
BALL'S
FORD
Cub Run

WHITE PLAINS

SALEM
(4 Miles)

MANASSAS GAP R.R.
BULL RUN

HOPEWELL

CHESTNUT LICK

O THORNTON

BLACKBURN'S
FORD
MITCHELL'S
FORD

GEORGETOWN

Thoroughfare Gap

Broad Run

HAYMARKET

Warrenton Turnpike

GROVETON

BALD
HILL

LONGSTREET

NEW MARKET

MT.
PONE

Bull Run

Situation at Dusk, 30 Aug. 1862

UNION
MILLS

FAIRFAX STA.

ORLEANS
(3 Miles)

NEW BALTIMORE

BUCKLAND MILLS

GAINESVILLE

North Fork

Dawkin's Branch

MANASSAS

MANASSAS-GAINESVILLE ROAD

MANASSAS GAP R.R.

South Run

Broad Run

MANASSAS
JUNCTION

ORANGE and ALEXANDRIA R.R.

Pope's Run

Occoquan River

WARRENTON

Cedar Run

GREENWICH

MILFORD

BRISTOE STA.

Kettle Run

BRENTSVILLE

Cedar Run

Slate Run

CATLETT'S STA.

ORANGE and ALEXANDRIA R.R.

WARRENTON JC.

Neabsco Creek

GERMANTOWN

Licking Run

Cedar Run

FAYETTEVILLE

RAPPAHANNOCK STA. (6 Miles)

SECOND BULL RUN
CAMPAIGN
SECOND DAY OF SECOND BATTLE OF BULL RUN
Situation at Dusk, 30 Aug. 1862

BATTLE OF CHANTILLY
1 Sept. 1862

0   1   2   3   4   5 Miles

SCALE

ANTIETAM CAMPAIGN: 1

After Chantilly, confusion reigned in the Union camp. Halleck refused to accept any responsibility; Pope wanted to reorganize, move out again, and fight; and McClellan sent his wife's silver to safety! Nevertheless, McClellan still maintained the confidence of his fellow officers and men, and so Lincoln made Pope's Army of Virginia part of McClellan's Army of the Potomac and sent Pope to command the Northwest Department. McClellan did a good job reorganizing (it was probably his best period of the war and made the best use of his bureaucratic talents).

Meanwhile, screened to the east by Stuart's cavalry, Lee began crossing the Potomac on 4 September 1862, and by the 7th was concentrated around Frederick, Maryland. A number of reasons led him to risk this invasion: the need to retain the initiative, the chance of winning foreign recognition for the Confederacy, the chance of sparking revolt in Maryland, and the desire to protect Virginia. His plan was opportunistic and vague—he would strike toward Harrisburg, Pennsylvania, and cut the North's major east–west railroads, then consider operations against Philadelphia, Baltimore, or Washington.

Lee's invasion, though, produced problems for the Confederates. Maryland did not rise, the hard northern roads crippled the feet of the shoeless soldiery, supplies of all sorts were lacking, and the men lived on green corn and developed diarrhea. But in morale and leadership, Lee's army was still formidable, and Lee again banked on McClellan's passivity, as he had done at Richmond.

On 6 September, McClellan began a slow northward move, and as usual overestimated the size of Lee's army fantastically. By the 13th, he had reached Frederick, where he was handed a captured copy of Lee's entire plan of operations; but he delayed sixteen hours before putting his troops in motion. On the night of the 13th, Burnside was ordered toward Turner's Gap, and Franklin toward Crampton's Gap.

Through a spy Lee learned that McClellan knew of his plans so, on 14 September, he started D. H. Hill and Longstreet to block Turner's Gap. Hill arrived in time to block Burnside. The Union attack in the ensuing engagement (battle of South Mountain) was conducted cautiously, again because McClellan had overestimated Confederate strength. Longstreet arrived to support Hill and heavy fighting continued into the night. Finally, the Confederates, roughly handled and enveloped on both flanks, left the field. Meanwhile, to the south, Franklin proceeded on his mission to seize Crampton's Gap and relieve Harper's Ferry, but after an initial success against Maj. Gen Lafayette McLaws, he was fooled by McLaws into thinking he faced a more formidable opponent than he actually did, and so stopped to consider the situation. While he pondered, the Confederates began bombarding Harper's Ferry (surrounded by hills, it was virtually indefensible), and its commander, Col. Miles, surrendered at 9:00 A.M. on 15 September 1862 (shortly afterward, he was mortally wounded by an artillery shell).

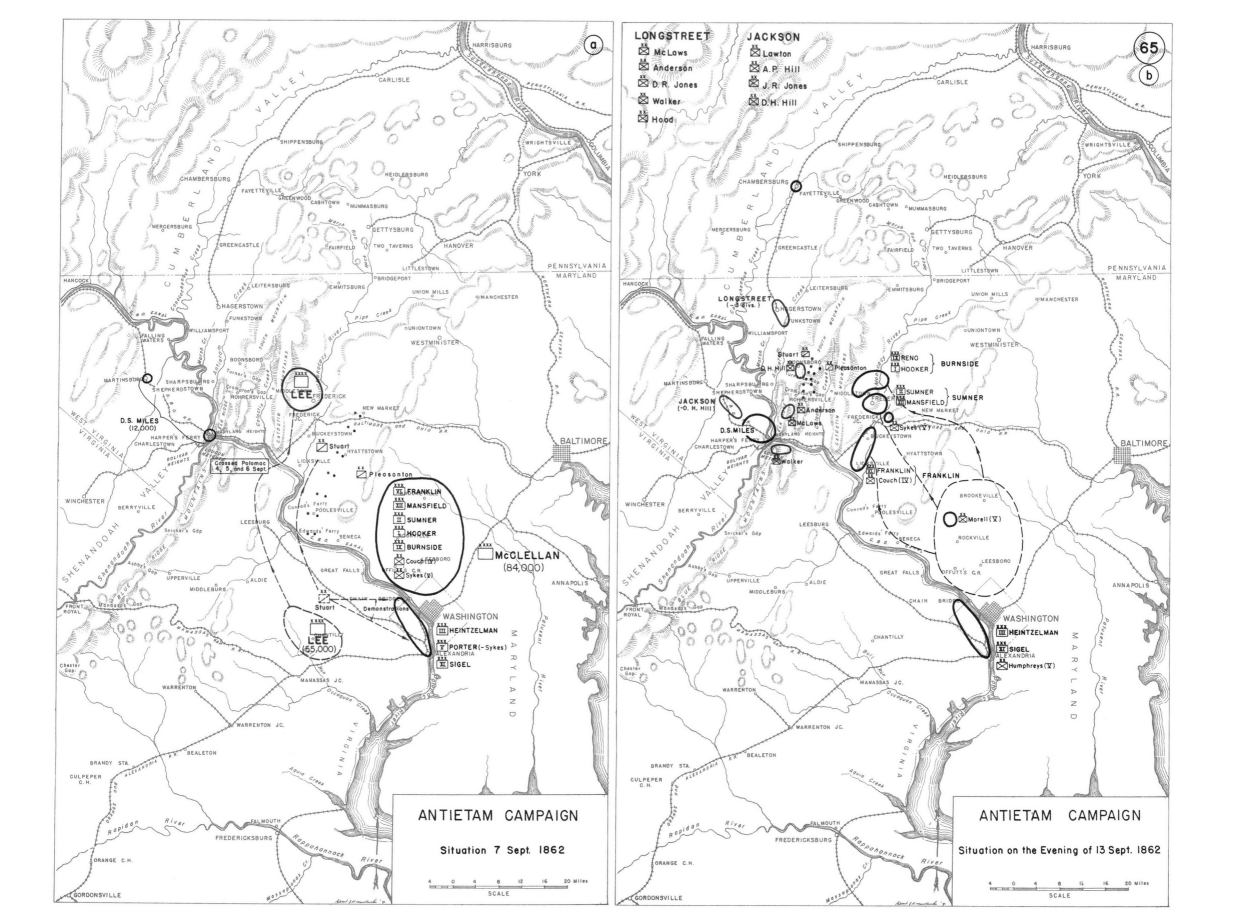

LONGSTREET
- McLaws
- Anderson
- D. R. Jones
- Walker
- Hood

JACKSON
- Lawton
- A. P. Hill
- J. R. Jones
- D. H. Hill

LEE

D.S. MILES
(12,000)

Crossed Potomac
4, 5, and 6 Sept.

Stuart

Pleasonton

FRANKLIN
MANSFIELD
SUMNER
HOOKER
BURNSIDE
Couch (IV)
Sykes (V)

McCLELLAN
(84,000)

Stuart
Demonstrations

LEE
(55,000)

WASHINGTON
HEINTZELMAN
PORTER (-Sykes)
SIGEL

ANTIETAM CAMPAIGN

Situation 7 Sept. 1862

LONGSTREET
(-3 Divs.)

Stuart
D. H. Hill
Pleasonton

RENO
HOOKER
BURNSIDE

SUMNER
MANSFIELD
SUMNER

JACKSON
(-D. H. Hill)

Anderson
McLaws

D.S. MILES

Sykes (V)

Walker

FRANKLIN
Couch (IV)
FRANKLIN

Morell (V)

BROOKEVILLE

ROCKVILLE

LEESBORO

WASHINGTON
HEINTZELMAN
SIGEL
Humphreys (V)

ANTIETAM CAMPAIGN

Situation on the Evening of 13 Sept. 1862

ANTIETAM CAMPAIGN: 2

Having lost the South Mountain passes, Lee planned to withdraw through Sharpsburg to the south bank of the Potomac and concentrate his forces there before McClellan could crush them in detail. McLaws was instructed to abandon Maryland Heights and likewise move south of the river. But when Jackson reported that Harper's Ferry might soon fall, Lee decided to halt temporarily at Sharpsburg. Then, once he learned that Jackson had indeed captured Harper's Ferry and was moving to rejoin him, his natural combativeness reasserted itself and he immediately took up position behind Antietam Creek and waited for McClellan.

The position was shallow and only moderately strong; Lee could retreat or receive reinforcements via Boteler's Ford, which was deep, rocky, and to the extreme of the Confederate line. Another major weakness of the position was that high ground along the east bank of Antietam Creek was of limited value as an obstacle, except below the Middle Bridge where its west bank was steep and rugged. In addition to the four bridges across it, there were several regular fords and, at this season, it could be waded in many other places. Lee failed to strengthen his line with field fortifications, but numerous irregularities in the ground and several small woods gave his troops considerable shelter.

McClellan's main body (Franklin had been left at Rohrersville to cover Harper's Ferry) arrived at the position shown during the early afternoon of 15 September. McClellan, however, thought it was too late in the day to launch an attack, and he spent the next day skirmishing and drawing up plans, although a determined attack, given his superior numbers, would have crushed the little force Lee had with him. Later in the day, Jackson and Walker rejoined Lee, and Maj. Gen. Richard H. Anderson and McLaws were prepared to follow. A. P. Hill remained at Harper's Ferry.

Eventually McClellan decided on left and right flanking attacks, but he made no effective reconnaissance of Lee's exact position or the points at which Antietam Creek could be forded.

In accordance with his plan, McClellan sent Hooker's corps across the Upper Bridge and a nearby ford on the afternoon of the 16th to get into position for the attack the next morning. Naturally, the movement was discovered and Gen. John B. Hood was sent to block it. After some brisk skirmishing, Hood was withdrawn and Hooker went into bivouac.

As soon as there was enough light on the morning of the 17th, Hooker delivered a powerful assault against Lee's left; Jackson's line gave way in heavy fighting but did not break. A savage counterattack by Hood and enfilading fire from Stuart's battery helped to check the Union attack. However, Confederate losses were heavy. Maj. Gen. Joseph K. Mansfield brought the XII Corps forward, but he was killed almost immediately, and shortly afterward, Hooker was wounded.

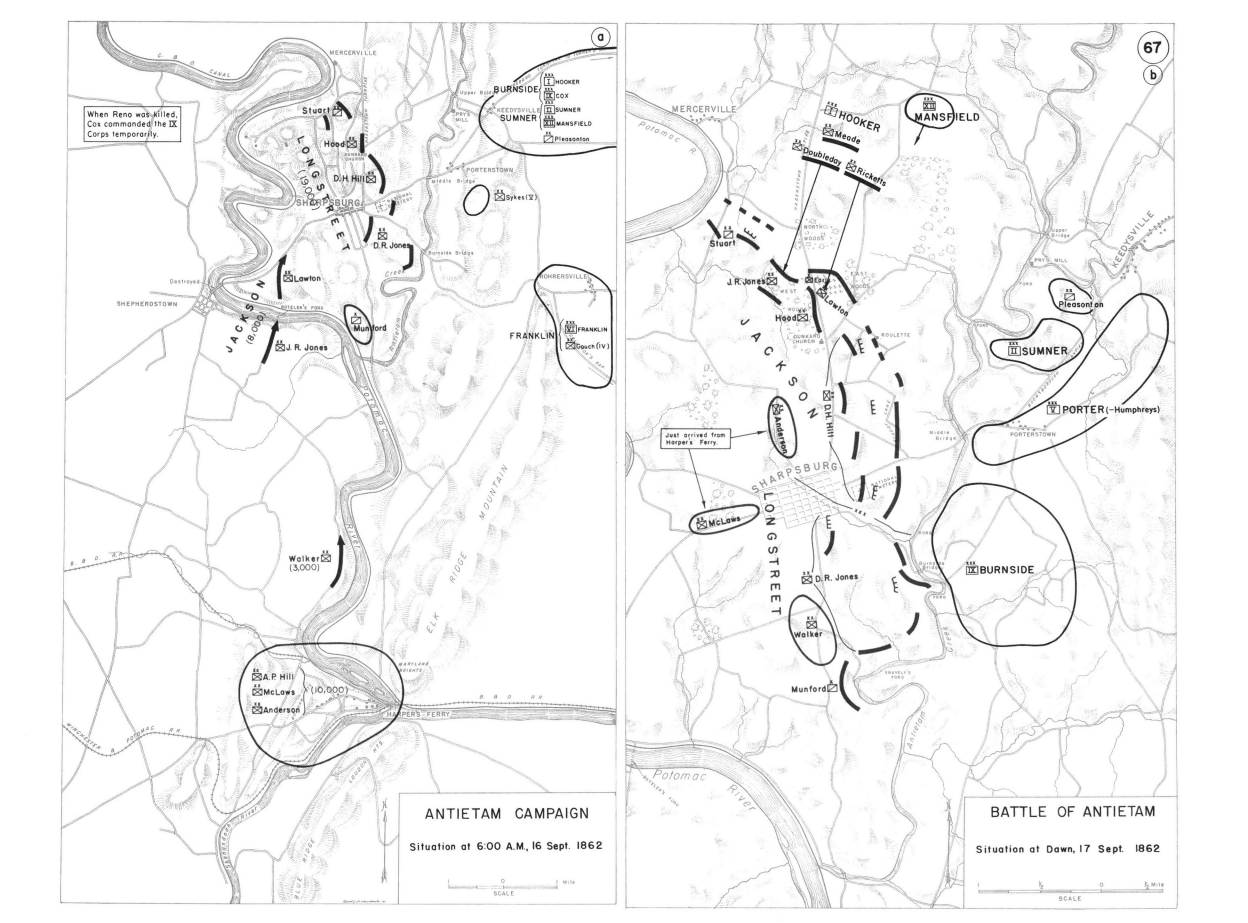

Map a

When Reno was killed, Cox commanded the IX Corps temporarily.

BURNSIDE
I HOOKER
IX COX
SUMNER
II SUMNER
XII MANSFIELD
Pleasonton

Stuart
Hood
D.H. Hill
SHARPSBURG
LONGSTREET (9,000)
D.R. Jones
Sykes (V)
Lawton
JACKSON (8,000)
Munford
J. R. Jones

FRANKLIN
VI FRANKLIN
Couch (IV)

Walker (3,000)

A.P. Hill
McLaws (10,000)
Anderson
HARPER'S FERRY

ANTIETAM CAMPAIGN

Situation at 6:00 A.M., 16 Sept. 1862

SCALE

67

Map b

MERCERVILLE

I HOOKER
XII MANSFIELD
Meade
Doubleday
Ricketts

Stuart
J. R. Jones
Early
Lawton
Hood
JACKSON
D.H. Hill

Anderson
Just arrived from Harper's Ferry.
McLaws

SHARPSBURG
LONGSTREET

Pleasonton
II SUMNER
V PORTER (-Humphreys)

D. R. Jones
Walker
Munford

IX BURNSIDE

BATTLE OF ANTIETAM

Situation at Dawn, 17 Sept. 1862

SCALE

ANTIETAM CAMPAIGN: 3

The loss of two fighting corps commanders, Hooker and Mansfield, left no one in overall control of McClellan's "main attack" on the Confederate left. Gen. George Gordon Meade rallied the remnants of the I Corps near North Woods, while the XII Corps division commanders, Brig. Gen. Alpheus Williams and Brig. Gen. George S. Greene, pressed the attack. They completed the shattering of the Confederate left and forced it back beyond the Dunkard Church and West Woods. Soon Williams had to withdraw his division to rest and replenish ammunition, but Greene clung to the Dunkard Church and part of the woods around it.

Sumner had been alerted the previous evening to be ready for action early the next morning, and he moved out with his II Corps, himself riding with Sedgwick's leading division. Flung into the action in column formation, it was soon trapped by Confederate troops sent forward by Jackson in a hasty counterattack from three directions. With the advantage of position and surprise, the outnumbered Confederates drove Sedgwick back in disorder with the loss of about 2,200 men. The Confederates pressed the pursuit and almost regained the ground lost earlier in the morning, until they were finally stopped by strong Union artillery fire. When Sedgwick's division left the field, he exposed Greene's right flank and forced him also to retire.

The second division of Sumner's corps, Brig. Gen. William H. French, had somehow missed the road taken by Sedgwick and so came into the line further south, against the left of Lee's center, where it became embroiled in a savage fight against D. H. Hill. Sumner's last division, that of Maj. Gen. Richardson, arrived later on French's left after having been delayed for an hour by McClellan. Together, the two divisions forced the Confederates back into the sunken, trenchlike Bloody Lane, which became the epicenter of carnage. Eventually Union forces managed to bring enfilading fire down the length of the lane, which forced the Confederates to flee.

Lee's artillery, though fighting gamely, had been overwhelmed by the expertly handled Union batteries. Sharpsburg was filled with demoralized Confederate soldiers, and famous commands, such as Hood's Texans, were completely shattered. Most of the left and center was held only by devoted handfuls, hanging on out of sheer courage. One more Federal attack and Lee's Army of North Virginia would have faced destruction. Meanwhile, on the Union left flank, Burnside started his attack on the Confederate right at 10:00 A.M., and Richardson drove the Confederates from the hills to the south of Bloody Lane, completely wrecking Lee's center, but McClellan forbade any further advances.

Further south, Burnside had failed to scout for alternative crossings of Antietam Creek and therefore funneled his men over the bridge that now bears his name, and it was not until the third bloody attempt that the bridge was taken. By 3:00 P.M., Burnside's IX Corps was deployed across the creek and, by 4:00 P.M., it had gained almost all of the high ground to the east and south of Sharpsburg; but they were struck in flank by A. P. Hill and driven back to the ridges along the creek. There the battle ended and Lee withdrew, although one determined drive by McClellan toward Boteler's Ford might well have trapped Lee up against the Potomac. But McClellan remained idle all day. Total Confederate casualties were about 10,318 (27 percent of his force); Union, 12,410 (16.4 percent).

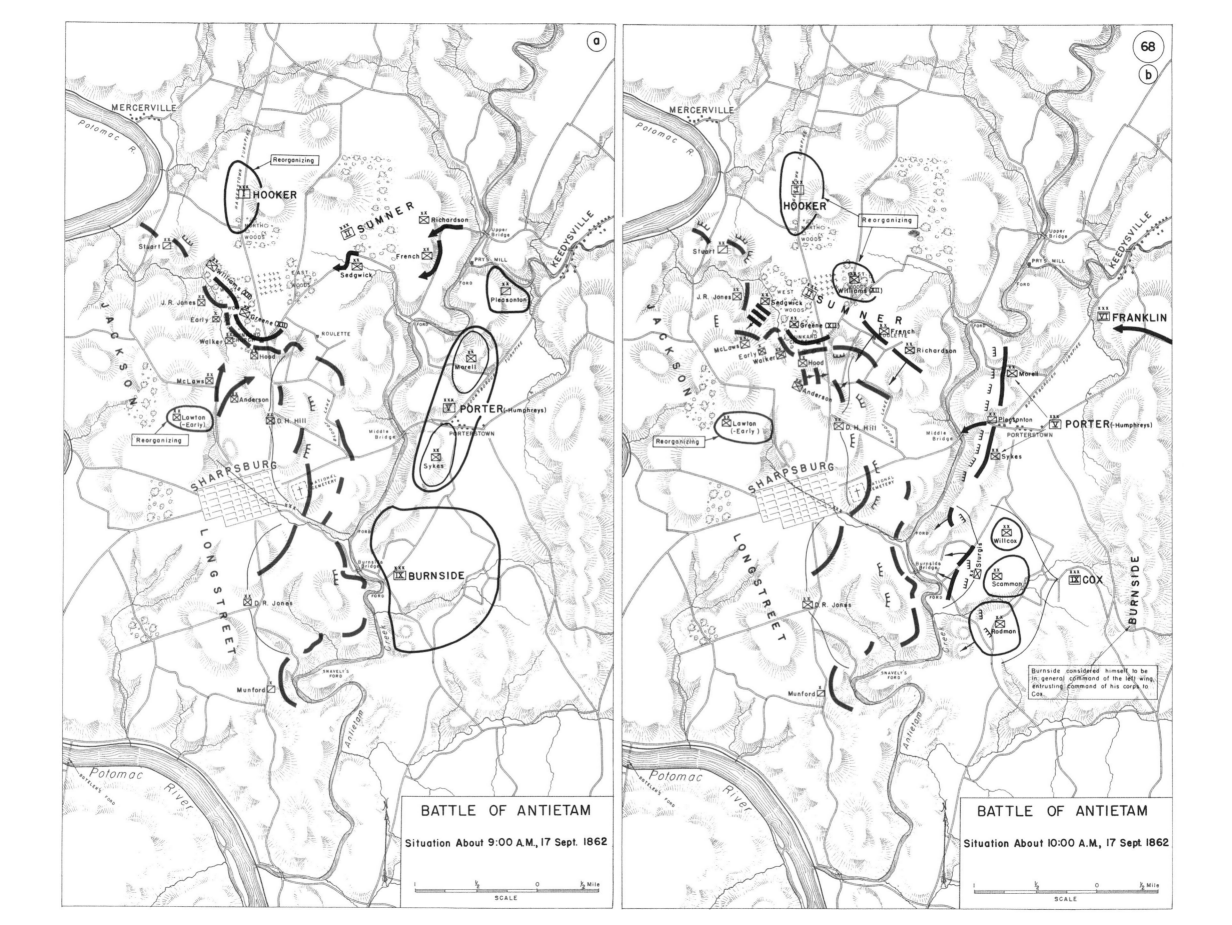

a

MERCERVILLE

Potomac R.

Reorganizing

□ HOOKER

Stuart ⊠

II SUMNER

⊠ Richardson

Upper Bridge

French ⊠

PRY'S MILL

KEEDYSVILLE

Williams XII ⊠

J.R. Jones ⊠

EAST WOODS

Sedgwick ⊠

FORD

⊠ Pleasonton

Early ⊠

Greene XII ⊠

ROULETTE

Walker ⊠

Hood ⊠

⊠ Morell

McLaws ⊠

⊠ Anderson

V PORTER (-Humphreys)

JACKSON

Lawton (-Early) ⊠

⊠ D.H. Hill

Middle Bridge

PORTERSTOWN

Reorganizing

⊠ Sykes

SHARPSBURG

NATIONAL CEMETERY

LONGSTREET

FORD

Burns Bridge

IX BURNSIDE

⊠ D.R. Jones

FORD

SNAVELY'S FORD

Munford ⊠

Potomac River

BATTLE OF ANTIETAM

Situation About 9:00 A.M., 17 Sept. 1862

SCALE

b

MERCERVILLE

Potomac R.

□ HOOKER

Reorganizing

Stuart ⊠

II SUMNER

WEST WOODS

Williams XII ⊠

Upper Bridge

PRY'S MILL

KEEDYSVILLE

VI FRANKLIN

J.R. Jones ⊠

Sedgwick ⊠

Greene XII ⊠

French ⊠

McLaws ⊠

DUNKARD

⊠ Richardson

Early ⊠

Walker ⊠

Hood ⊠

⊠ Morell

JACKSON

⊠ Anderson

⊠ D.H. Hill

Pleasonton ⊠

V PORTER (-Humphreys)

Lawton (-Early) ⊠

Reorganizing

Middle Bridge

PORTERSTOWN

⊠ Sykes

SHARPSBURG

NATIONAL CEMETERY

LONGSTREET

FORD

⊠ Willcox

Burnside Bridge

⊠ Scammon

IX COX

FORD

⊠ Rodman

BURNSIDE

⊠ D.R. Jones

SNAVELY'S FORD

Munford ⊠

Potomac River

Burnside considered himself to be in general command of the left wing, entrusting command of his corps to Cox.

BATTLE OF ANTIETAM

Situation About 10:00 A.M., 17 Sept. 1862

SCALE

FREDERICKSBURG CAMPAIGN: 1

After his withdrawal from Antietam, Lee moved his battered army west to Opequan Creek and, by November 1862, its strength had risen to 85,000 (McClellan, also reinforced, had 120,000). Confederate discipline tightened and the army was organized for the first time into permanent corps. Meanwhile, McClellan sat north of the Potomac and feuded by telegraph with Halleck, frittering away the good campaigning weather of October. In the west, Bragg's invasion of Kentucky made a brief sensation before it ebbed, and Gen. William S. Rosencrans gained successes at Iuka and Corinth.

There were only minor interruptions of the peace along the Potomac. The irrepressible Stuart led a 1,500-cavalry unit right around McClellan's army. It was great theater, but militarily not too useful except to boost morale. By late October 1862, McClellan decided to advance on Warrenton, east of the Blue Ridge Mountains, leaving the XII Corps at Harper's Ferry and Morell's division to guard the upper Potomac. It took McClellan from 26 October until 2 November for his army to cross the river, and then it moved slowly south. Lee countered by dividing his army, again leaving Jackson in the Shenandoah Valley, while he himself retired deliberately and slowly before McClellan. In the late evening of 7 November, McClellan received a War Department order directing that he hand over his command to Burnside.

Burnside was a loyal and dedicated soldier who, unlike McClellan, had no interest in politics. On 9 November, Burnside transmitted his plan of operations to Halleck. He proposed concentrating on Warrenton as if for an attack on either Culpeper or Gordonsville. Then he was going to shift to Fredericksburg with a view to moving on Richmond. An advance through Fredericksburg, though it would have wider rivers to cross, would be easier to support logistically, since Burnside could use Aquia Creek, which was at the end of a secure line of water transportation from Washington.

On 25 November, the first pontoons arrived for the crossing of the Rappahannock but the moment had passed, for, on the 21st, Longstreet's corps had arrived at Fredericksburg, and Jackson would join him on the 30th. Lee had not had not overlooked the possibility of Burnside's march to Fredericksburg, but he had been surprised by the speed with which it was carried out. At first he thought of making a stand behind the North Anna River, but when Burnside delayed his crossing, Lee moved directly to Fredericksburg.

Still, Burnside had one more opportunity. Longstreet was at Fredericksburg, but Jackson could not possibly join him for several days. A swift march back up the Rappahannock would have enabled Burnside to place his entire army between the two Confederate corps. But Burnside's thoughts were focused on Richmond, rather than his true objective—Lee's army.

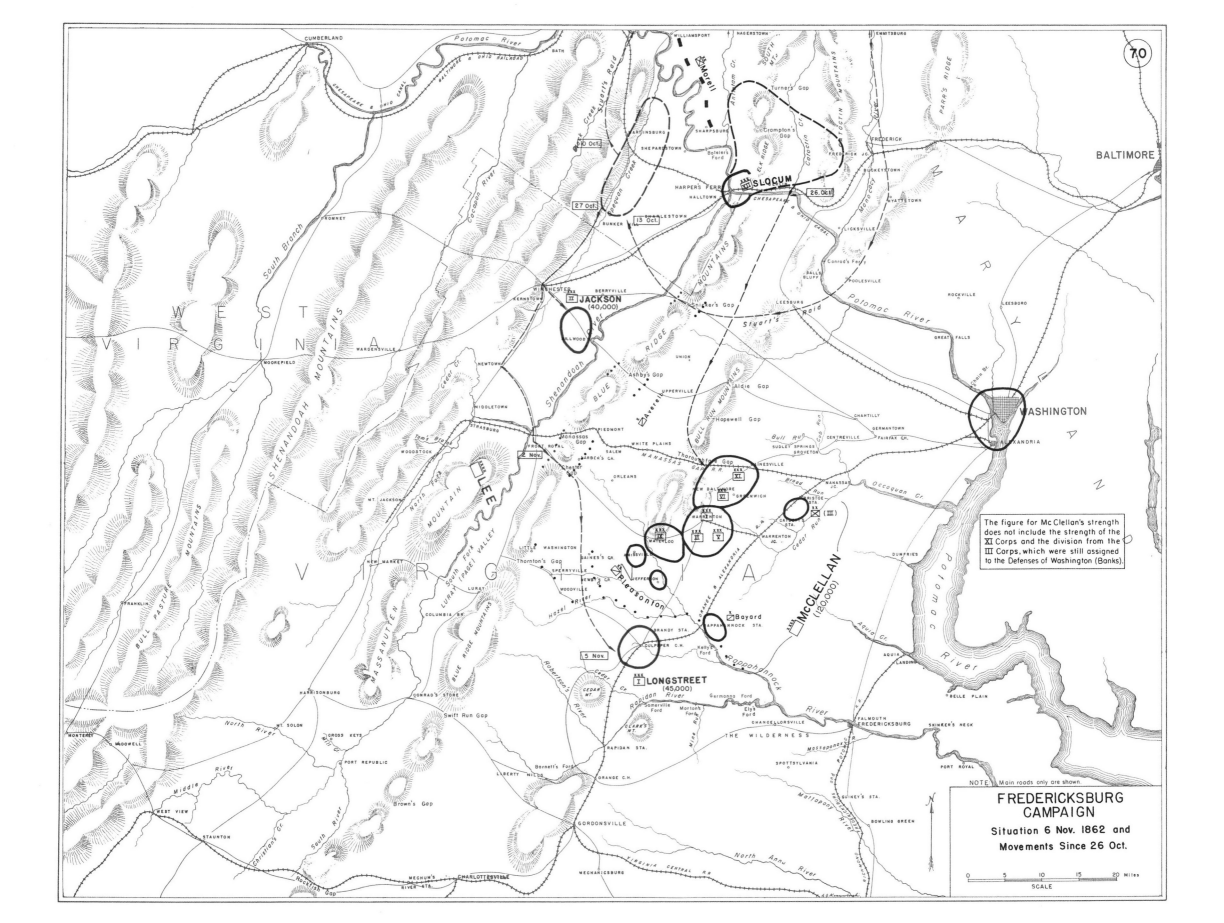

FREDERICKSBURG
CAMPAIGN

Situation 6 Nov. 1862 and
Movements Since 26 Oct.

The figure for McClellan's strength
does not include the strength of the
XI Corps and the division from the
III Corps, which were still assigned
to the Defenses of Washington (Banks).

NOTE: Main roads only are shown.

FREDERICKSBURG CAMPAIGN: 2

With insufficient pontoons to cross his whole army, Burnside had to delay his intended crossing and was now confronted by the whole Confederate army. Again, as at Antietam, he failed to scout Lee's positions aggressively, depending instead on balloon observation, which was ineffective in such wooded countryside.

The Union crossings began on the night of 10 December, and on the Union left met with little opposition. At Fredericksburg, Brig. Gen. William Barksdale's Mississippians, firing from houses along the river, repeatedly stopped the bridge-building, and even Union artillery fire failed to dislodge the sharpshooters. Eventually, Union volunteers crossed in boats and cleared the town. By then it was almost dark and Burnside suspended operations for the day.

On 12 December, Burnside's orders were for Franklin and Hooker to make the main attack, while Sumner would make a secondary attack on Marye's Heights. Between them, it was hoped, they could push the Confederates off the ridge overlooking the town. The attack on Franklin's front was spearheaded by Meade's division. It drove forward through a weak spot and routed Brig. Gen. Maxcy Gregg's brigade in the Confederate second line. Jackson attempted a counterattack, but halted it when it brought down a storm of Union artillery fire. On Sumner's front the attack was made at 11:00 A.M. by French's division, followed in quick succession by those of Hancock, Howard, and Gen. John Sturgis, but by 1:30 P.M. they had all been beaten back with heavy losses.

After Jackson's abortive counterattack, Franklin remained inactive despite at least one direct order to attack with his full force, and on the Union right the initial attack had been delayed until 11:00 A.M., due to fog. When it lifted, the Union troops in Fredericksburg came under intense artillery fire, to which their own artillery could not respond because it was too far away. The Union advance had to be made across an open plain, cut by a steep-banked drainage ditch some thirty feet wide and six deep. At the foot of Marye's Hill, a sunken road with stone retaining walls on either side formed a natural trench for Confederate riflemen.

Burnside now called on Hooker to resume the assault on Marye's Hill, and on Franklin to attack on his front. Lee had already taken advantage of Franklin's inactivity to shift Pickett's division and one of Hood's brigades to Marye's Hill. Griffin's and Brig. Gen. Andrew Atkinson Humphreys' divisions made their attacks at 3:30 and 4:00 P.M. respectively, and met the same bloody fate as those who had preceded them. Gen. George W. Getty was also repulsed, and Hooker decided to suspend the assault and withdraw his troops. And although Burnside wanted to renew the attack the next morning he was dissuaded by his grand division commanders. Both sides stood off each other on the 14th, and although Lee hoped Burnside would again batter his army against the impregnable Confederate positions, Burnside skillfully withdrew back across the river during the night. All the Union troops and supplies (down to the last foot of telegraph wire) got across, and the pontoon bridges were taken up undetected.

The Confederate casualties were about 5,580, whereas the Federals suffered 12,600, of whom about 6,300 occurred at the foot of Marye's Hill. On 25 January, Lincoln relieved Burnside, Sumner, and Franklin, and gave command of the Army of the Potomac to Hooker.

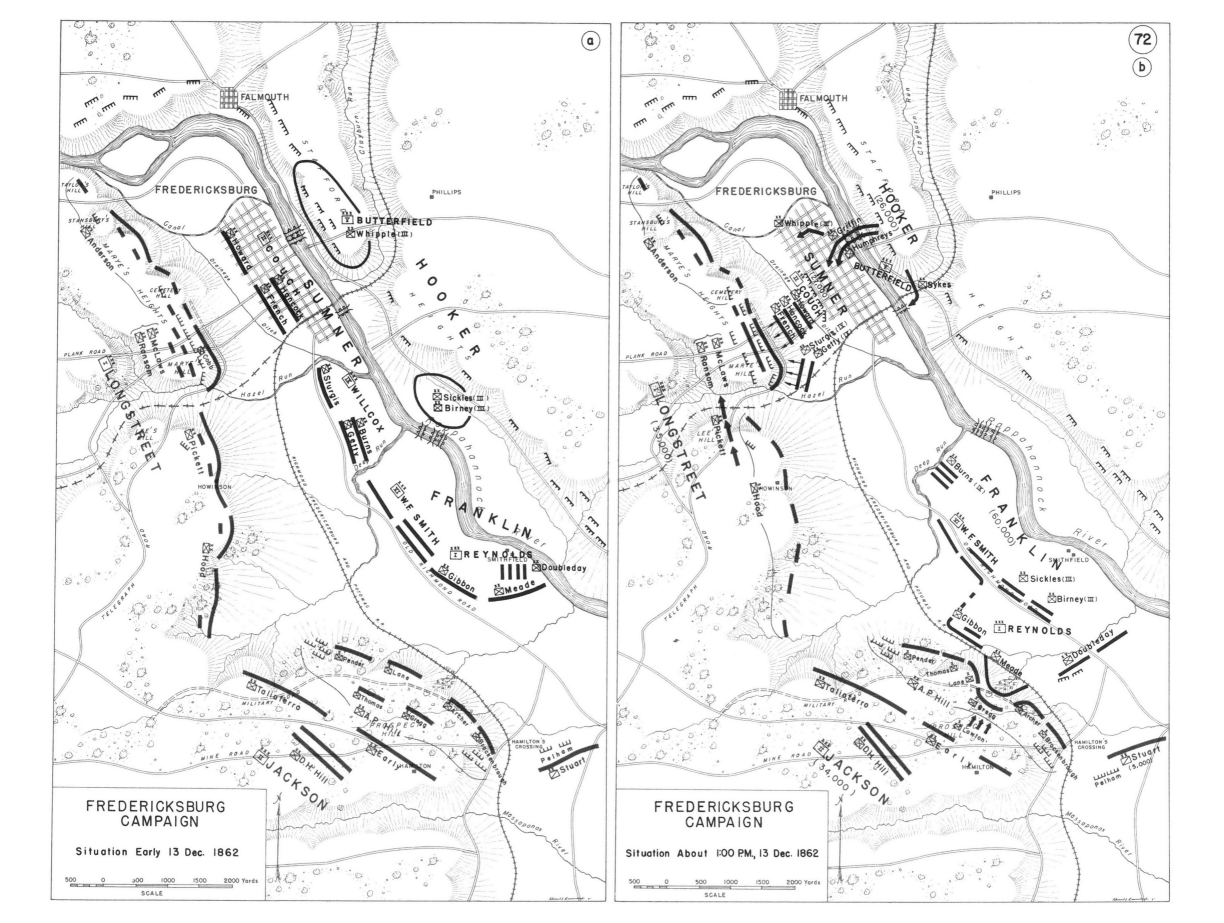

FREDERICKSBURG
CAMPAIGN

Situation Early 13 Dec. 1862

FREDERICKSBURG
CAMPAIGN

Situation About 1:00 P.M., 13 Dec. 1862

STONES RIVER CAMPAIGN: 1

After the battle of Shiloh (6–7 April 1862), Halleck moved his headquarters to Pittsburg Landing and began concentrating his forces. To the south, at Corinth, Beauregard likewise was summoning all available reinforcements, including troops from Arkansas under Maj. Gen. Sterling Price and Maj. Gen. Earl Van Dorn.

Halleck reorganized his army into a right wing, under Thomas (now a major general); a center, under Buell; a left wing, under Pope; and a reserve, under McClernand. Grant he appointed his second in command, and thereafter ignored him. Then, on 30 April 1862, his army began its advance to the railroad hub of Corinth. The twenty miles took him a month of deliberate and inexorable progress. Corinth was heavily fortified and formed a strong defensive position. Nevertheless, Beauregard wisely chose not to risk a battle that would most likely have seen him shut up in the city. Covering his actions with an elaborate program of deception, he steadily evacuated his troops and supplies and marched safely to Tupelo. But Jefferson Davis was furious over yet another Confederate withdrawal in the west, and Beauregard resigned his command and handed it over to Bragg.

Halleck now dispersed his own army. On 10 June, Buell was sent east to take Chattanooga; Sherman was sent to Memphis (already captured by naval forces); Pope held a covering position south of Corinth; and one division was sent as reinforcements to Arkansas. But Halleck was recalled to Washington to serve as general in chief, and so his command was split between Buell and Grant.

At first, Buell based himself on Corinth, later moving to Athens, where he discovered how effective Confederate guerrillas could be in disrupting his supply line via the Nashville & Decatur Railroad. Repair work was done on the Nashville and Charleston Railroad, and Buell enjoyed an excellent rail supply to Nashville and Louisville, although he was still constantly plagued by Confederate raids on his communications (Forrest at Murfreesboro on 13 July, and Brig. Gen. John Hunt Morgan at Gallatin on 12 August, for example) and he did not have the necessary cavalry to deal with them.

Bragg, meanwhile, had decided that an advance north from Tupelo was not practicable, and so he left Price and Van Dorn to fix Grant in place and shifted 35,000 men to Chattanooga, which he reached before Buell did. His general plan was to invade Kentucky with Kirby Smith, hoping to cut Buell's line of communications, defeat him, and then turn on Grant. Bragg left Chattanooga as Kirby Smith approached Lexington. Thomas urged Buell to concentrate at McMinnville and to strike Bragg as he emerged from the Sequatchie River valley. Instead, Buell, somewhat confused, withdrew to Murfreesboro and then to Nashville, where he left a garrison and moved back to his supply depot at Bowling Green.

Bragg continued on to Munfordville (whose garrison surrendered) and was now squarely across Buell's supply lines to Louisville. In this crisis, Buell shied away from attacking Bragg, and Louisville and Cincinnati braced themselves for a Confederate attack. Grant now sent Brig. Gen. Gordon Granger's division to Louisville to assist Buell. By aggressive marching and maneuvering, Bragg had forced Buell back almost to the Ohio River.

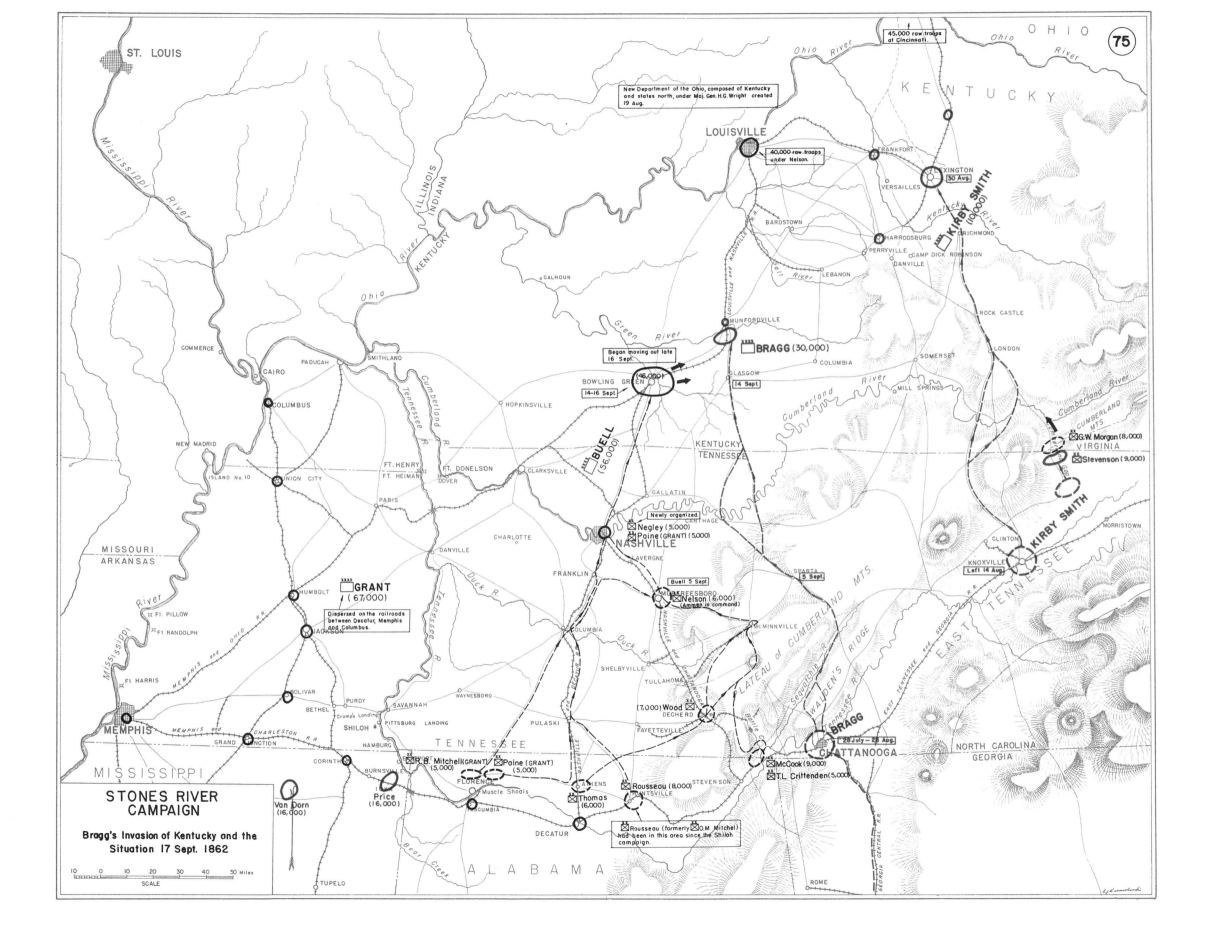

STONES RIVER
CAMPAIGN

Bragg's Invasion of Kentucky and the
Situation 17 Sept. 1862

10 0   10   20   30   40   50 Miles
SCALE

OHIO

KENTUCKY

ST. LOUIS

45,000 raw troops
at Cincinnati.

New Department of the Ohio, composed of Kentucky
and states north, under Maj. Gen. H.G. Wright created
19 Aug.

LOUISVILLE

40,000 raw troops
under Nelson.

FRANKFORT

VERSAILLES

LEXINGTON
30 Aug.

KIRBY SMITH

RICHMOND
(10,000)

BARDSTOWN

HARRODSBURG

PERRYVILLE

CAMP DICK ROBINSON

DANVILLE

LEBANON

ROCK CASTLE

LONDON

COLUMBIA

SOMERSET

MILL SPRINGS

ILLINOIS

INDIANA

KENTUCKY River

Ohio River

COMMERCE

CAIRO

PADUCAH

SMITHLAND

Green River

MUNFORDVILLE

BRAGG (30,000)

Began moving out late
16 Sept.

BOWLING GREEN (46,000)
14-16 Sept.

GLASGOW
14 Sept.

Cumberland River

Cumberland Island

Cumberland River

CUMBERLAND MTS.

COLUMBUS

NEW MADRID

ISLAND No. 10

UNION CITY

HOPKINSVILLE

Tennessee R.

Cumberland R.

FT. HENRY
FT. HEIMAN

FT. DONELSON

DOVER

CLARKSVILLE

BUELL
(56,000)

KENTUCKY
TENNESSEE

G.W. Morgan (8,000)
VIRGINIA
Stevenson (9,000)

KIRBY SMITH

PARIS

GALLATIN

CARTHAGE

Newly organized

Negley (5,000)
Paine (GRANT) (5,000)

CLINTON

KNOXVILLE
Left 14 Aug.

MORRISTOWN

MISSOURI
ARKANSAS

HUMBOLT

JACKSON

GRANT
(67,000)

Dispersed on the railroads
between Decatur, Memphis
and Columbus.

DANVILLE

CHARLOTTE

NASHVILLE

FRANKLIN

LAVERGNE

MURFREESBORO
Nelson (6,000)
(Ammen in command)

Buell 5 Sept.

SPARTA
5 Sept.

McMINNVILLE

PLATEAU of CUMBERLAND MTS.

EAST TENNESSEE

FT. PILLOW

FT. RANDOLPH

Mississippi River

FT. HARRIS

BOLIVAR

BETHEL

PURDY

SAVANNAH

Duck R.

COLUMBIA

SHELBYVILLE

TULLAHOMA

Duck R.

Sequatchie R.

WALDEN'S RIDGE

NORTH CAROLINA
GEORGIA

MEMPHIS

Memphis and Ohio R.R.

CRUMP'S LANDING

SHILOH

PITTSBURG LANDING

HAMBURG

WAYNESBORO

PULASKI

FAYETTEVILLE

(7,000) Wood
DECHERD

Tennessee R.

BRAGG
28 July-28 Aug.

CHATTANOOGA

MISSISSIPPI

Memphis and Charleston R.R.

GRAND JUNCTION

CORINTH

BURNSVILLE

Price
(16,000)

Van Dorn
(16,000)

R.B. Mitchell (GRANT)
(5,000)

FLORENCE

Muscle Shoals

Paine (GRANT)
(5,000)

ATHENS

Thomas
(6,000)

HUNTSVILLE

Rousseau (8,000)

STEVENSON

McCook (9,000)

T.L. Crittenden (5,000)

Rousseau (formerly O.M. Mitchel)
had been in this area since the Shiloh
campaign.

TENNESSEE

TUSCUMBIA

DECATUR

Bear Creek

ALABAMA

GEORGIA CENTRAL R.R.

ROME

STONES RIVER CAMPAIGN: 2

Although Bragg had put himself in a powerful strategic position, he felt he did not have a large enough force to attack Buell. Running short of supplies, he moved north to Bardstown on the road to Lexington. Buell then moved rapidly to Louisville. The Confederate invasion was not achieving the expected results; Bragg and Kirby Smith acted as independent commanders, and their failure to unite denied the Confederates sufficient mass to contest the issue with Buell. In addition, few Kentuckians joined the Confederate forces; likewise, an attempt at conscription in eastern Tennessee failed completely.

On 1 October, Buell (who had come close to being fired by Lincoln) advanced slowly on Bardstown, sending two detached divisions toward Frankfort in an attempt to confuse the Confederates. On 7 October, the Union advance approached Perryville and found Confederate forces present in some strength. On the 8th, fighting began over possession of water, and Gen. Philip Henry Sheridan's division of Gilbert's corps forced the Confederates away from one creek and dug in. Early in the afternoon, Maj. Gen. Alexander M.

McCook's corps arrived and began forming into a line, at which moment Polk attacked, pushing McCook back about a mile with heavy losses; Sheridan, however, held his ground. Col. William P. Carlin's brigade counterattacked and drove the Confederates out of Perryville. Buell, who had not left his headquarters and was unaware of the battle until it was half over, failed to pursue Bragg, who had ordered a retreat to Harrodsburg, and from there through the Cumberland Gap, where he eventually regained Murfreesboro, completely disheartened. Buell was fired and replaced by Rosencrans.

Rosencrans, who had received much credit for his recent victories at Iuka and Corinth, started by reorganizing his cavalry and concentrating his army at Nashville. On 26 December, he started his march south. He was so continually harried by the Confederate cavalry under Gen. Joseph Wheeler that his advance became a constant skirmish, one in which the Union infantry was forced to deploy at every piece of strong terrain. It was not until the evening of the 29th that the leading Union corps—Crittenden's—approached Murfreesboro, where Bragg had concentrated his force and had decided to make his stand.

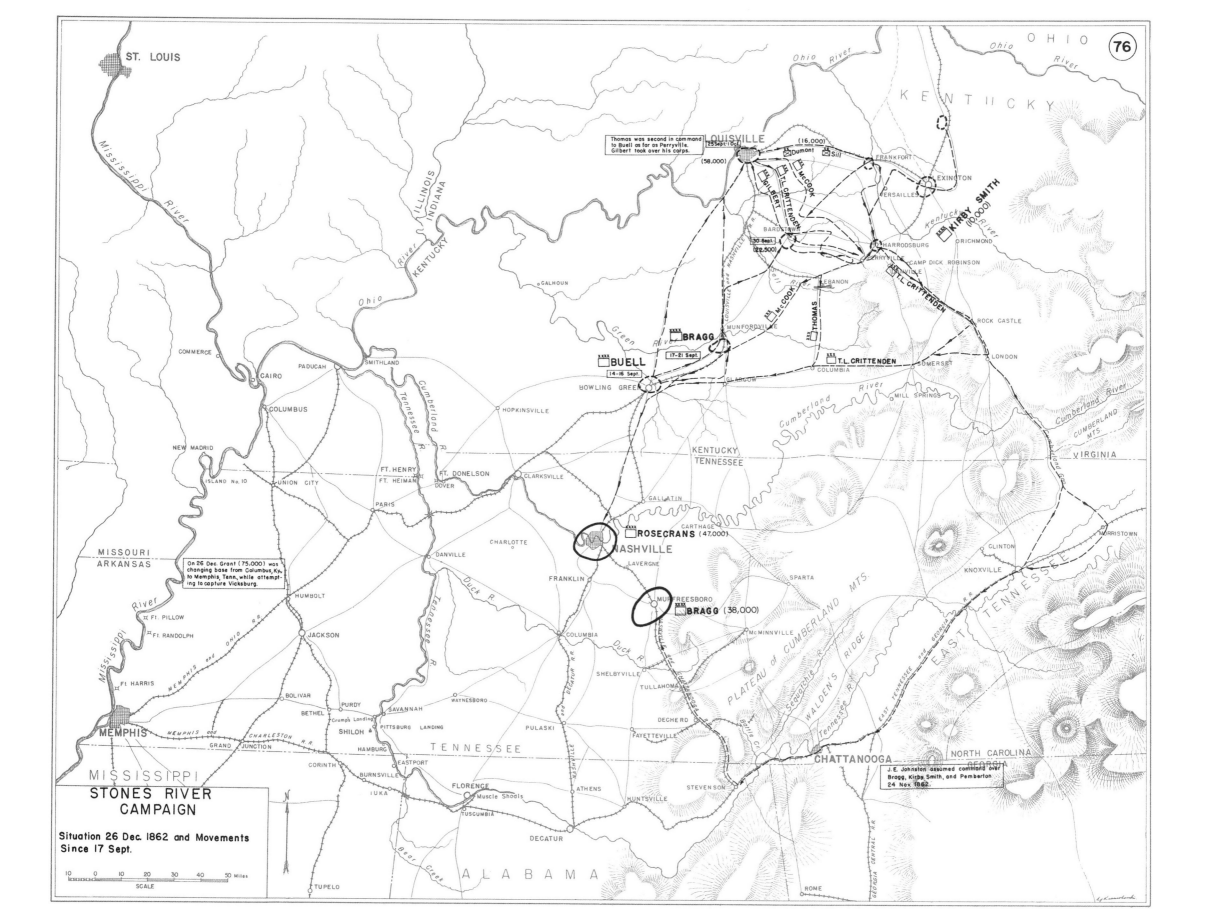

OHIO

Ohio River

KENTUCKY

ST. LOUIS

Mississippi River

ILLINOIS
INDIANA

Thomas was second in command to Buell as far as Perryville. Gilbert took over his corps.

LOUISVILLE 25 Sept.–1 Oct. (16,000)

(58,000)

Dumont   Sill   FRANKFORT

McCOOK

GILBERT

T.L. CRITTENDEN

LEXINGTON

VERSAILLES

KIRBY SMITH (10,000)

BARDSTOWN

30 Sept.
(22,500)

HARRODSBURG

RICHMOND

PERRYVILLE CAMP DICK ROBINSON

DANVILLE

T.L. CRITTENDEN

ROCK CASTLE

LEBANON

LONDON

McCOOK

THOMAS

Green River

BRAGG

MUNFORDVILLE

BUELL

17–21 Sept.

14–16 Sept.

T.L. CRITTENDEN

SOMERSET

COLUMBIA

BOWLING GREEN

GLASGOW

Cumberland River

MILL SPRINGS

CUMBERLAND MTS.

VIRGINIA

o GALHOUN

HOPKINSVILLE

KENTUCKY
TENNESSEE

COMMERCE

CAIRO

PADUCAH   SMITHLAND

Tennessee R.

Cumberland R.

COLUMBUS

NEW MADRID

FT. HENRY
FT. HEIMAN   FT. DONELSON

DOVER

CLARKSVILLE

GALLATIN

CARTHAGE

MORRISTOWN

ISLAND No. 10

UNION CITY

PARIS

ROSECRANS (47,000)

NASHVILLE

CHARLOTTE o

LAVERGNE

SPARTA

CLINTON

MISSOURI
ARKANSAS

On 26 Dec. Grant (75,000) was changing base from Columbus, Ky., to Memphis, Tenn., while attempting to capture Vicksburg.

DANVILLE

FRANKLIN

MURFREESBORO

BRAGG (38,000)

McMINNVILLE

KNOXVILLE

EAST TENNESSEE

HUMBOLT

Mississippi River

JACKSON

COLUMBIA

Duck R.

Plateau of Cumberland Mts.

WALDEN'S RIDGE

Ft. PILLOW
Ft. RANDOLPH

BOLIVAR

PURDY

Crump's Landing

SAVANNAH

SHELBYVILLE

TULLAHOMA

Sequatchie R.

BETHEL

SHILOH   PITTSBURG LANDING

WAYNESBORO

PULASKI

DECHERD

FAYETTEVILLE

Ft. HARRIS

MEMPHIS

HAMBURG

TENNESSEE

CHATTANOOGA

NORTH CAROLINA
GEORGIA

MISSISSIPPI

CORINTH

EASTPORT

J. E. Johnston assumed command over Bragg, Kirby Smith, and Pemberton 24 Nov. 1862.

STONES RIVER
CAMPAIGN

BURNSVILLE

IUKA

FLORENCE   Muscle Shoals

ATHENS

HUNTSVILLE

STEVENSON

GEORGIA CENTRAL R.R.

Situation 26 Dec. 1862 and Movements
Since 17 Sept.

N

TUSCUMBIA

DECATUR

ALABAMA

Bear Creek

ROME

10 0 10 20 30 40 50 Miles
SCALE

TUPELO

STONES RIVER CAMPAIGN: 3

Bragg had taken up a defensive position astride the West Fork of Stones River, his front strengthened in laces by light entrenchments. The river was not a major obstacle at this time, because it could be crossed by several bridges and numerous fords. However, if rains caused the river to rise, Polk's corps would be dangerously isolated. The ground between the river and Overall Creek to the west was generally level; there were many clearings, but most of the area was covered with scrub cedar that limited visibility but was not a great obstacle to troop movements. The dominating terrain was the group of hills east of the river and north of Murfreesboro, held by Breckinridge.

On the evening of 30 December, the opposing forces were drawn up as shown on the map below. Polk occupied the west bank and Hardee the east. On that day the Confederate cavalry had ridden completely around the Union army, doing considerable damage to its supply trains. Bragg had apparently anticipated a Union attack but, when it failed to materialize, he initiated his own early on 31 December. Hardee's corps (less Breckinridge's division) was to move to the south, cross Stones River and, with the help of Brig. Gen. John A. Wharton's cavalry, envelop the Union right flank. Polk would then join the attack, pivoting on his own right flank. The overall object was to wheel Rosencrans and pin him against the river. Bragg had no fear that Breckinridge on the east bank would be attacked, and he looked on him as a reserve.

Ironically, Rosencrans was planning a mirror image of Bragg's plan. He would envelop the Confederate right wing and swing Bragg around, to trap *him* against the river. Since the two plans were basically identical, victory would probably go to the commander who struck first and hardest. Bragg issued his orders on the 30th, whereas Brig. Gen. Horatio P. Van Cleve and Brig. Gen. Wood did not receive their orders to advance until the morning of the 31st. In addition, Rosencrans failed to inspect McCook's position to learn if his troops were properly posted.

At dawn on the 31st, Hardee and Wharton drove suddenly against the Union right flank and the Union outposts were quickly driven in; Johnson's division, caught preparing breakfast, was broken up and forced back, although they eventually rallied about three miles to the rear. The leading Confederate division (Maj. Gen. John P. McCown) now began to meet stubborn resistance and was pushed off to the left, which created a gap that Cleburne promptly filled. Union Brig. Gen. Jefferson C. Davis, however, held firm against the pressure of McCown and Cleburne. Withers's division and the reserve division of Cheatham were committed but failed to break the Union line.

On the Federal left flank, Van Cleve began to cross the Stones River at about 7:00 A.M., while Wood was about to cross the ford directly in front of him. Rosencrans suddenly became anxious and ordered Wood to suspend his assault and Van Cleve to bring back his men that had already crossed (which he did skillfully). Breckinridge, though, had seen Van Cleve's initial crossing and assumed he was about to be attacked.

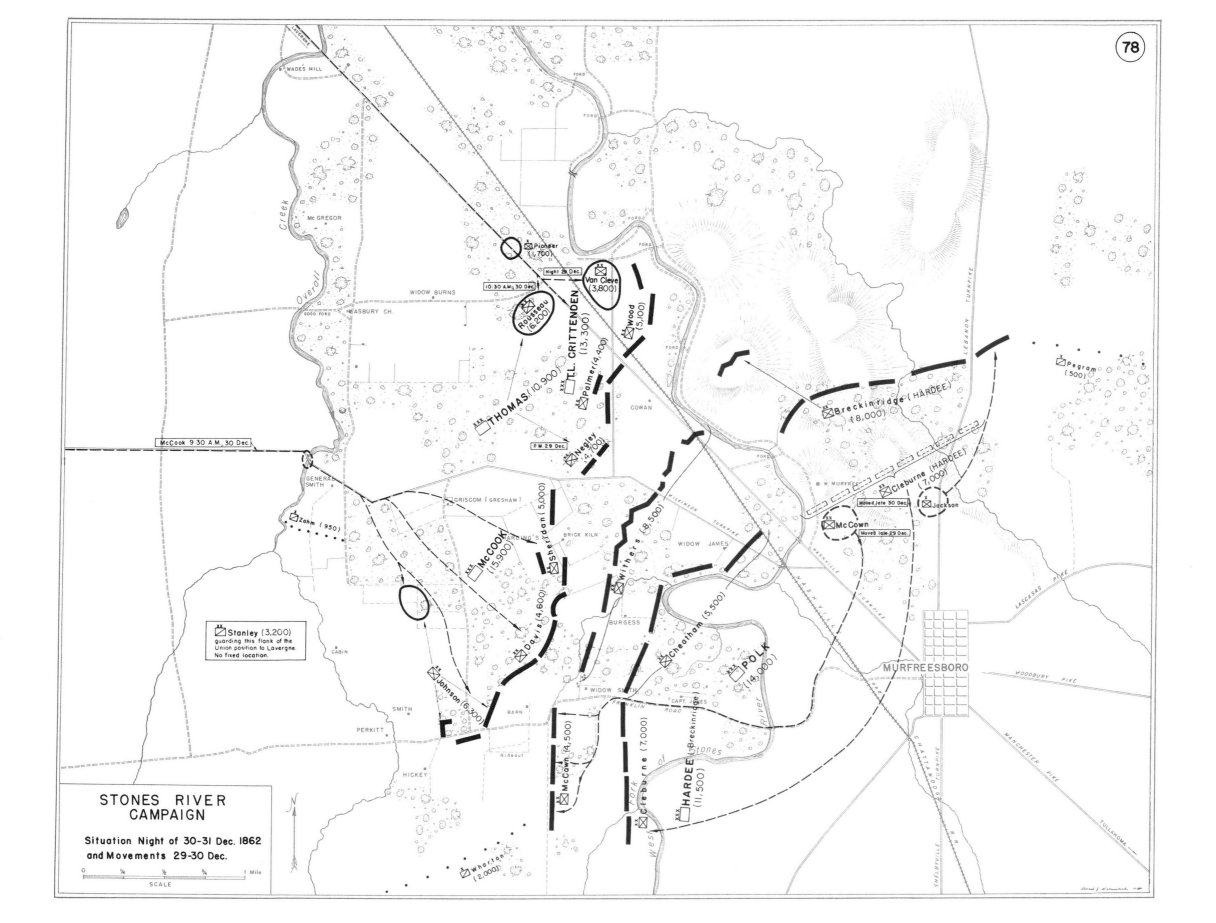

WADES MILL

McGREGOR

Creek

Overall

Pioneer (1,700)

Night 29 Dec

Van Cleve (3,800)

10:30 A.M., 30 Dec.

WIDOW BURNS

Rousseau (6,200)

GOOD FORD ASBURY CH.

T.L. CRITTENDEN (13,300)

Wood (5,100)

Palmer (4,400)

THOMAS (10,900)

FORD

COWAN

Breckinridge (HARDEE) (8,000)

Pegram (500)

McCook 9:30 A.M., 30 Dec.

P.M. 29 Dec.

Negley (4,700)

W. MURFREE

Cleburne (HARDEE) (7,000)

GENERAL SMITH

Moved late 30 Dec

Jackson

Zahm (950)

GRISCOM (GRESHAM)

Sheridan (5,000)

Withers (8,500)

WILKINSON

McCown

Moved late 29 Dec

HARDING'S

BRICK KILN

WIDOW JAMES

Cheatham (5,500)

Stanley (3,200)
guarding this flank of the
Union position to Lavergne.
No fixed location.

McCOOK (15,900)

Davis (4,600)

BURGESS

POLK (4,000)

MURFREESBORO

WOODBURY PIKE

CABIN

WIDOW SMITH

Johnson (6,300)

CAPT. JONES

SMITH

BARN

FRANKLIN ROAD

PERKITT

RIDEOUT

HICKEY

McCown (4,500)

Cleburne (7,000)

HARDEE (11,500)

STONES RIVER
CAMPAIGN

Situation Night of 30-31 Dec. 1862
and Movements 29-30 Dec.

N

0   1/4   1/2   3/4   1 Mile
SCALE

Wharton (2,000)

West Fork of Stones River

SHELBYVILLE R.R.

CHATTANOOGA & TULLAHOMA R.R.

MANCHESTER PIKE

STONES RIVER CAMPAIGN: 4

Persistent Confederate pressure on Davis's right flank eventually made his position untenable. In addition, Wharton's cavalry was deep in the Union rear, and Davis had to retire, sometimes in considerable disorder.

The full force of Hardee's ably handled attack thus fell on Sheridan's division, the toughest the Confederates had yet encountered. It had been alert and ready by 4:00 A.M., and repeated and costly attacks by Polk failed to dislodge it. Now, with his right flank exposed by Davis's retreat, Sheridan moved his extreme left brigade across the rear of his position and launched it in a vigorous counterattack against Hardee, checking the latter's advance. Having gained time, Sheridan now fell back to a position parallel to the Nashville Turnpike.

Maj. Gen. Lovell Harrison Rousseau's division came into the action on the right of Sheridan's position and a new line, perpendicular to the original front, was thus established on the Union right. Rosencrans now rapidly extended this line by adding a brigade from each of Wood's and Van Cleve's divisions. In the center, Brig. Gen. James S. Negley's division continued to hold off Polk's assaults, but by now Sheridan's men were almost out of ammunition. Temporarily, the battle had been stabilized. Hardee's and Polk's units had become badly intermingled and their men were beginning to tire. Rosencrans, displaying inspiring personal courage and energy, was working furiously to gain control of the action.

By 10:00 A.M., Bragg realized he was losing the initiative and ordered Breckinridge to send two brigades across the river to reinforce Hardee, but Breckinridge, under the false impression that Van Cleve intended to attack him, begged off. Bragg also was under a misapprehension that he was about to be attacked down the Lebanon Pike. Although considerable disorder existed in places immediately behind the reconstructed Union front, vigorous efforts by Rosencrans and his subordinates kept practically all the units intact.

By noon, Rosencrans had completed the reorganization of his front line and repeated Confederate attacks against it were uniformly unsuccessful. Bragg now decided that his best chance for a decisive victory now lay in an overwhelming attack against the Union left flank, which he felt had been weakened to bolster the Union right. As the only fresh troops were those of Breckinridge, Bragg again ordered him across the river, but again he was slow to respond. Meanwhile, by 2:00 P.M. Hardee had been fought to a standstill and had even been pushed back in places. At about 4:00 P.M. Breckinridge's first two brigades came into the line opposite Col. William B. Hazen's brigade, and Polk immediately committed them to battle, as he did the rest of Breckinridge's corps. It was a bloody and complete failure.

That night Rosencrans held a council of war, and the decision was made to stay and fight. Union morale rose, and Van Cleve's division (now under Col. Samuel Beatty, Van Cleve having been wounded) was once more sent over the river. Bragg, for his part, was convinced he'd won, but his troops were less optimistic and began digging in.

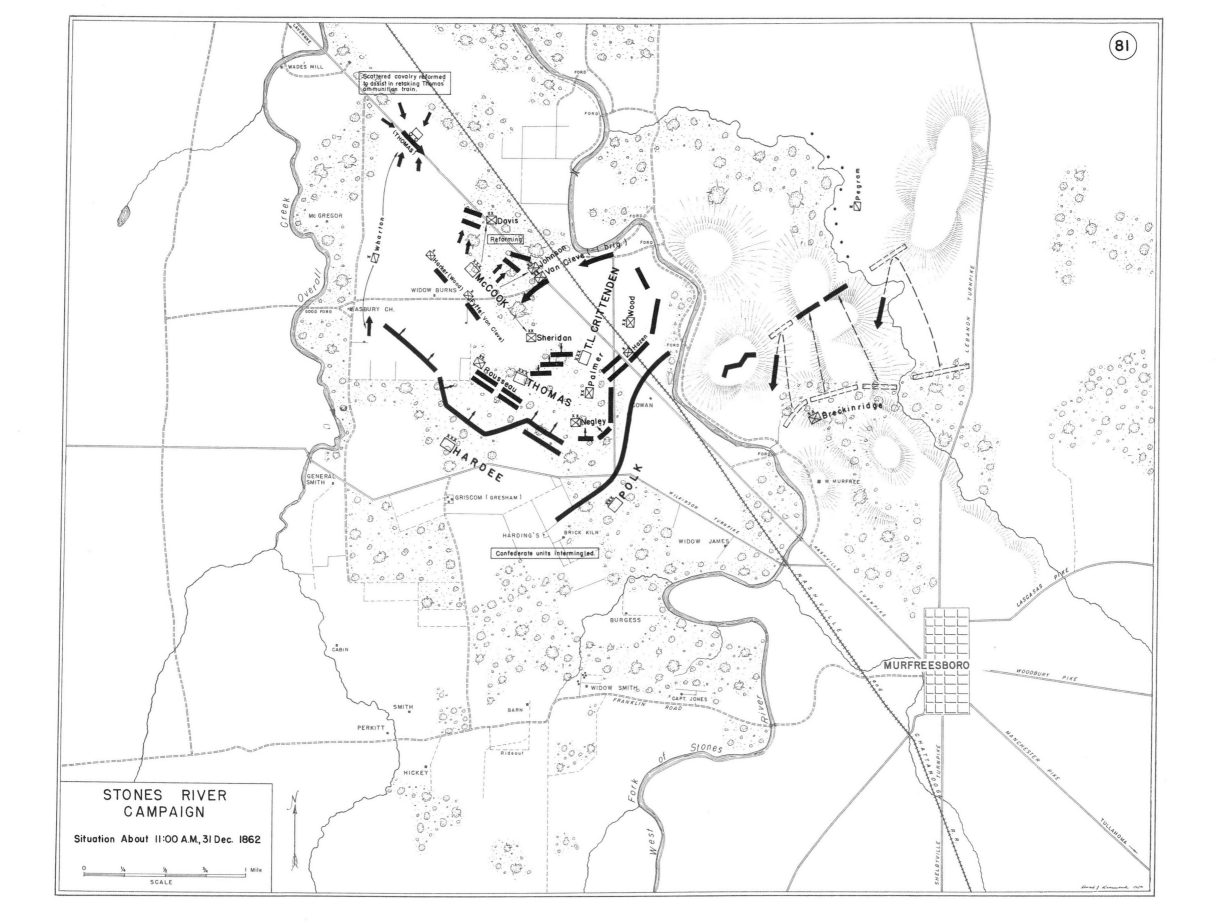

STONES RIVER
CAMPAIGN

Situation About 11:00 A.M., 31 Dec. 1862

0   1/4   1/2   3/4   1 Mile
SCALE

Scattered cavalry reformed
to assist in retaking Thomas'
ammunition train.

Confederate units intermingled.

MURFREESBORO

STONES RIVER CAMPAIGN: 5

On the battleground of Murfreesboro, New Year's Day 1863 was relatively quiet. Polk closed on the new Union line, occupying ground relinquished by Rosencrans as he straightened his front, and sent testing attacks against Thomas, which brought him nothing but casualties. Meanwhile Beatty, heading Van Cleve's division, completed the occupation of the hill east of the river and confronted Breckinridge, who had also returned to the far bank.

Wheeler's cavalry was very active and effectively harassing the Union rear, so much so that the Union wounded and supply trains had to be escorted to the rear, which Wheeler mistook as a sign that the Federals were in a general retreat—misinformation that he duly reported to Bragg who, glad to have his fervent hopes confirmed, allowed his men to rest and collect any available booty. But to Bragg's disappointment, 2 January revealed Rosencrans to be very much still in position, and so once more Bragg ordered Breckinridge with four brigades to push the Federals back across the river. Breckinridge protested that the mission was suicidal, but nevertheless did his duty and attacked with determination. He succeeded in dislodging Beatty, but massed Union artillery firing into the Confederate flank from the west bank stopped Breckinridge's division, whereupon Union infantry stormed across the river, driving the Confederates back to their line of departure.

Early on the morning of 3 January, a large supply train reached Rosencrans, and, later that evening, Thomas, on his own initiative, attacked the center of the opposing line with two brigades and drove the Confederates from their entrenchments. That night, Bragg made a skillful withdrawal through Murfreesboro and began his retreat to Tullahoma, thirty-six miles to the south. He had fought courageously, if not capably. Perhaps his army was too small for the attack he attempted. Still, more than were most other battles of the war, this was a conflict between the wills of the opposing commanders. Rosencrans, powerfully supported by Thomas and others, would not admit himself beaten, and so—in the end—won a victory of sorts.

Rosencrans occupied Murfreesboro but made no effort to pursue Bragg. Murfreesboro had been the scene of one of the bloodiest battles of the war: each side had suffered about 12,000 casualties (the Confederates, perhaps a shade fewer but, given a smaller population base, they could not replenish losses like the North. As a percentage of the men involved, these high casualty rates were devastating to the South).

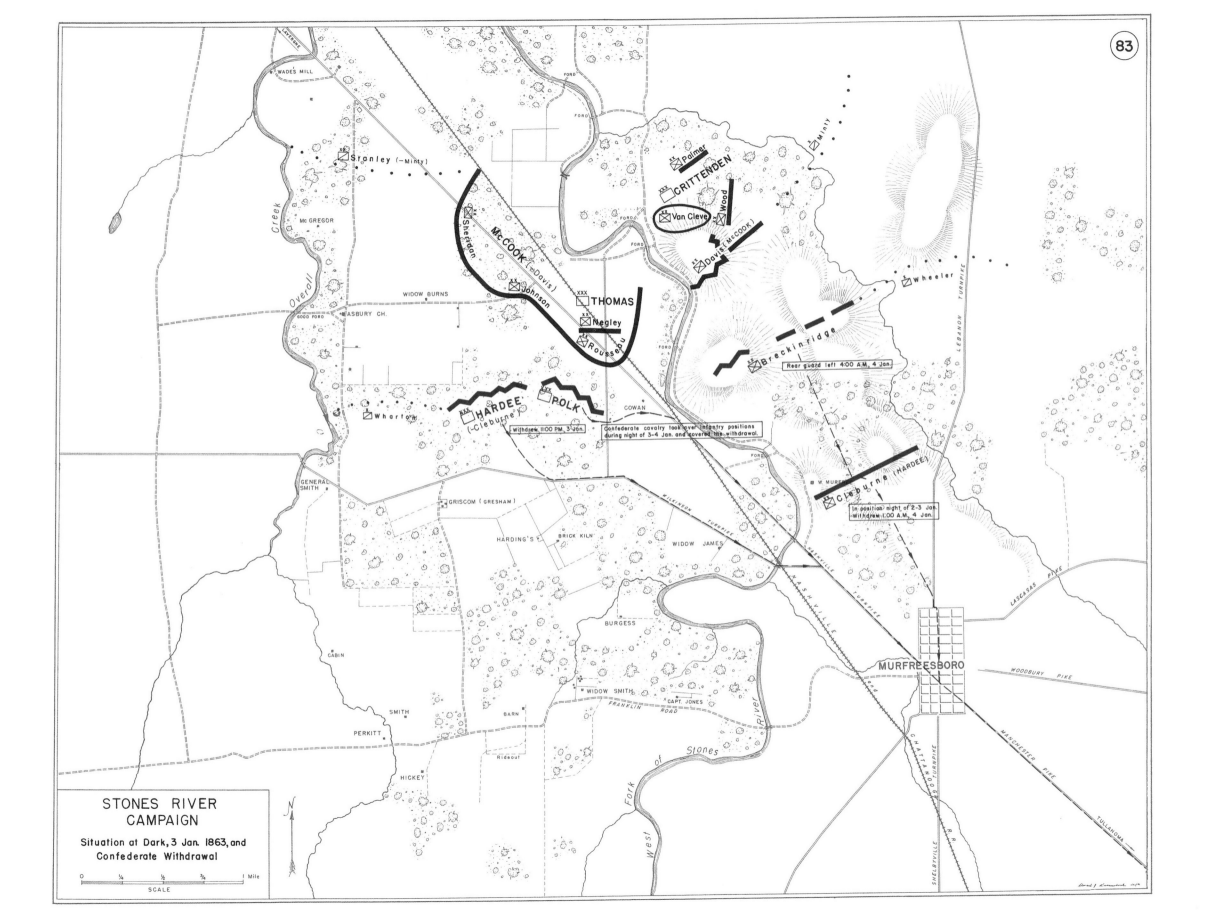

83

WADES MILL

LAVERGNE

FORD

FORD

Stanley (-Minty)

Creek

Overall

McGREGOR

Palmer

CRITTENDEN

Minty

FORD

Wood

Van Cleve

Sheridan

McCOOK (-Davis)

Davis (McCOOK)

WIDOW BURNS

Johnson

THOMAS

Wheeler

ASBURY CH.

GOOD FORD

Negley

Rousseau

Breckinridge

FORD

Rear guard left 4:00 A.M., 4 Jan.

HARDEE (-Cleburne)

POLK

COWAN

Wharton

Withdrew 11:00 P.M. 3 Jan.

Confederate cavalry took over infantry positions during night of 3-4 Jan. and covered the withdrawal.

LEBANON TURNPIKE

WILKINSON TURNPIKE

FORD

W. MURFR.

GENERAL SMITH

Cleburne (HARDEE)

GRISCOM (GRESHAM)

In position night of 2-3 Jan. Withdrew 1:00 A.M., 4 Jan.

HARDING'S

BRICK KILN

WIDOW JAMES

NASHVILLE TURNPIKE

CABIN

BURGESS

LASCASAS PIKE

MURFREESBORO

WOODBURY PIKE

SMITH

WIDOW SMITH

CAPT. JONES

FRANKLIN ROAD

PERKITT

BARN

West Fork of Stones River

NASHVILLE R.R.

HICKEY

Rideout

CHATTANOOGA TURNPIKE

SHELBYVILLE R.R.

MANCHESTER PIKE

TULLAHOMA

STONES RIVER
CAMPAIGN

Situation at Dark, 3 Jan. 1863, and
Confederate Withdrawal

N

0   ¼   ½   ¾   1 Mile
SCALE

CHANCELLORSVILLE CAMPAIGN: 1

When Hooker had relieved Burnside after the disastrous Fredericksburg campaign, he found the Army of the Potomac in a sorry state: desertion was increasing and the army's own interior administration had deteriorated. Hooker was a boastful, ambitious man, and an intriguer, but he was brave and aggressive as a combat leader. Now, he also unexpectedly showed himself to be an able administrator and organizer. Training and discipline tightened and an efficient military intelligence organization was established. Hooker reorganized his forces into seven infantry corps and one cavalry corps, a consolidation of the mounted arm that rapidly increased the effectiveness of the Federal horsemen.

In planning his offensive, Hooker had the problem of crossing the Rappahannock against a dangerous opponent. Lee had carefully fortified the south bank, from Port Royal to Banks's Ford, but Hooker knew he had a numerical superiority because he had learned that Lee had sent Longstreet south with two divisions to guard the Virginia-Carolina coast. And so, Hooker began to revise his plan. Slocum marched on 27 April 1863, with the V, XI, and XII Corps. At Kelley's Ford, he surprised the Confederate outposts and continued across the Rapidan. The day after Slocum's departure, Sedgwick took the I and VI Corps ostentatiously toward the river, crossing just below Fredericksburg on the 29th. The III Corps, under Brig. Gen. Daniel E. Sickles, was kept in reserve. The cavalry was tasked to destroy Lee's communications.

Lee himself had been planning an offensive movement in the Shenandoah Valley, but now the extent of Hooker's actions temporarily baffled him. On 29 April, Lee moved the three divisions on his right flank closer to Fredericksburg and sent Anderson to occupy a position near Chancellorsville.

By 3:00 P.M. Hooker had three corps in Lee's rear near Chancellorsville, and Maj. Gen. Darius Nash Couch's two divisions were close behind. A prompt advance would have gotten this force into more open ground, clearing Banks's Ford, and halved the distance between it and Sedgwick. Hooker, however, halted the three corps to await reinforcements.

Chancellorsville was a lone brick house at a minor crossroads in a waste area appropriately called "the Wilderness." Thick, second-growth pine and oak tangled with undergrowth, severely limited visibility and made movement away from the few roads highly problematic; the area was further cut up by many swampy little streams, all of which militated against the deployment of large numbers of troops. And so the Union's numerical advantage was cancelled out. Nevertheless, Hooker delayed there until about 11:00 A.M. on 1 May.

Lee was still uncertain as to which wing of the Union army he could more profitably attack, and as usual it did not occur to him to stand on the defensive. Leaving Early's division to hold Sedgwick, he moved the rest of his army against Hooker. The initial clashes were indecisive. Maj. Gen. George Sykes forced McLaws back until he himself was enveloped by Confederate reinforcements and was driven back through Hancock's division. Hancock stopped the advance, and Slocum, too, held his ground. But with a real chance of a victory in sight, Hooker's nerve failed him, and he ordered a pull-back.

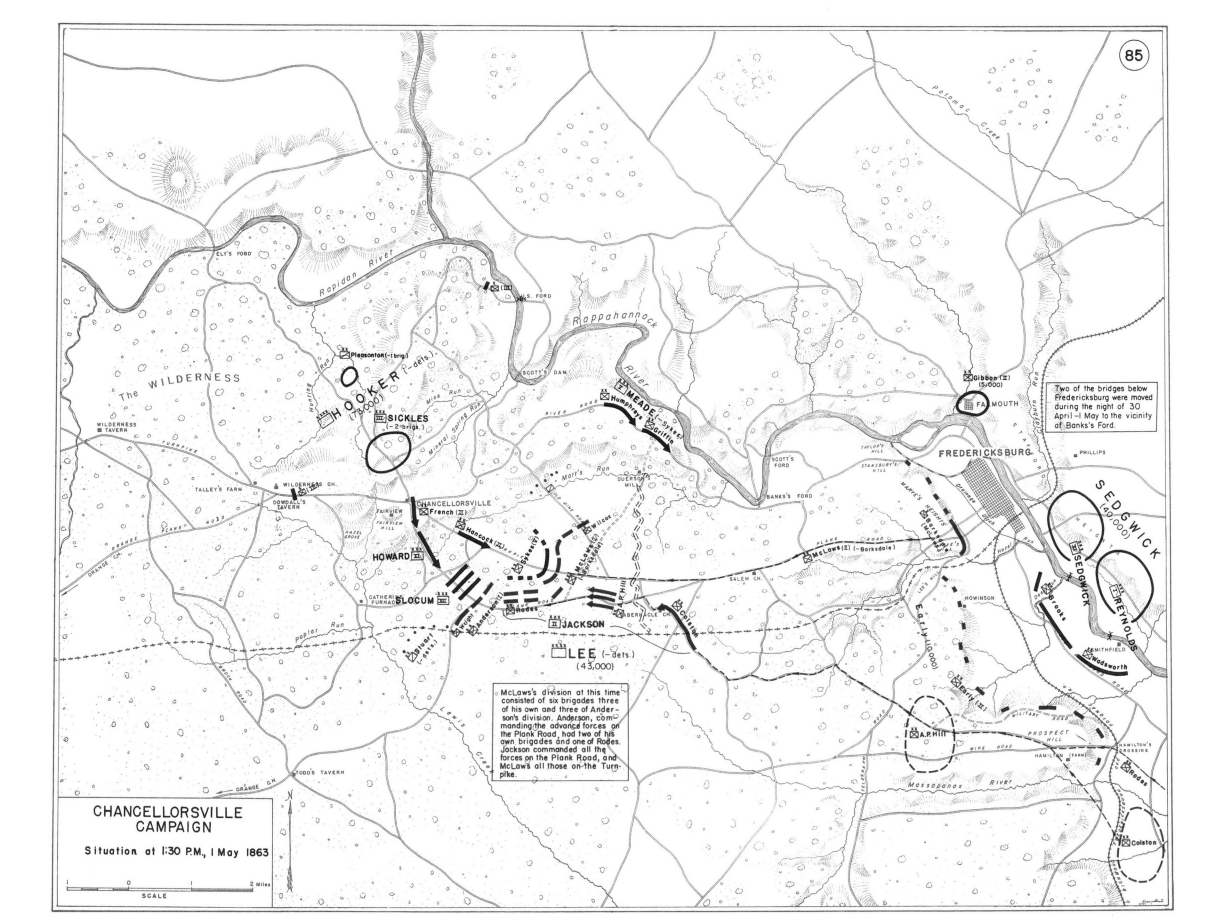

85

CHANCELLORSVILLE
CAMPAIGN

Situation at 1:30 P.M., 1 May 1863

SCALE

Two of the bridges below
Fredericksburg were moved
during the night of 30
April—1 May to the vicinity
of Banks's Ford.

McLaws's division at this time
consisted of six brigades three
of his own and three of Anderson's division. Anderson, commanding the advance forces on
the Plank Road, had two of his
own brigades and one of Rodes.
Jackson commanded all the
forces on the Plank Road, and
McLaws all those on the Turnpike.

HOOKER
(73,000)

SICKLES
(—2 brigs.)

MEADE (—Sykes)
Humphreys
Griffin

Gibbon (II)
(5,000)

FALMOUTH

FREDERICKSBURG

SEDGWICK
(40,000)

SEDGWICK

REYNOLDS

HOWARD

FRENCH (II)

Hancock (II)

Wilcox

Sykes

McLaws (II) (—Barksdale)

SLOCUM

Anderson

Rodes

JACKSON

LEE (—dets.)
(43,000)

Stuart (—dets.)

Colston

A. P. Hill

Early (10,000)

Wadsworth

Colston

Rodes

THE WILDERNESS

WILDERNESS TAVERN

TALLEY'S FARM

DOWDALL'S TAVERN

WILDERNESS CH.

FAIRVIEW

CHANCELLORSVILLE

HAZEL GROVE

CATHARINE FURNACE

TODD'S TAVERN

Pleasonton (—1 brig.)

ELY'S FORD

U.S. FORD

SCOTT'S DAM

SCOTT'S FORD

BANKS'S FORD

Rapidan River

Rappahannock River

Poplar Run

Lewis Creek

Massaponax River

PROSPECT HILL

HAMILTON'S CROSSING

SMITHFIELD

CHANCELLORSVILLE CAMPAIGN: 2

Lee began to consider an attack on Hooker's right, and at that moment Stuart returned from a reconnaissance to confirm a weakness on the Union right. Lee now sent Jackson with some 26,000 men, screened by Stuart's cavalry, to circle around the Union position and attack it from the west; Lee, meanwhile, would with approximately 17,000 remaining men keep Hooker engaged on the existing front. The problem was that Lee was already outnumbered; by splitting his army into three segments, none of which could support the other, he risked being destroyed in detail.

Jackson began his march at about 6:00 A.M. on 2 May and began forming for the attack about 2:30 P.M. Heavy brush made it slow work; not until more than three hours later was he satisfied with his deployment, all of which was carefully observed by the Union officers of XI Corps. Sickles, in particular, urged an attack against Jackson's columns moving across his front and finally got permission to make an attack, which did some damage but could not halt Jackson's march. For some unfathomable reason, Sickles's slight success convinced Hooker that Jackson was actually retreating toward Gordonsville, so he gave orders to prepare for a pursuit and ordered Sedgwick and Gibbon to attack on their fronts.

At approximately 6:00 P.M. (only two hours before dark) Jackson attacked. The right flank brigades of XI Corps were quickly routed and fled to the rear in disorder. Col. Adolphus Buschbeck's brigade, however, held the line and held Jackson for over half an hour before withdrawing in good order. The time it gained allowed Howard and Hooker to build a new line comprising the hard core of the XI Corps, two brigades from Maj. Gen. Hiram G. Berry's division, another brigade from II Corps, and all available artillery. Reynolds hurried forward to anchor the right flank. Rough terrain, hard fighting, and a series of errors by subordinate commanders had taken most of the sting out of Jackson's attack, and his rush was finally stopped west of Fairview Hill. Darkness fell, but Jackson, seeking a way to exploit his success, rode out into the gloom with a small entourage in searching for a route that would enable him to cut Hooker off from United States Ford. Returning, he was shot down by his own men who were jumpy from an earlier chance clash with Union cavalry. Shortly after, A. P. Hill was wounded, and Confederate operations against the Union right came to a confused halt. Jackson died on 10 May.

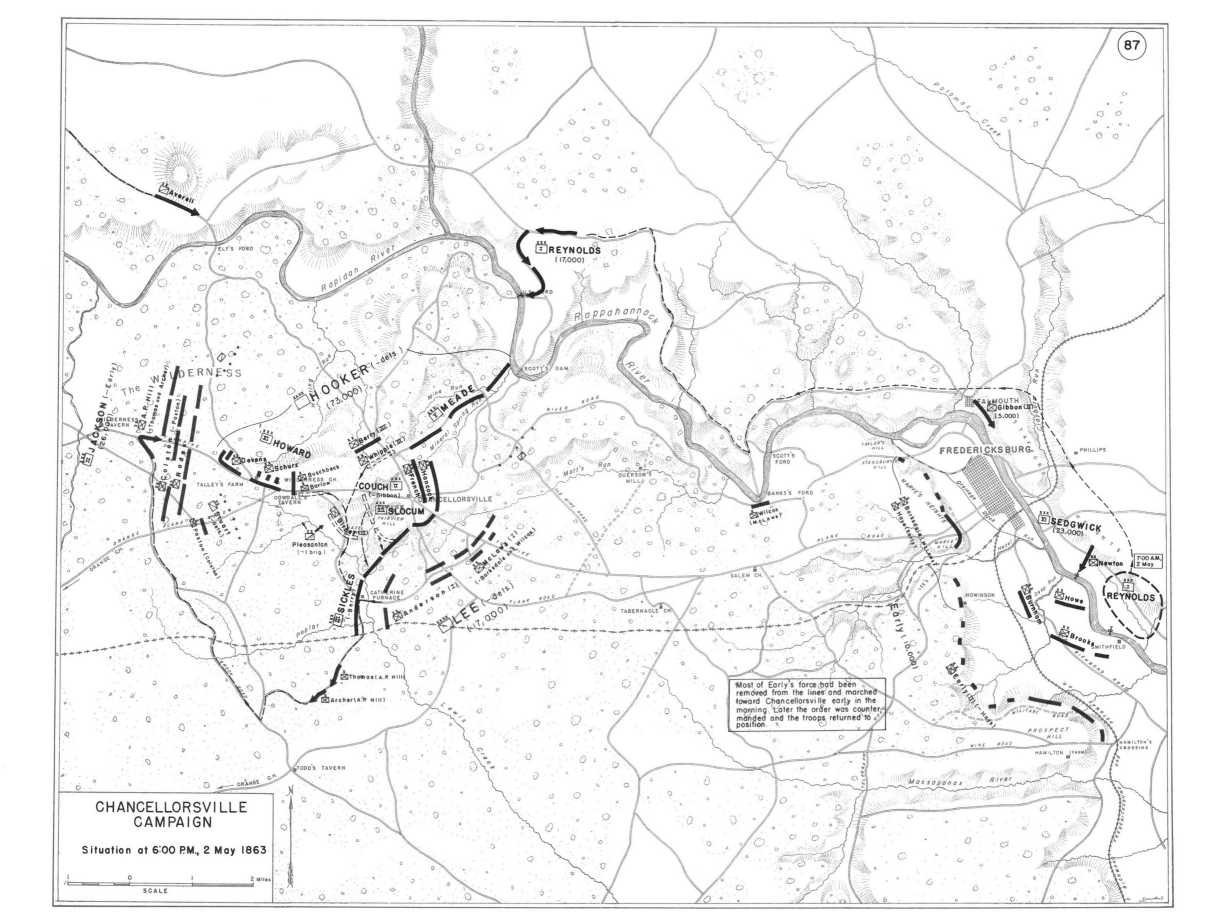

87

CHANCELLORSVILLE
CAMPAIGN

Situation at 6:00 P.M., 2 May 1863

SCALE

Most of Early's force had been removed from the lines and marched toward Chancellorsville early in the morning. Later the order was countermanded and the troops returned to position.

CHANCELLORSVILLE CAMPAIGN: 3

On the morning of 3 May, Hooker again had a splendid opportunity to defeat Lee. The Confederate army around Chancellorsville was completely split, with its two halves almost a day's march apart. Furthermore, the arrival of Reynolds's I Corps and the relatively prompt rally of most of Howard's XI Corps gave Hooker an approximately two-to-one numerical superiority in the area. Nevertheless, he made no effort to regain the initiative, but instead ordered a second line of defense prepared north of Chancellorsville.

The night before, after Jackson's attack had been stopped just west of Fairview Hill, Sickles had returned from Catherine Furnace and had taken up a position that included the high ground at Hazel Grove, which dominated Fairview Hill and the surrounding area. Hooker had visited Hazel Grove and should have appreciated that a Federal attack from there would have struck the flank of Lee's army. Nevertheless, he ordered the position abandoned, a blunder of staggering magnitude. It left the Confederates to use the Dowdall's Tavern–Catherine Furnace road, thus reuniting their separated army. It also gave up the dominating terrain of the area. Stuart, who had taken over Jackson's army, advanced at daybreak on the 3rd and got fifty guns on to the top of Hazel Grove from which he directed a devastating fire on Sickles and Slocum. At the same time, the Confederates attacked both sides of the Union perimeter, where after numerous attacks they began to gain ground.

Hooker had been hit by a Confederate shell, but although badly shocked and in great pain, refused to relinquish command. Couch, next in command after Hooker, was a fighter, and had I and V Corps fresh and ready to attack; IX Corps, too, had only been lightly engaged. Lee's troops, by comparison, were fully committed and exhausted, but Hooker refused to relinquish command, and in fact ordered Couch to pull back north of Chancellorsville. Lee, in response, urged his exhausted troops forward and occupied Chancellorsville.

To the east, Sedgwick had received Hooker's order to attack about midnight on 2–3 May. Pushing back some light Confederate outposts, he occupied Fredericksburg by 5:00 A.M., and shortly after the Federals attacked the thinly held position. Despite Wilcox's arrival to strengthen the Confederate left, Sedgwick managed to take Marye's Heights at the fourth attempt and overran part of the Confederate artillery, forcing Early to retreat southward along Telegraph Road. Wilcox fell back toward Chancellorsville, trying to hold up the Union advance as he did so. He joined up with McLaws at Salem Church where they were vigorously attacked by Sedgwick. The Union attackers were eventually checked and both forces bivouacked on the battlefield.

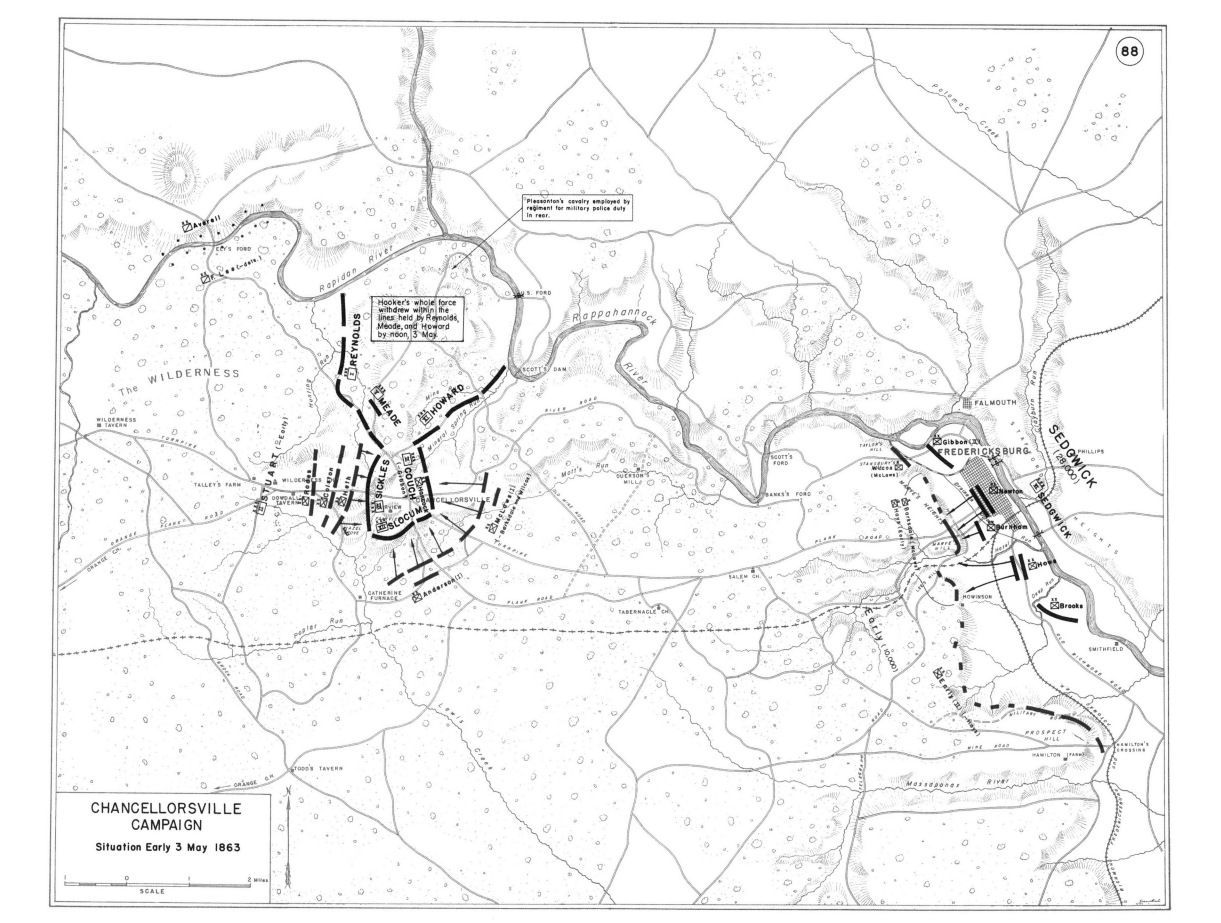

Pleasonton's cavalry employed by regiment for military police duty in rear.

Hooker's whole force withdrew within the lines held by Reynolds, Meade, and Howard by noon, 3 May.

The WILDERNESS

WILDERNESS TAVERN

Rapidan River

Rappahannock River

U.S. FORD

SCOTT'S DAM

ELY'S FORD

Hunting Run

Mine Spring Run

Mineral Spring Run

RIVER ROAD

FALMOUTH

SCOTT'S FORD

Mott's Run

DUERSON'S MILL

BANKS'S FORD

TAYLOR'S HILL

STANSBURY'S HILL

FREDERICKSBURG

PHILLIPS

Averell

R. Lee (dets.)

REYNOLDS

MEADE

HOWARD

STUART (Early)

Hooker

Colston

Hill

SICKLES

COUCH

Hancock

Geary

SLOCUM

FAIRVIEW

CHANCELLORSVILLE

HAZEL GROVE

McLaws (I)

Barksdale and Wilcox

Anderson (I)

CATHERINE FURNACE

TALLEY'S FARM

DOWDALL'S TAVERN

TURNPIKE

PLANK ROAD

ORANGE C.H.

ORANGE PLANK ROAD

TABERNACLE CH.

SALEM CH.

Poplar Run

BROCK ROAD

Lewis Creek

TODD'S TAVERN

ORANGE C.H.

Wilcox

Gibbon (II)

McLaws

STANSBURY'S HILL

MARYE'S HEIGHTS

Hays (Early)

Barksdale (McLaws)

Newton

Burnham

SEDGWICK (28,000)

SEDGWICK

Howe

Brooks

HOWINSON

Early (10,000)

Early (Hoke)

SMITHFIELD

PROSPECT HILL

HAMILTON (FARM)

HAMILTON'S CROSSING

MINE ROAD

MILITARY ROAD

TELEGRAPH ROAD

OLD RICHMOND ROAD

Massaponax River

Deep Run

Hazel Run

Potomac Creek

Aquia Creek

CHANCELLORSVILLE CAMPAIGN

Situation Early 3 May 1863

SCALE

1   0   1   2 Miles

CHANCELLORSVILLE CAMPAIGN: 4

During the night, Hooker's troops had strengthened their already strong position, and Lee, judging this to be an indication that Hooker intended to remain on the defensive, decided to concentrate against Sedgwick in the hopes of destroying his corps. Consequently, he left Stuart with 25,000 men to contain Hooker's 75,000, while he moved with 21,000 against Sedgwick's 19,000. During the night, Sedgwick established communication with the north bank of the Rappahannock across a pontoon bridge laid by the Army of Potomac engineers at Scott's Ford, and a detached brigade from II Corps set up a protective bridgehead on the south bank.

As Lee's concentration got under way, Early returned along Telegraph Road and advanced against Marye's Heights. Gibbon, heavily outnumbered, retired into Fredericksburg. Sedgwick set up a horseshoe-shaped defense and prepared hasty fortifications, hoping to hold out until night and then withdraw. His skillful organization of the ground that denied the Confederates the use of Plank Road greatly delayed Lee's deployment, and it was not until about 5:30 P.M. that Lee attacked. It was gallant but piecemeal, and Sedgwick gave at least as good as he got, allowing him to make an unmolested crossing at Scott's Ford during the night. Meanwhile, even though he could hear Sedgwick's cannon, Hooker, still groggy from his injury, made no effort to advance. During the early morning of 5 May, Gibbon skillfully recrossed to the north bank of the Rappahannock, and all the pontoon bridges downstream from United States Ford were taken up.

Lee now decided to crush Hooker, even though Hooker was embedded in a formidable mass of field fortifications. Lee concentrated every man for an assault at sunrise on the 6th, but Hooker had already decided on a withdrawal. Meade's V Corps was given the mission of serving as rear guard covering the withdrawal, and the rest of the army crossed the Rappahannock during the night of the 5th and morning of the 6th. The withdrawal took Lee completely by surprise, and only a few of his advance scouts ever made contact with the Federals.

Confederates losses were approximately 13,000; Federal, 17,000. Proportionately, however, Lee suffered the worse damage (even without taking Jackson's loss, which was grievous, into account).

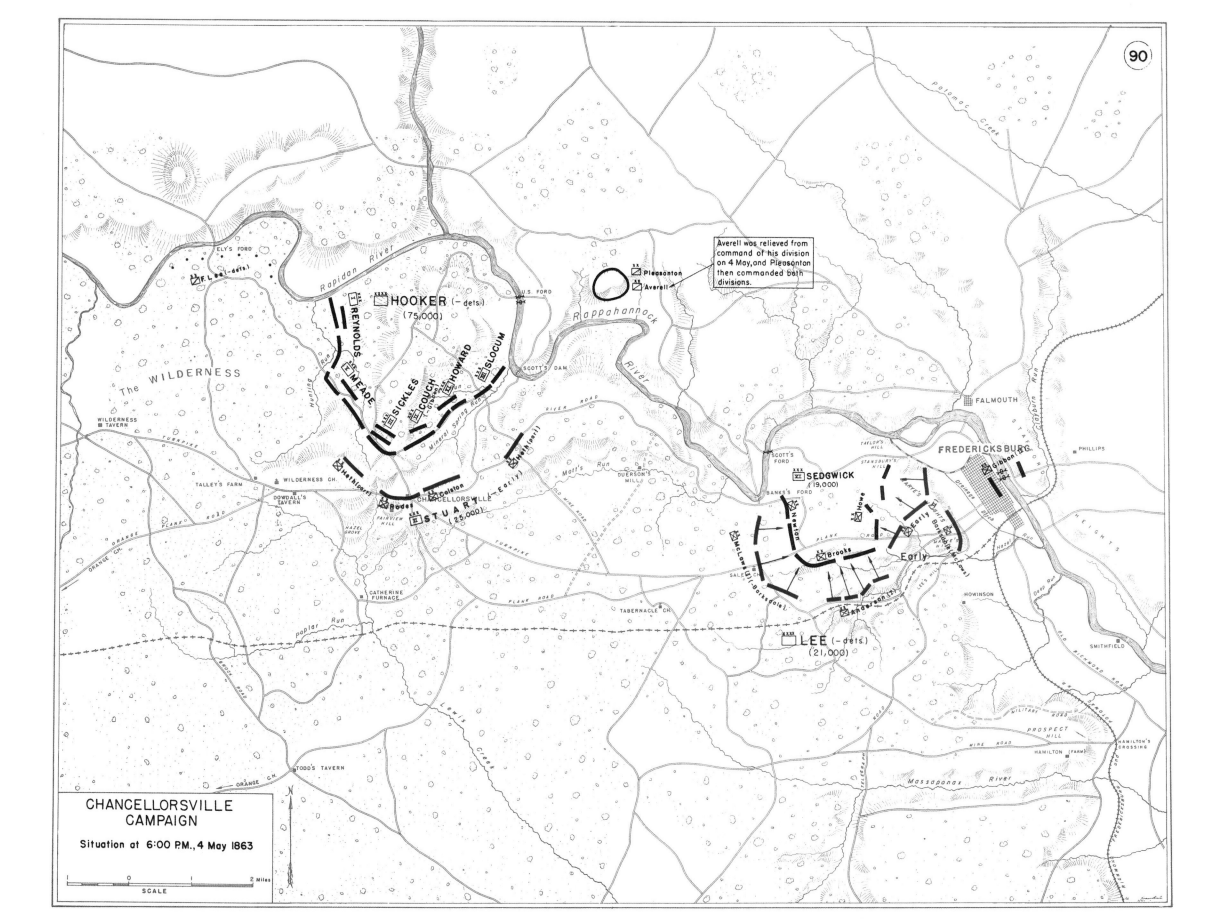

90

Averell was relieved from
command of his division
on 4 May, and Pleasonton
then commanded both
divisions.

XX Pleasonton
XX Averell

Rapidan River

ELY'S FORD
F. Lee (-dets.)

The WILDERNESS

WILDERNESS
TAVERN

HOOKER (-dets.)
(75,000)

REYNOLDS
MEADE
SICKLES
COUCH (-dets.)
HOWARD
SLOCUM

U.S. FORD
SCOTT'S DAM
Rappahannock River

Hunting Run
Mineral Spring Run

Hazel Run

TURNPIKE

TALLEY'S FARM
DOWDALL'S TAVERN
WILDERNESS CH.
Hazel Grove
FAIRVIEW HILL
Rodes
CHANCELLORSVILLE (-Early)
STUART
(25,000)
Colston

RIVER ROAD

Mott's Run
DUERSON'S MILL

SCOTT'S FORD

BANKS'S FORD
SEDGWICK
(19,000)

FALMOUTH

TAYLOR'S HILL
STANSBURY'S HILL

FREDERICKSBURG

PHILLIPS

Gibbon
HEIGHTS

Newton
Howe
Early
Marye's
Barksdale
Early

ORANGE
PLANK
ROAD

CATHERINE FURNACE

McLaws
Barksdale
Brooks
Anderson

SALEM CH.

PLANK ROAD

TABERNACLE CH.

LEE (-dets.)
(21,000)

HOWINSON

SMITHFIELD

Poplar Run

Lewis Creek

Brock Road

ORANGE CH.
TODD'S TAVERN

ORANGE CH.

N

PROSPECT HILL

HAMILTON (FARM)
HAMILTON'S CROSSING

MINE ROAD

Massaponax River

MILITARY ROAD

OLD RICHMOND ROAD

CHANCELLORSVILLE
CAMPAIGN

Situation at 6:00 P.M., 4 May 1863

SCALE
2 Miles

GETTYSBURG CAMPAIGN: 1

Following Chancellorsville, Hooker and Lee resumed their former positions along the Rappahannock. Hooker's main aim was to defend Harper's Ferry and Washington, while on the Confederate side Chancellorsville was seen as a solid victory and a feeling of euphoria spread through the Army of Northern Virginia. It was now a far stronger army than the one Hooker had faced at Chancellorsville, and conscription enabled Lee to fill out his weaker units. Accordingly, he reorganized the army into three infantry corps, commanded respectively by Longstreet, Ewell, and A. P. Hill, together with Stuart's oversized cavalry division. (Throughout the first three years of the war, the average Southern corps and division had almost twice as many men as did their Northern counterparts.)

However, the overall military situation was not promising for the Confederacy. The Army of the Potomac was still strong, and Lee knew that it was only a matter of time before it launched a new offensive. The Federal naval blockade continued to throttle Southern ports. In the center, Rosencrans and Bragg neutralized one another for the time being, but the war along the Mississippi was definitely being lost by the Confederacy. Grant held Lt. Gen. John C. Pemberton under siege at Vicksburg, and New Orleans had been captured by Rear Admiral David G. Farragut in April 1862.

On 9 June 1863, the opposing forces were disposed as shown below (*left*). Lee's own plan was simple: he could never win the war by defensive strategy; therefore he had to invade the North once again. Hooker's position was too strong to attack, but the threat of an invasion would force him to leave it. So Lee began shifting his army quietly westward for an advance down the Shenandoah and up the Cumberland Valleys. By holding the passes in the Blue Ridge and South Mountains, he could both screen his advance and protect his supply line. A. P. Hill's corps remained around Fredericksburg, spread thinly to deceive Hooker that whole Confederate army was there.

By late May, Hooker had an inkling of Lee's plan, and he sent Sedgwick across the river on 5–6 June to test the Confederate strength in the Fredericksburg area; Hill reacted aggressively, trying to convince Sedgwick that the whole army was there. Hooker was not convinced and sent Gen. Alfred Pleasanton (commander of the Cavalry Corps) off on a reconnaissance toward Culpeper. Early on 9 June, Pleasanton surprised Stuart, his Confederate counterpart, at Brandy Station, and the largest cavalry action in American history began with some 10,000 sabers on each side. Stuart, supported by infantry, began to get the upper hand, and Pleasanton withdrew, having discovered what he needed to.

Hooker began shifting his forces further west. On the 13th, certain that Lee was moving into the Shenandoah, he moved his army swiftly toward Manassas. By 17 June, the Confederates were strung out over a distance of one hundred miles, as shown, and by 24 June, they had closed up north of the Potomac. On that day, Hooker set his army in motion toward Frederick, Maryland.

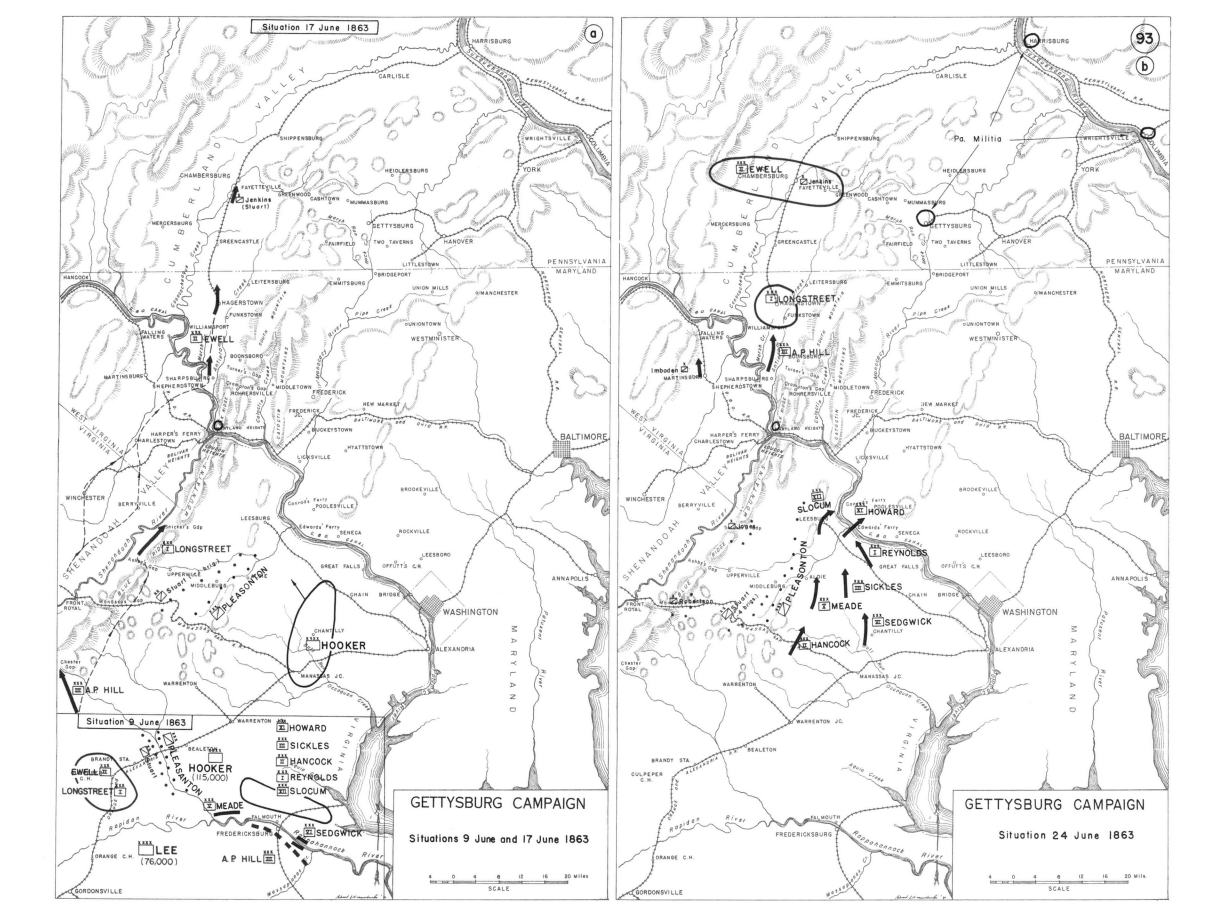

Situation 17 June 1863

a

93

b

GETTYSBURG CAMPAIGN

Situations 9 June and 17 June 1863

GETTYSBURG CAMPAIGN

Situation 24 June 1863

GETTYSBURG CAMPAIGN: 2

On 27 June, Hooker had the Army of the Potomac concentrated between Frederick and South Mountain and had ordered cavalry sent forward toward Emmitsburg and Gettysburg. He appears to have planned an operation against Lee's lines of communications but had issued no definite orders. The United States could not afford another Chancellorsville, especially one fought on Northern soil, so the administration had given Hooker all available reinforcements, including a large part of the Washington garrison, yet Hooker was complaining that he undermanned, and asked to be relieved. Lincoln acquiesced, and Meade became the new commander of the Army of the Potomac.

Lee was short of information about Union dispositions, partly because J. E. B. Stuart (the "eyes" of the army) had taken it upon himself to take his three favorite brigades on a raid east, where they became entangled in Union columns and could not return until 27 June. Lee, therefore, was under the misapprehension that Meade's army was still sitting south of the Potomac. On the 28th, he discovered that his opponent was, in fact, around Frederick, and preparing to march. At 4:00 P.M. on 29 June, Meade began moving north.

Meade was a cautious, canny fighter, fully aware that he was about to face Lee, the champion, and sensitive to the enormous burden that rested on his shoulders. But he did have the advantage of a group of seasoned corps commanders with an excellent knowledge of Lee's position and actual strength. Halleck gave him no instructions other than to maneuver to cover the capital and Baltimore "as far as circumstances will admit."

The night of 28/29 June had been a busy one for Lee's staff; orders went out at the gallop for all Confederate units to concentrate at Cashtown because it offered a strong defensive position, and a concentration there would put Lee's army on the flank of the Union advance from Frederick. Stuart was struggling northward toward Hanover, doing minor skirmishing, and Lee took a while to galvanize his other cavalry resources.

Meade's earlier determination to find and fight Lee began to weaken. He lost sleep, missed meals, frequently changed orders, and became highly agitated at times. On the 30th, while his engineers reconnoitered a defensive position along Big Pipe Creek, he ordered Reynolds to advance the next day with I and XI Corps to Gettysburg, and III Corps to Emmitsburg, while leaving VI Corps far to the rear at Manchester. Also on the 30th, Buford, with two brigades of cavalry, rode through Gettysburg toward the Cashtown Gap, where they briefly clashed with Brig. Gen. James J. Pettigrew's infantry as they came in the opposite direction in search of shoes at Gettysburg. Pettigrew fell back to Cashtown and reported Buford's position to his immediate commander, Maj. Gen. Henry Heth, and his corps commander, A. P. Hill. Heth received permission to go to Gettysburg next day and "get those shoes." Buford, meanwhile, had examined the road network around Gettysburg and came to the conclusion that the town was a key position, which he reported to Meade and Reynolds, and then prepared to hold the town.

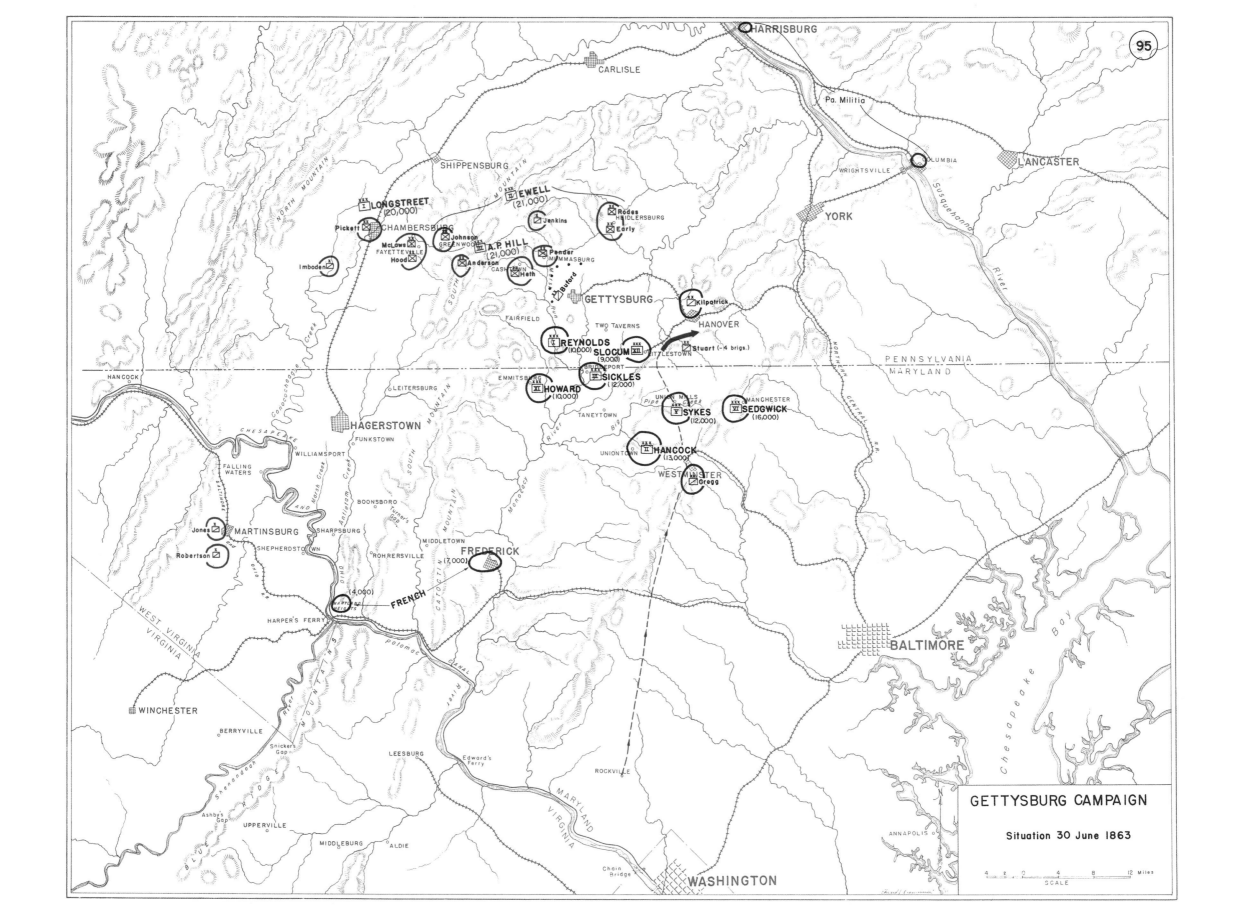

HARRISBURG

CARLISLE

Pa. Militia

LANCASTER

COLUMBIA

WRIGHTSVILLE

YORK

SHIPPENSBURG

LONGSTREET
(20,000)

EWELL
(21,000)

Pickett

CHAMBERSBURG

Johnson
GREENWOOD

Jenkins

Rodes
HEIDLERSBURG

Early

McLaws
FAYETTEVILLE
Hood

A.P. HILL
(21,000)

Anderson

Pender
MUMMASBURG

CASHTOWN
Heth

Imboden

Buford

GETTYSBURG

Kilpatrick

FAIRFIELD

TWO TAVERNS

HANOVER

REYNOLDS
(10,000)
SLOCUM
(9,000)

LITTLESTOWN

Stuart (~4 brigs.)

PENNSYLVANIA
MARYLAND

HANCOCK

EMMITSBURG

Pipe Creek

HOWARD
(10,000)

SICKLES
(12,000)

UNION MILLS

MANCHESTER

SYKES
(12,000)

SEDGWICK
(16,000)

TANEYTOWN

Big

HAGERSTOWN

FUNKSTOWN

HANCOCK
(13,000)

UNIONTOWN

WILLIAMSPORT

WESTMINSTER

Gregg

FALLING
WATERS

BOONSBORO

Turner's
Gap

CHESAPEAKE

Jones

MARTINSBURG

SHARPSBURG

SHEPHERDSTOWN

Robertson

MIDDLETOWN

FREDERICK
(7,000)

(4,000)
FRENCH

HARPER'S FERRY

WEST
VIRGINIA
VIRGINIA

WINCHESTER

BERRYVILLE

ROHRERSVILLE

LEESBURG

Edward's
Ferry

ROCKVILLE

BALTIMORE

Chesapeake
Bay

MARYLAND
VIRGINIA

Snicker's
Gap

Ashby's
Gap

UPPERVILLE

MIDDLEBURG

ALDIE

ANNAPOLIS

Chain
Bridge

WASHINGTON

GETTYSBURG CAMPAIGN

Situation 30 June 1863

SCALE
12 Miles

GETTYSBURG CAMPAIGN: 3

The terrain around Gettysburg shaped the battle, so is worth examining.

Northwest of Gettysburg is the dominating height of Oak Hill, southward from which ran two high ridges: Seminary Ridge, the longer one, extends to the Peach Orchard and along the Emmitsburg Road beyond; just to the left is McPherson's Ridge (not on map), wider but lower. North of Gettysburg, the ground is relatively open and level, while south of the town, Cemetery Hill rises abruptly some eighty feet. A lower ridge runs eastward from Cemetery Hill, ending in the rugged, wooded mass of Culp's Hill, while Cemetery Ridge extends for approximately a mile to the south. At its southern tip, Cemetery Ridge dwindles away into a low, timbered area, after which come the bold elevations of Little Round Top and Round Top. From Round Top to Culp's Hill, along this "fishhook" line, is approximately four miles. Seminary Ridge and Cemetery Ridge run parallel, about a mile apart across open fields, whereas the ground between Seminary Ridge and the Round Tops is rough and broken.

About 8:00 A.M. on 1 July 1863, Heth's division, followed by that of Maj. Gen. W. Dorsey Pender, encountered Buford, who had deployed a dismounted brigade under Brig. Gen. William Gamble along McPherson's Ridge, and Maj. Gen. Thomas C. Devin's brigade across the Carlisle Road considerably north of Gettysburg, awaiting Ewell. Although Buford was outmanned, his positions were good, and his repeating carbines gave him good firepower. For almost two hours this single brigade with one battery of artillery held up the Confederate attack. By 9:30, Reynolds was on the field, the divisions of his I Corps (temporarily under Maj. Gen. Abner Doubleday) strung out along the road behind him. Buford had been pushed back to Seminary Ridge. Reynolds did not know of Meade's intention to defend at Big Pipe Creek, but he was a fighter and Gettysburg looked like a good place for a battle. He ordered Gen. Oliver O. Howard's XI Corps to advance.

Around 11:00 A.M., Heth's attack on Seminary Ridge was wrecked by a counterattack led by Brig. Gen. James S. Wadsworth, but Reynolds was killed by a sharpshooter. To the north, Ewell was pressing in, and about noon Howard arrived and took command, and called for help from Slocum and Sickles. Recognizing the importance of Cemetery Hill, he dropped one of his divisions there as a reserve and began moving the other two toward Oak Hill on Doubleday's right flank. However, the arrival of Ewell's leading division forced him to form them in line directly north of the town. Confederate pressure was building up and A. P. Hill renewed his attack from the west; Early arrived from York and outflanked the Union right, while Confederate artillery on Oak Hill enfiladed both Union corps, despite good counterbattery work. The Union lines gave, slowly and stubbornly in most places, but more and more rapidly on the right, as Early's attack gathered momentum.

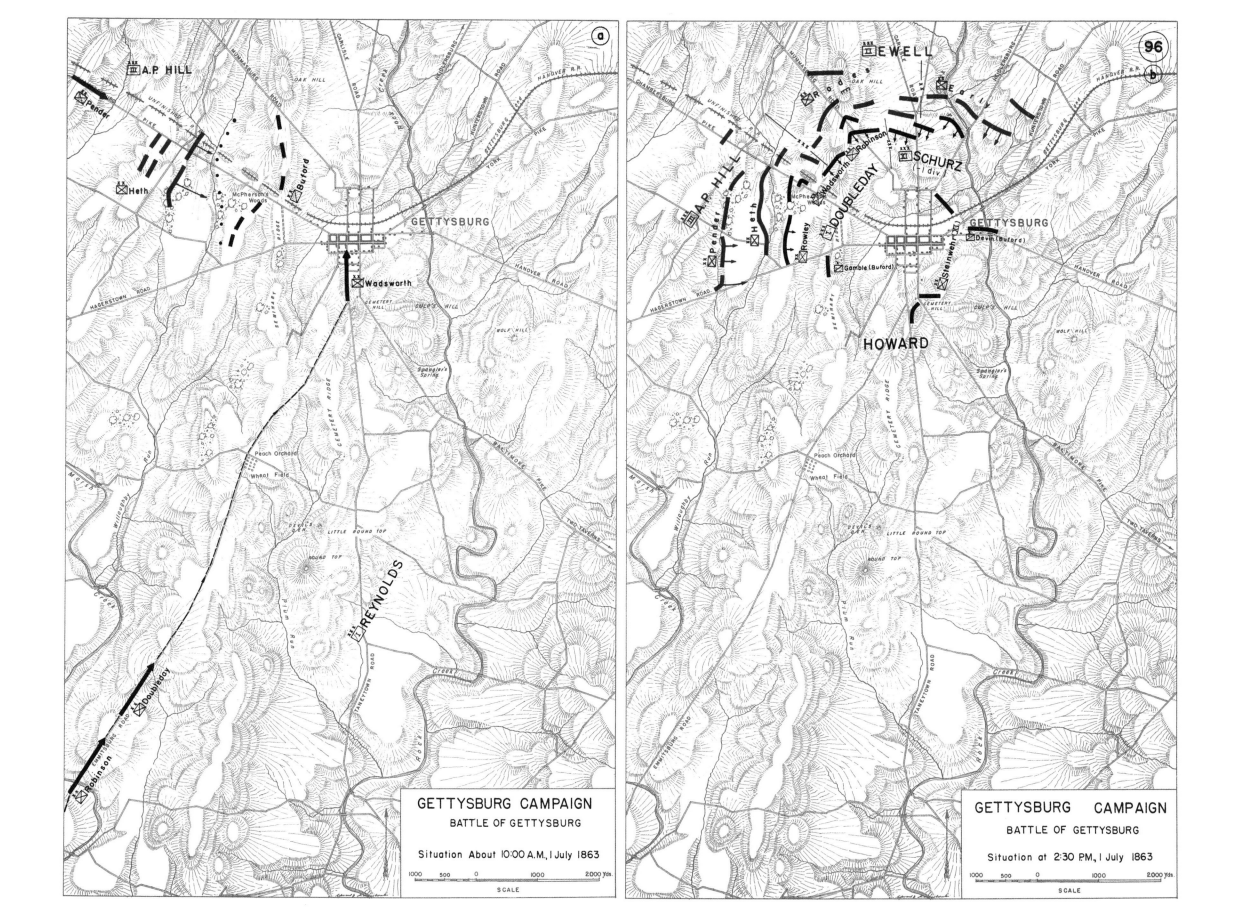

A.P. HILL

Pender

Heth

McPherson's Woods

Buford

CARLISLE ROAD

OAK HILL

MUMMASBURG ROAD

HANOVER R.R.

UNFINISHED PIKE

YORK ROAD

HUNTERSTOWN ROAD

GETTYSBURGH PIKE

GETTYSBURG

HAGERSTOWN ROAD

SEMINARY RIDGE

CEMETERY RIDGE

Wadsworth

CEMETERY HILL

CULP'S HILL

HANOVER ROAD

WOLF HILL

Spangler's Spring

Peach Orchard

Wheat Field

DEVIL'S DEN

LITTLE ROUND TOP

ROUND TOP

TANEYTOWN ROAD

BALTIMORE PIKE

TWO TAVERNS

REYNOLDS

MARSH CREEK

WILLOUGHBY RUN

PLUM RUN

ROCK CREEK

Doubleday

EMMITSBURG ROAD

Robinson

GETTYSBURG CAMPAIGN

BATTLE OF GETTYSBURG

Situation About 10:00 A.M., 1 July 1863

1000 500 0 1000 2000 Yds.

SCALE

EWELL

Rodes

Early

A.P. HILL

Pender

Heth

Robinson

Wadsworth

McPherson's Woods

Rowley

SCHURZ
(I div)

DOUBLEDAY

Devin (Buford)

GETTYSBURG

Gamble (Buford)

Steinwehr

HOWARD

CARLISLE ROAD

OAK HILL

MUMMASBURG ROAD

HANOVER R.R.

UNFINISHED RY.

YORK ROAD

HUNTERSTOWN ROAD

GETTYSBURGH PIKE

HAGERSTOWN ROAD

SEMINARY RIDGE

CEMETERY RIDGE

CEMETERY HILL

CULP'S HILL

HANOVER ROAD

WOLF HILL

Spangler's Spring

Peach Orchard

Wheat Field

DEVIL'S DEN

LITTLE ROUND TOP

ROUND TOP

TANEYTOWN ROAD

BALTIMORE PIKE

TWO TAVERNS

MARSH CREEK

WILLOUGHBY RUN

PLUM RUN

ROCK CREEK

EMMITSBURG ROAD

GETTYSBURG CAMPAIGN

BATTLE OF GETTYSBURG

Situation at 2:30 P.M., 1 July 1863

1000 500 0 1000 2000 Yds.

SCALE

GETTYSBURG CAMPAIGN: 4

While XI Corps was driven back through the town in something like a rout, I Corps withdrew in fairly good order. While A. P. Hill sat on Seminary Ridge, Ewell's command flowed into the town. Howard rallied XI Corps on Cemetery Hill, which had been turned into a strong point by Brig. Gen. Adolph von Steinwehr. Both Union Corps had suffered losses of over 50 percent, but at least they could count on a strong artillery presence on Cemetery Hill and Ridge.

Shortly after 4:00 P.M. Hancock arrived, under orders to take over command, and he and Howard rapidly organized the position; Hancock grasped the importance of Culp's Hill and browbeat Doubleday into sending the survivors of the Iron Brigade to occupy it. XII Corps began arriving shortly after 5:00 P.M.; and elements of III Corps, an hour later.

Lee had been overtaken by events at Gettysburg. His army was scattered across south-central Pennsylvania; Stuart, typically, was headed in the wrong direction; and now aggressive subordinate commanders had plunged him into a major battle. He had won partial success against a weaker enemy but did not know where the rest of the Union army might be. Now, eager to destroy the weakened Union forces at Gettysburg, he ordered Ewell to take Cemetery Hill, "if practicable." Ewell, whose own men had taken a battering, decided it was not, and an attack on Culp's Hill was beaten off by the Iron Brigade. That night and next morning, both armies massed around Gettysburg; and with Meade's having arrived at midnight, Lee's numerical superiority was beginning to erode.

Lee's plan for 2 July was for Longstreet to get around the Federal left (which Lee mistakenly thought extended from Cemetery Hill along Cemetery Road) and attack north. Anderson's division would then join the assault, and Ewell would attack when he heard Longstreet's guns. Lee had wanted an early attack, but it was 11:00 A.M. before his orders were issued—orders of which Longstreet did not approve. He had wanted to take a defensive position and let Meade attack him. Disgruntled, he moved forward over strange ground, his lead units taking heavy casualties from the sharpshooters of III Corps. The Federal line was not where Lee had expected it; there was trouble forming for the attack, so it was not until 3:00 P.M. that Longstreet's artillery opened up.

There were three flaws in the Union position at this time: the Round Tops remained unoccupied, although they were crucial to the security of the left flank; Pleasanton had ordered Buford from the south flank back to Westminster, but had forgotten to replace him; and Sickles had moved his corps forward from the ground just north of the Round Tops without permission from Meade. Sickles's new position (which was too extensive for his one corps) was on higher ground, but its shape permitted Confederate artillery to take it under fire from two directions. Meade furiously attempted to have Sickles reposition, but it was too late. Confederate infantry was advancing.

84

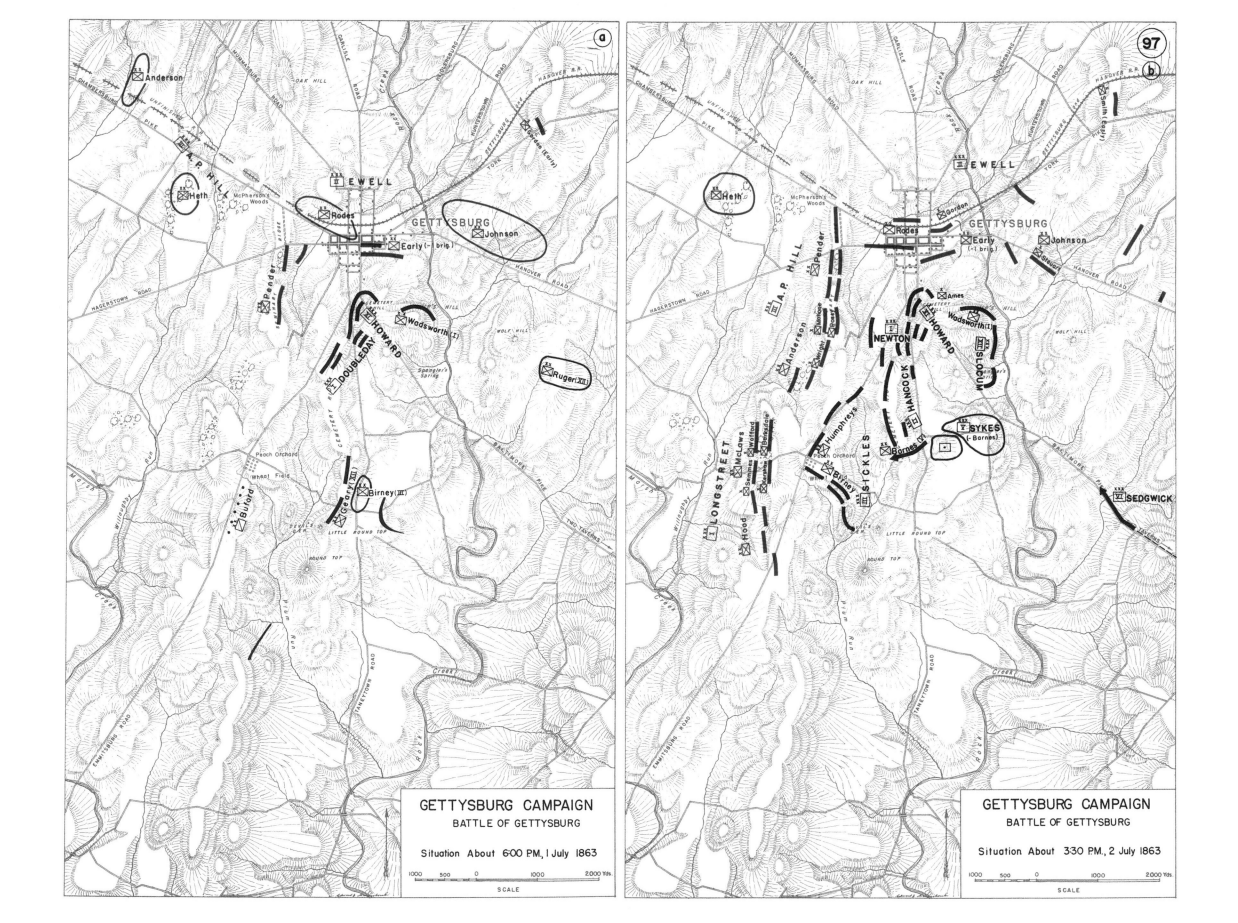

GETTYSBURG CAMPAIGN

BATTLE OF GETTYSBURG

Situation About 6:00 P.M., 1 July 1863

1000 500 0 1000 2000 Yds.

SCALE

GETTYSBURG CAMPAIGN

BATTLE OF GETTYSBURG

Situation About 3:30 P.M., 2 July 1863

1000 500 0 1000 2000 Yds.

SCALE

GETTYSBURG CAMPAIGN: 5

Meade had already ordered Sykes's V Corps to support the left flank, and also now began shift most of Slocum's XII Corps to the left. The lead units of Sedgwick's VI Corps were also arriving on the left, but they were exhausted from a thirty-four-mile march.

Longstreet's attack was a jumbled affair from the start; divisions and brigades went in piecemeal, but with a savage enthusiasm. Hood's division quickly smashed Sickles's left flank, overran the Devil's Den, and went clawing up the west side of Little Round Top. This was the key to the Union position because, from its crest, enfilading fire could be directed down the whole Union line. At this desperate moment, Brig. Gen. Gouverneur K. Warren, chief engineer of the Army of the Potomac, reached Little Round Top and found it occupied by only a small signal detail. On his own responsibility, he ordered two V Corps brigades and a battery on to its summit, and they got there just a few yards ahead of Hood's men and drove off the Confederates in hand-to-hand fighting.

Sickles's center and right flank held longer than his left, but was eventually driven back; and although one of Anderson's brigades broke through the Federal center, it was soon expelled. To the north, Ewell's artillery open up at the sound of Longstreet's guns but was soon silenced, and it was almost dark when Ewell committed his infantry. Johnson failed to carry Culp's Hill, and although two of Early's brigades got up the east side of Cemetery Hill to the top, only their dead stayed there.

Meade took council on the night of 2 July with his corps commanders: should they withdraw or should they fight? His commanders voted to stay, and so Meade placed Hancock in charge of II, II, and part of I Corps, forming the Union center. Slocum reformed XII Corps and prepared to recover his former positions around Culp's Hill. Johnson attacked at 11:00 A.M. on the 3rd, but Slocum beat him off.

Longstreet now urged Lee to reduce the Union left, get across Meade's lines of communication and force him to attack. But Lee knew he had little time. He could not delay and maneuver because his army was living off the country and would soon strip it bare; his own communications were highly vulnerable; and besides, the enemy in front of him engaged his natural combativeness. He gave his orders: Longstreet would penetrate the Federal center, while Stuart with all the army's cavalry, would strike the enemy's rear. Longstreet protested, but made the necessary preparations. He had 159 guns massed opposite the Union center, and about 15,000 infantry under Pickett readied for the assault. At 1:00 P.M., the Confederate artillery opened up, and was answered by only a brief Union artillery response (they had stopped to conserve ammunition), and, believing they had won the duel, urged Pickett to advance while they could still support him. As Pickett's men advanced, Union cannon tore huge gaps in their ranks, and Union infantry attacked their flanks. Yet they crashed into the first Union line. Then the Federal closed in. Well behind the battle, Brig. Gen. David M. Gregg intercepted Stuart and drove him back.

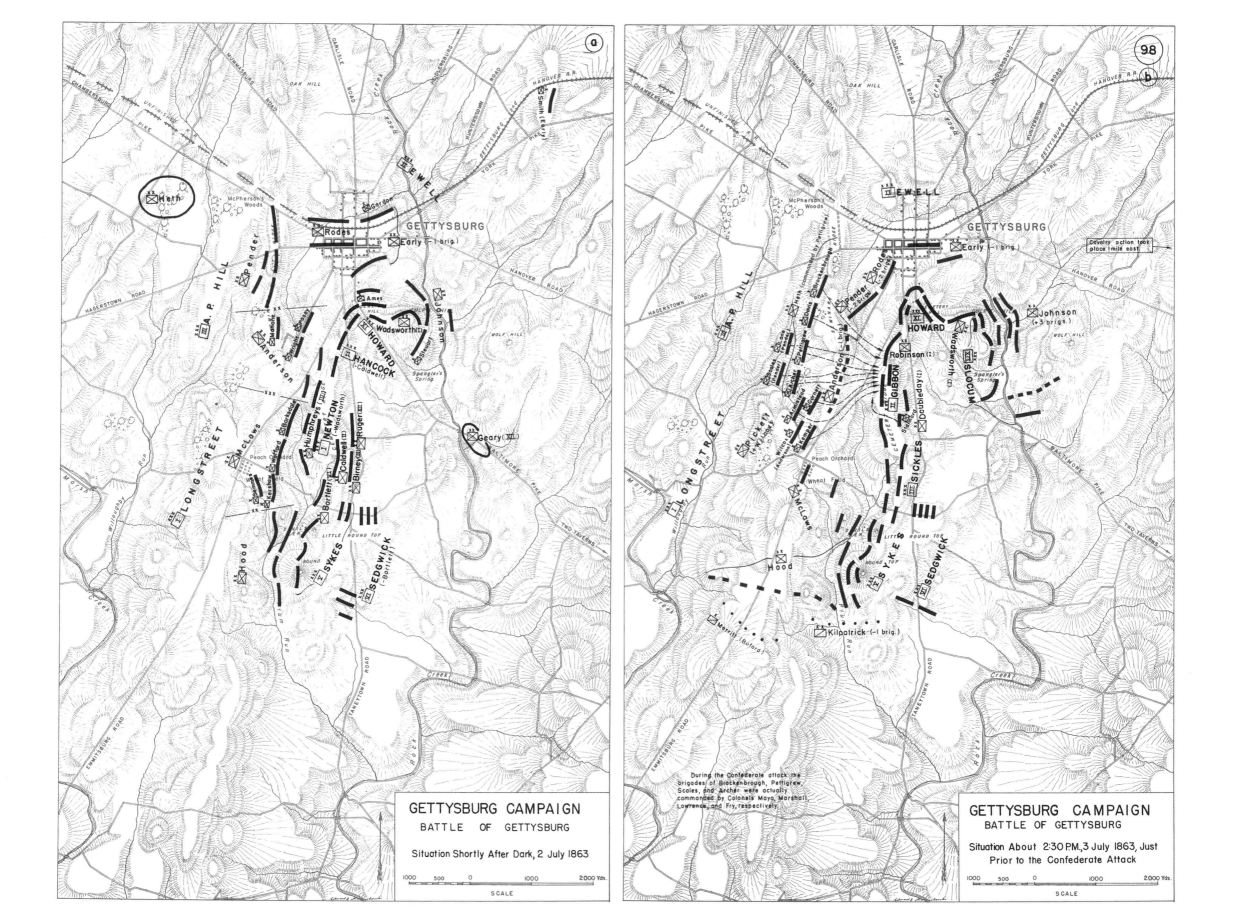

GETTYSBURG CAMPAIGN

BATTLE OF GETTYSBURG

Situation Shortly After Dark, 2 July 1863

1000   500   0   1000   2000 Yds.

SCALE

GETTYSBURG CAMPAIGN

BATTLE OF GETTYSBURG

Situation About 2:30 P.M., 3 July 1863, Just
Prior to the Confederate Attack

During the Confederate attack the
brigades of Brockenbrough, Pettigrew,
Scales, and Archer were actually
commanded by Colonels Mayo, Marshall,
Lowrence, and Fry, respectively.

Cavalry action took
place 1 mile east.

1000   500   0   1000   2000 Yds.

SCALE

GETTYSBURG CAMPAIGN: 6

lthough urged to counterattack after Pickett's attack had failed, Meade was content to fight defensively. Instead of keeping VI Corps concentrated for a decisive counterstroke, he scattered behind the lines as a reserve, and forfeited his chance to destroy Lee's army. On the night of the 3rd, Lee pulled his army together and dug in on a line running from Oak Hill to the Peach Orchard. Both armies were badly mauled; the Federals had lost 23,049 killed, wounded, and missing—approximately 25 percent of their total forces. The Confederates reported losses totaling 20,451, although their returns are incomplete. It is likely their actual losses were 28,000, about one-third of their troops.

Undoubtedly, Gettysburg was the lowest point of Lee's generalship (he accepted the blame for Pickett's defeat—"It's all my fault," he told the survivors). He was careless, his orders were vague, he merely suggested when he should have commanded, and he foredoomed his infantry in an attempt to win a battle that was already lost. But, on 4 July, he reasserted himself. All day (as he had before at Antietam), he held his army in position, defying Meade to attack. Meanwhile, his long convoy of wounded started to the rear, and that night, in driving rain, the rest of the Army of Northern Virginia followed.

Meade spent the 4th reorganizing. He planned a reconnaissance in force for the 5th. But by the 5th, Lee had gone. A slow pursuit did get under way, but Meade constantly fretted that Lee might turn on him and force another battle. Actually, Lee had arrived at Williamsport on the 7th, almost out of ammunition and his ranks thinned by desertion (his army now stood at about 35,000). In desperation, he entrenched with his back to the Chesapeake, and tried to improvise pontoons to get his army across. Meade approached cautiously with his 85,000 men and then called a council of war. His most aggressive commanders—Reynolds, Hancock, and Sickles—were dead or wounded, a majority of the council voted not to attack. So, on 13–14 July, Lee got his men across. He had escaped, but his army would never be the same.

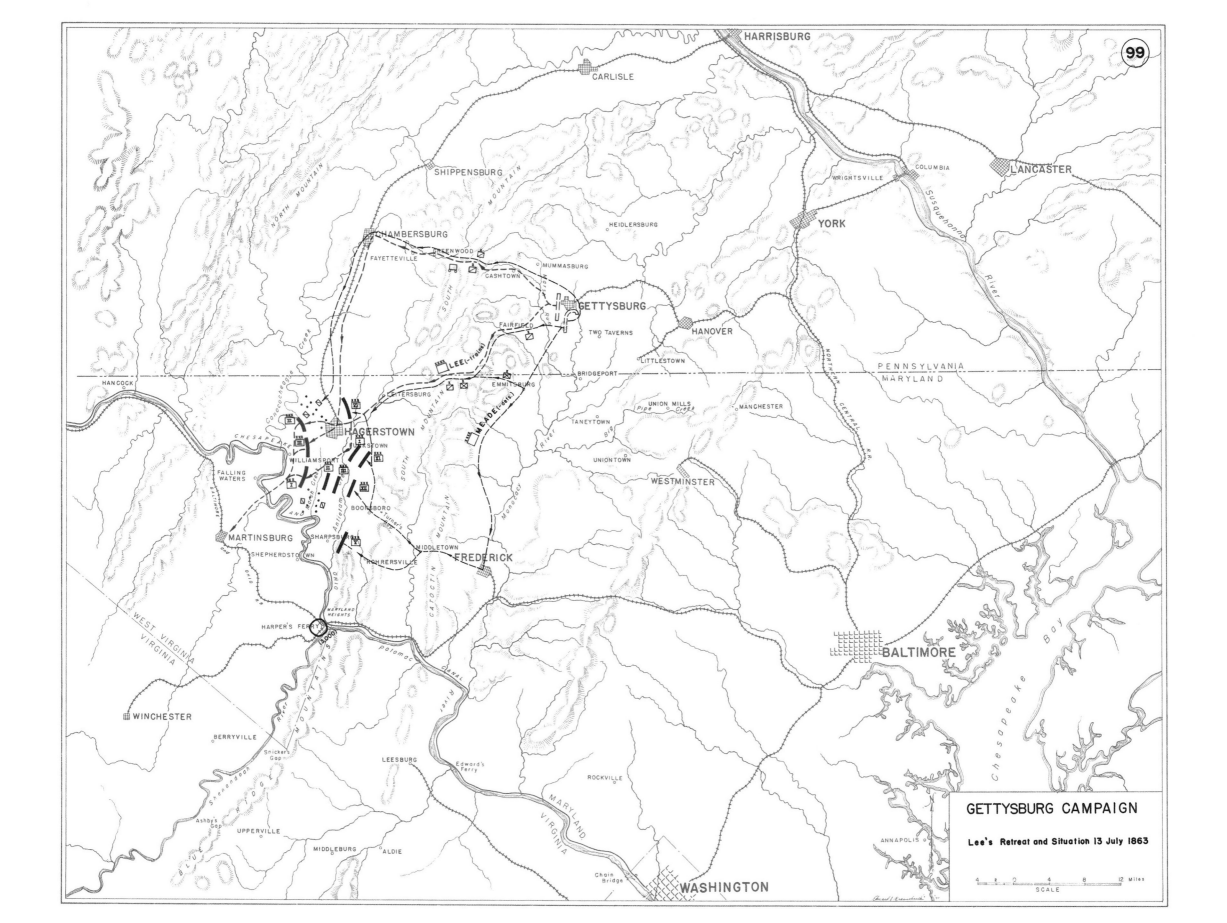

HARRISBURG

CARLISLE

SHIPPENSBURG

COLUMBIA

LANCASTER

WRIGHTSVILLE

HEIDLERSBURG

YORK

CHAMBERSBURG

FAYETTEVILLE

GREENWOOD

MUMMASBURG

CASHTOWN

GETTYSBURG

HANOVER

FAIRFIELD

TWO TAVERNS

LEE(-1 corps)

LITTLESTOWN

BRIDGEPORT

PENNSYLVANIA

MARYLAND

LEITERSBURG

EMMITSBURG

HANCOCK

UNION MILLS

Pipe

Creek

MANCHESTER

HAGERSTOWN

FUNKSTOWN

MEADE (-2 corps)

TANEYTOWN

Big

WILLIAMSPORT

UNIONTOWN

WESTMINSTER

FALLING
WATERS

BOONSBORO

Turner's

MARTINSBURG

SHARPSBURG

MIDDLETOWN

FREDERICK

SHEPHERDSTOWN

ROHRERSVILLE

MARYLAND
HEIGHTS

HARPER'S FERRY
13,000

BALTIMORE

WEST VIRGINIA

VIRGINIA

WINCHESTER

BERRYVILLE

LEESBURG

Edward's
Ferry

ROCKVILLE

Snicker's
Gap

Chesapeake Bay

UPPERVILLE

MIDDLEBURG

ALDIE

MARYLAND

VIRGINIA

ANNAPOLIS

Chain
Bridge

WASHINGTON

GETTYSBURG CAMPAIGN

Lee's Retreat and Situation 13 July 1863

4 2 0 4 8   12 Miles
SCALE

VICKSBURG CAMPAIGN: 1

Vicksburg was the decisive campaign in the western theater. It divided the Confederacy in two and brought Grant the reputation that eventually led to his selection as commander in chief of the Union armies.

To recap: after Shiloh, Halleck had advanced to Corinth and, on his recall to Washington on 17 July 1862, he had divided his army between Buell and Grant. In accordance with Halleck's plans, Grant's army was therefore dispersed to guard communications in western Tennessee. Buell was near Nashville, trying to counter Bragg's invasion of Kentucky, and had been reinforced with three of Grant's divisions. Opposing Grant were Price and Van Dorn, acting under Bragg's overall command.

Vicksburg was of great strategic importance to the Confederacy because it blocked Union navigation down the Mississippi and, perhaps more important, allowed communication with the states west of the river that were so essential for Confederate supplies. The natural defenses of the city were ideal for the warfare of the period: it sat high on a bluff overlooking a bend of the river, with a maze of swamps and bayous protecting its northern approaches.

Vicksburg had been attacked before—unsuccessfully by Farragut in May 1862. In June, under orders to try again, he returned; but by now the city had been strongly reinforced and the batteries strengthened. Farragut called on Capt. Charles H. Davis (succes-

sor to Admiral Foote, who had been wounded in the assault on Fort Donelson), to join his operations against Vicksburg.

Their attempt to bombard the fortress into surrender on 26–28 June failed, and throughout July they were reduced to bombardment and minor skirmishing with Confederate vessels because the contingent of infantry they transported, under Brig. Gen. Thomas Williams, was far too small to attempt a landing. In late July, Farragut returned to New Orleans, leaving part of Williams's command behind at Baton Rouge, while Davis went upstream to Memphis, which went back and forth between Confederate and Union occupiers.

The Union failure to capture Vicksburg in early July 1862 has seen the subject of much debate. Halleck has been criticized for not moving promptly, but he had actually expected the navy to take the city without too much difficulty. This was an overly optimistic appraisal, given Williams's small force. Halleck should have dispatched a sizable force to Memphis to accompany Davis downstream to Vicksburg, but so should the Union administration have given Farragut enough troops to accomplish the task assigned to him. In June, such an operation might have succeeded but, by December 1862, Vicksburg was heavily garrisoned and would be able to withstand anything but a major offensive.

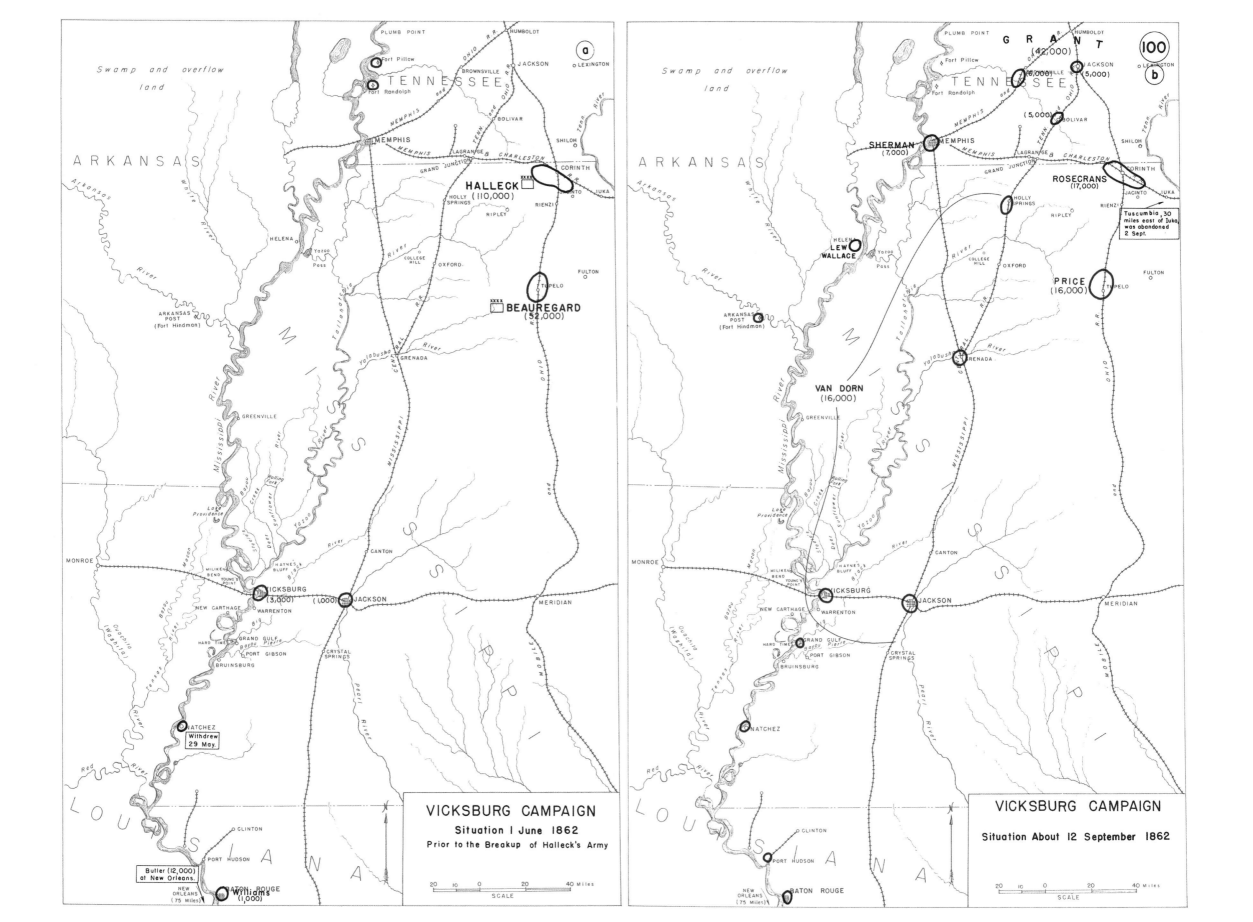

VICKSBURG CAMPAIGN

Situation 1 June 1862

Prior to the Breakup of Halleck's Army

VICKSBURG CAMPAIGN

Situation About 12 September 1862

VICKSBURG CAMPAIGN: 2

When Bragg departed with his main army for Chattanooga, he left Price to prevent Grant from sending reinforcement to Buell, and left Van Dorn to guard Vicksburg. Under the erroneous impression that Rosencrans had left Corinth to join Buell, Bragg ordered Price to move to Nashville to balance the scales. Price reached Iuka on 14 September 1862, where he learned Rosencrans was still at Corinth. There Grant decided to attack him; but as often happens in war, the plans went awry. Rosencrans was delayed, the battle continued until dark, and Price managed to get away to join Van Dorn. The joint force attacked Rosencrans at Corinth; the two-day battle resulted in Van Dorn's withdrawing toward Chewalla. The battle cost the Confederates 4,838 casualties; the Union, 3,090. A period of watchful waiting now followed. Sherman's attempted investment of Vicksburg had failed, and on 29 January 1863, Grant himself took over command of the siege, and decided to come down through the bayous until his force was south of the city, and then it would be transported to the east bank by barges. By 29 April,

McPherson's and McClernand's corps were at Hard Times, south of Vicksburg; and by 7 May, Sherman had joined them.

Grant was faced with the possibility that if he waited too long, Pemberton, the commander of the Vicksburg garrison, might be reinforced. So, in one of the most daring decisions of the war, he decided to cut loose from his base and operate without a supply line. On May 11, he began his advance from Rocky Springs; and by the 14th, Sherman and McPherson had reached Jackson; while McClernand, at Raymond and Clinton, blocked any Confederate advance from the west. The confederate situation on the night of the 14th approached the ludicrous. Johnston was retreating to the northeast, while Pemberton was preparing to advance to the southeast in search of a nonexistent Union supply line. Grant, well concentrated, was squarely between them. On 18 May, Grant pushed on to Vicksburg and then, hoping for an opportunistic victory, he attacked on the 19th, unsuccessfully.

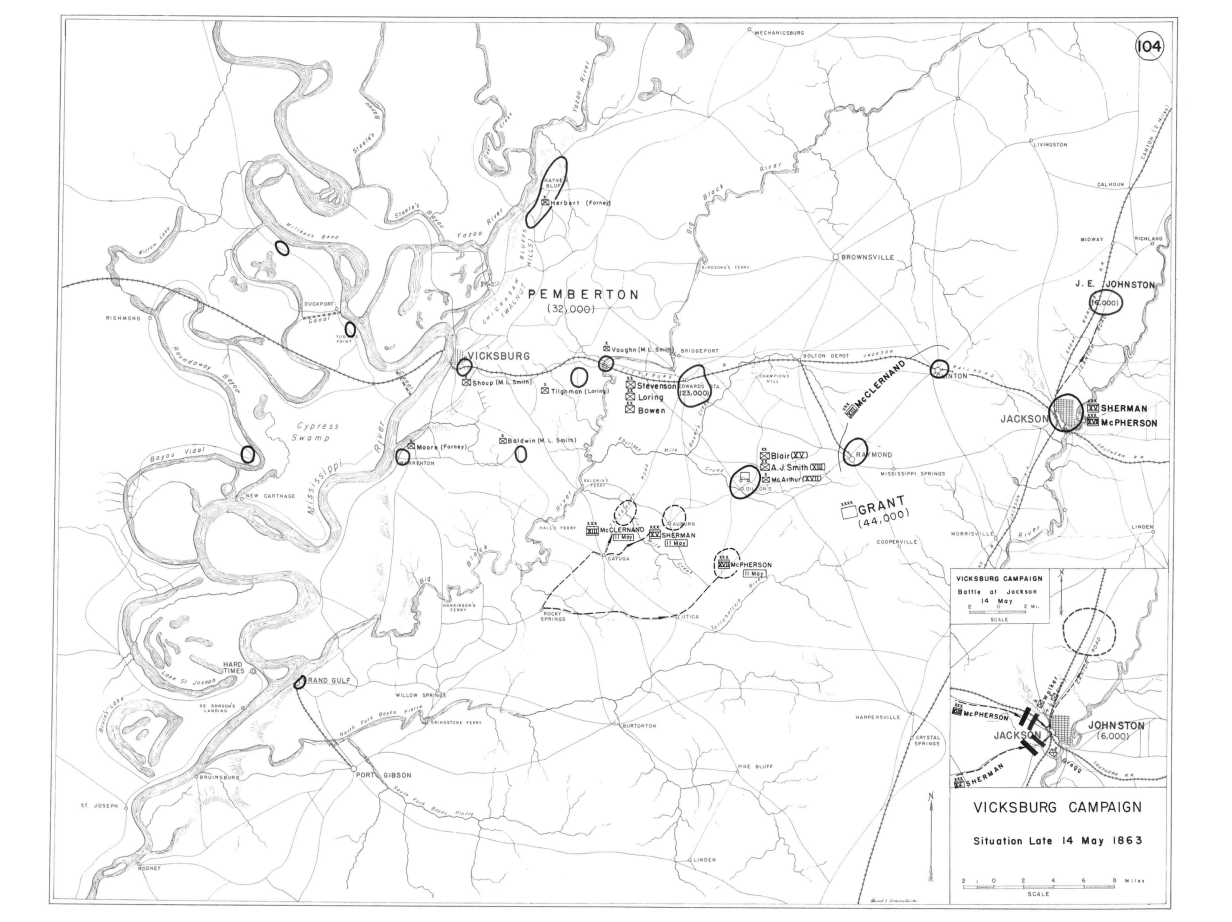

MECHANICSBURG

LIVINGSTON

CALHOUN

MIDWAY   RICHLAND

BROWNSVILLE

J. E. JOHNSTON
(6,000)

PEMBERTON
(32,000)

HAYNES
BLUFF
⊠ Herbert (Forney)

BIRDSONG'S FERRY

BOLTON DEPOT

CANTON

Vaughn (M.L.Smith)   BRIDGEPORT

CHAMPIONS
HILL

⊠ McCLERNAND

JACKSON   ⊠ SHERMAN
⊠ McPHERSON

VICKSBURG

⊠ Shoup (M.L.Smith)

Stevenson   EDWARDS
Loring   (23,000)
Bowen

⊠ Tilghman (Loring)

Cypress
Swamp

RAYMOND

MISSISSIPPI SPRINGS

⊠ Moore (Forney)

WARRENTON

⊠ Baldwin (M.L.Smith)

Blair (XV)
A. J. Smith (XIII)
McArthur (XVII)
DILLON'S

GRANT
(44,000)

MORRISVILLE

LINDEN

NEW CARTHAGE

BALDWIN'S
FERRY

HALL'S FERRY

McCLERNAND
(11 May)

AUBURN
SHERMAN
(11 May)

COOPERVILLE

McPHERSON
(11 May)

CAYUGA

HANKINSON'S
FERRY

ROCKY
SPRINGS

UTICA

VICKSBURG CAMPAIGN
Battle at Jackson
14 May
2 0   2 Mi.
SCALE

HARD
TIMES

GRAND GULF

WILLOW SPRINGS

DE SHROON'S
LANDING

GRINDSTONE FERRY

BURTONTON

HARPERSVILLE

CRYSTAL
SPRINGS

McPHERSON
JACKSON   JOHNSTON
(6,000)

SHERMAN

PINE BLUFF

BRUINSBURG

PORT GIBSON

N

VICKSBURG CAMPAIGN

ST. JOSEPH

RODNEY   LINDEN

Situation Late 14 May 1863

2 0 2 4 6 8 Miles
SCALE

VICKSBURG CAMPAIGN: 3

On 22 May, Grant decided to assault Vicksburg, and although his troops advanced gallantly, it was only at a few points that they managed to reach the parapet, and the morale of the defenders remained high. By 11:30 A.M., Grant had convinced himself that the attack had failed, but he now began to receive optimistic messages from McClernand, and so he decided to persevere. He ordered Sherman and McPherson to renew the assault. McClernand's earlier optimism proved ill founded and the assault was comprehensively repulsed, at the cost of about 3,200 casualties.

Nevertheless, Grant continued his methodical siege; reinforcements were brought in; and mines and countermines were dug, with men dying daily from the mining, sniping, and constant artillery fire. Eventually, Pemberton's garrison was reduced to starvation and, before Grant could put in a final assault, Pemberton capitulated, on 4 July.

Grant's casualties, from 1 May until Vicksburg surrendered, totaled 9,362, exceeding the total by one man those suffered by Grant (but not including Buell) at Shiloh. It was a cheap price to pay for the strategic results achieved—the splitting of the Confederacy and the control of the Mississippi River. In the eighteen days from the time he had crossed the river at Bruinsburg until he arrived at Vicksburg, Grant had marched almost two hundred miles, keeping his army concentrated, and had defeated the Confederates on four separate occasions. Well could Sherman say as he looked down the Mississippi on 19 May, that until then he had not been certain the operation would succeed, but that even if Vicksburg had never been taken, it could be considered a successful campaign. The turning point of the war had been reached, for as Grant tended to the business of feeding Pemberton's starved troops, Lee's shattered army was retreating from Gettysburg.

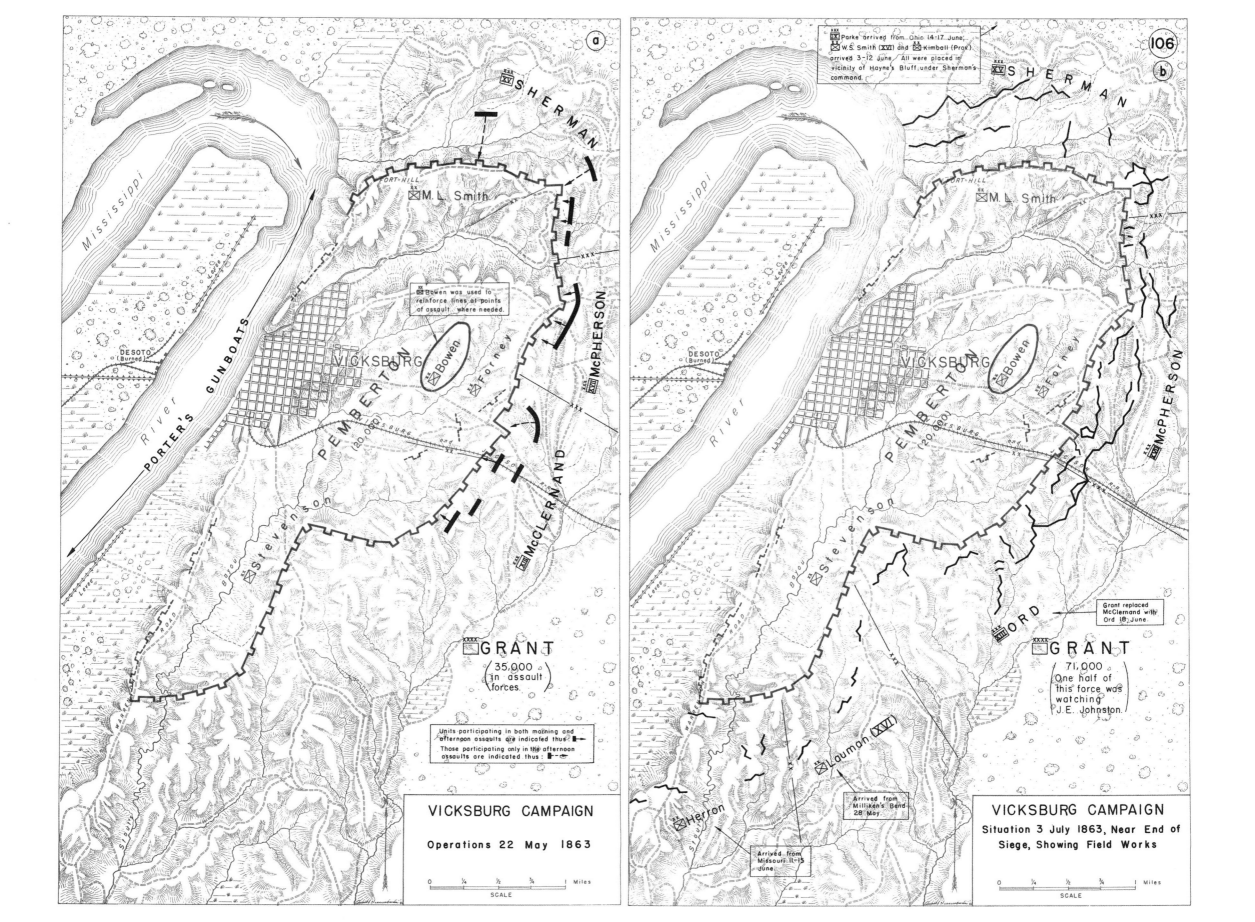

Map a:

SHERMAN

Parke arrived from Ohio 14-17 June;
W.S. Smith (XVI) and Kimball (Prov)
arrived 3-12 June. All were placed in
vicinity of Hayne's Bluff under Sherman's
command.

FORT HILL

M.L. Smith

Mississippi River

Bowen was used to
reinforce lines at points
of assault where needed.

DESOTO
(Burned)

VICKSBURG

Bowen

Forney

McPHERSON

XVI

PORTER'S GUNBOATS

River

PEMBERTON
(20,000)

Stevenson

McCLERNAND
XIII

GRANT
35,000
in assault
forces.

Units participating in both morning and
afternoon assaults are indicated thus:
Those participating only in the afternoon
assaults are indicated thus:

VICKSBURG CAMPAIGN

Operations 22 May 1863

0 ¼ ½ ¾ 1 Miles
SCALE

Map b:

SHERMAN

FORT HILL

M.L. Smith

Mississippi River

DESOTO
(Burned)

VICKSBURG

Bowen

Forney

McPHERSON
XVI

River

PEMBERTON
(20,000)

Stevenson

ORD
XIII

Grant replaced
McClernand with
Ord 18 June.

GRANT
71,000
One half of
this force was
watching
J.E. Johnston.

Lauman XVI

Herron

Arrived from
Milliken's Bend
28 May.

Arrived from
Missouri 11-15
June.

VICKSBURG CAMPAIGN

Situation 3 July 1863, Near End of
Siege, Showing Field Works

0 ¼ ½ ¾ 1 Miles
SCALE

CHICKAMAUGA CAMPAIGN: 1

After the battle of Murfreesboro in January 1863, Bragg withdrew and took up position to the south, around Fairfield-Wartrace-Shelbyville. Outnumbered as he was, and with Vicksburg receiving priority for troops, he had to remain on the defensive, while making every effort to deny Chattanooga, an essential railroad supply hub for the Confederacy, to the Union. Rosencrans, in Murfreesboro, was under great pressure from Washington to break out, which he resisted until 26 June. Maj. Gen. David S. Stanley was on the move around Bragg's open flank at Shelbyville, while Rosencrans's infantry corps would transverse the rugged country to the east and turn the Confederate right flank. By 30 June, after some small and stiff fights, Rosencrans had reached Manchester and Bragg had retreated to Tullahoma. Rosencrans then seized the crossings over the Elk River and Bragg withdrew all the way back to Chattanooga. In nine days of skillful maneuvering Rosencrans, at the cost of only 560 casualties, had forced Bragg across the Tennessee.

On 4 July, Rosencrans stopped pursuing Bragg at the Fayetteville-Decherd-McMinnville line, and there he stopped for a month and a half (much to the chagrin of the administration in Washington). On 16 August, he started his advance toward the Tennessee River, with the general plan to turn Bragg above or below Chattanooga; he elected below. Once he had crossed the river the terrain was formidably rough going: poor roads,

with few gaps through the mountains. Bragg, meanwhile, had been preparing himself and had sent Buckner to Chattanooga, while Longstreet's corps was temporarily detached from Lee's army and started westward.

While Rosencrans advanced across the mountains, Bragg concentrated his forces. On 8 September, he learned that the entire Federal army had crossed the river and was moving against his rear. So Bragg quit Chattanooga and moved his army south to Lafayette, where he saw an opportunity to destroy Rosencrans, who had divided his forces into three separate groups to transverse three roads leading forty miles apart from one another. On 9 September, Rosencrans realized he had been misinformed that Bragg was utterly demoralized and fleeing toward Dalton. Without proper cavalry screening, he was about to blunder into a trap. But whether Bragg could take advantage of the Union mistake would depend on how quickly he could strike.

Still seeking to defeat his foe in detail, Bragg decided to attack Crittenden, about whose movements Forrest had kept him well informed. But twice in three days Bragg's subordinate commanders—Polk, in particular—failed him. Rosencrans now began to concentrate his force, thus reducing Bragg's targets of opportunity.

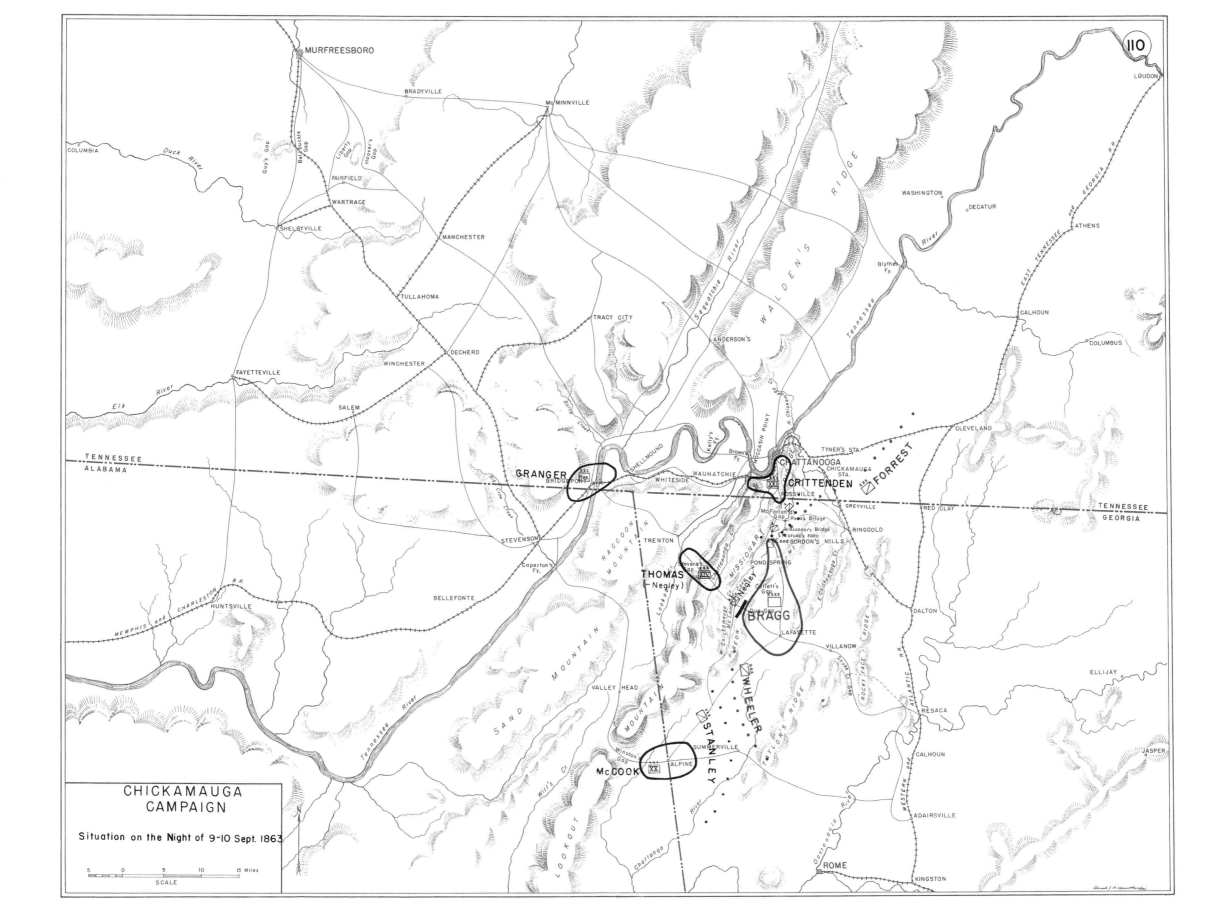

MURFREESBORO

BRADYVILLE

McMINNVILLE

COLUMBIA

Duck River

Guy's Gap

Liberty Gap

Hoover's Gap

Bell Buckle Gap

FAIRFIELD

WASHINGTON

DECATUR

WALDEN'S RIDGE

ATHENS

WARTRACE

Sequatchie River

Tennessee River

SHELBYVILLE

MANCHESTER

Elk River

TULLAHOMA

TRACY CITY

ANDERSON'S

CALHOUN

COLUMBUS

FAYETTEVILLE

WINCHESTER

DECHERD

SALEM

Battle Creek

CLEVELAND

TENNESSEE
ALABAMA

GRANGER

Shellmound

WHITESIDE

WAUHATCHIE

TYNER'S STA.

FORREST

CHATTANOOGA
CHICKAMAUGA STA.

CRITTENDEN

ROSSVILLE

Greyville

RED CLAY

TENNESSEE
GEORGIA

STEVENSON

TRENTON

McFarland's Gap

Reed's Bridge

Alexander's Bridge

Lee and Gordon's Mills

RINGGOLD

Memphis and Charleston R.R.

BELLEFONTE

HUNTSVILLE

Caperton's Fy.

RACCOON MOUNTAIN

Stevens's Gap

THOMAS
—(Negley)

Pond Spring

Gillett's Gap

Catlett's Gap

DALTON

BRAGG

Dug Gap

LAFAYETTE

VILLANOW

WHEELER

ELLIJAY

SAND MOUNTAIN

VALLEY HEAD

LOOKOUT MOUNTAIN

Winston Gap

STANLEY

RESACA

McCOOK

ALPINE

SUMMERVILLE

Will's Cr.

Chattooga River

CALHOUN

JASPER

Oostanaula River

ADAIRSVILLE

ROME

KINGSTON

CHICKAMAUGA
CAMPAIGN

Situation on the Night of 9-10 Sept. 1863

5 0 5 10 15 Miles
SCALE

CHICKAMAUGA CAMPAIGN: 2

Bragg, having moved most of his army north to launch his abortive attack on Crittenden, realized that if he moved quickly he might still have a chance to defeat a portion of Rosencrans's army before the remainder could interfere. Such was the situation on the eve of the battle of Chickamauga.

Early on 18 September, Longstreet's first three brigades from Virginia arrived, commanded by Hood; Longstreet himself and two more brigades were due on the 19th. Bragg decided on the morning of the 18th to advance on Crittenden's left, sever the routes to McFarland's Gap and Rossville, and thus cut off the three Union corps to the south from their base camps at Chattanooga. But Rosencrans, alerted by the dust raised by the marching Confederates, seems to have guessed at Bragg's plan, and he ordered Thomas and McCook to march to Crittenden's support.

Bragg had not reckoned with the speed by which Rosencrans would reinforce Crittenden and was unaware that Thomas's divisions were to the north of Crittenden. He believed that, except for cavalry, Crittenden's corps formed the extreme left of the Union line. The Federal commanders were equally unaware of Confederate dispositions and had no idea that the bulk of Bragg's army had crossed the creek.

The fighting of the 19th started when Thomas dispatched Brig. Gen. John M. Brannan toward Alexander's Bridge to destroy a Confederate brigade that he believed was the only

force across the stream. Brannan encountered Forrest, who was soon assisted by Walker. In what can be best described as very confused fighting, the battle raged all day, with most of Bragg's force engaged, often in piecemeal attacks that came to nothing, while Bragg himself seemed strangely detached from the events of the day.

By 11:00 P.M. on 19 September, Bragg had most of his army across the creek, reorganized into two wings under Polk and Longstreet. Bragg seems to have been still determined to envelop Rosencrans's left, and Breckinridge was ordered to attack next morning, with each division to the south joining in sequence (an attack known as "oblique order").

During the night of the 19th, Thomas erected log breastworks around Kelly Field, and asked for his north flank to be reinforced. Bragg's attack came about 9:30 A.M. on the 20th but, as was true of other assaults in this campaign, it had been delayed—by Polk. Breckinridge's assault on the Union left (north) was repulsed by Negley's division. Next in the rolling attack came Cleburne at about 10:00 A.M., but he was stopped by solid Union musketry from the log breastworks at Kelly Field. Bragg, now frustrated with his difficulties to the north, ordered the rest of his line to attack.

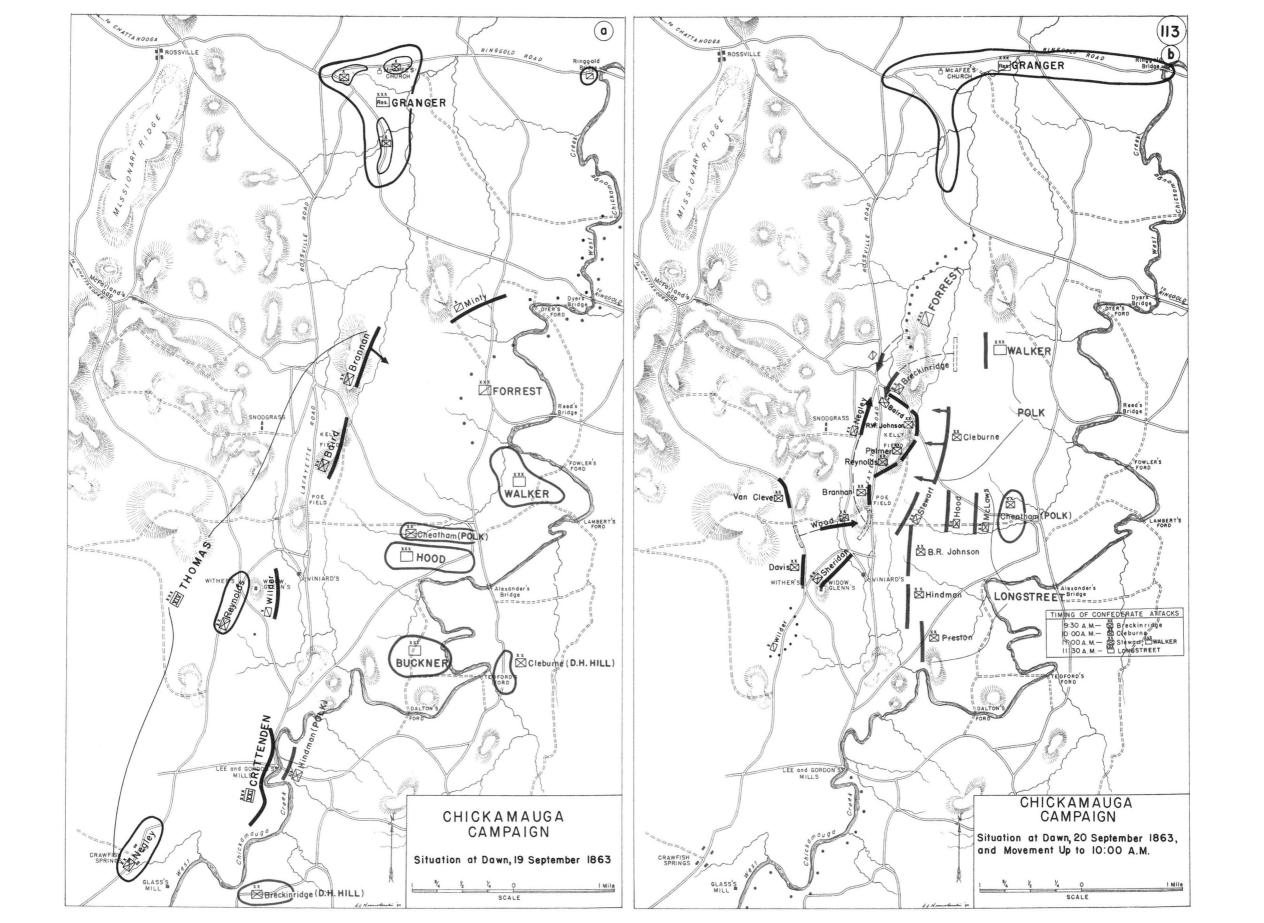

a

RINGGOLD ROAD

ROSSVILLE

McAFEE'S CHURCH

Ringgold Bridge

XXX
Res. GRANGER

MISSIONARY RIDGE

to CHATTANOOGA

ROSSVILLE ROAD

West Chickamauga Creek

Dyer's Bridge

DYER'S FORD

to RINGGOLD

Minty

Brannan

XXX FORREST

Reed's Bridge

SNODGRASS

KELL FIELD

Baird

FOWLER'S FORD

XXX WALKER

LAFAYETTE ROAD

POE FIELD

Cheatham (POLK)

XXX HOOD

LAMBERT'S FORD

THOMAS

WITHERS

W. GLENN'S

Reynolds

Wilder

VINIARD'S

Alexander's Bridge

XX
Negley

BUCKNER

Cleburne (D.H. HILL)

CRITTENDEN

Hindman (Polk)

LEE and GORDON'S MILLS

TEDFORD'S FORD

DALTON'S FORD

Chickamauga Creek

West Chickamauga

CRAWFISH SPRINGS

GLASS'S MILL

Negley

Breckinridge (D.H. HILL)

CHICKAMAUGA CAMPAIGN

Situation at Dawn, 19 September 1863

SCALE 3/4 1/2 1/4 0 1 Mile

b · 113

RINGGOLD ROAD

ROSSVILLE

McAFEE'S CHURCH

Res. GRANGER

Ringgold Bridge

MISSIONARY RIDGE

to CHATTANOOGA

ROSSVILLE ROAD

West Chickamauga Creek

Dyer's Bridge

DYER'S FORD

to RINGGOLD

XXX FORREST

Reed's Bridge

Breckinridge

XXX WALKER

Negley

Baird

R.W. Johnson

KELLY

SNODGRASS

Cleburne

FIELD

POLK

Palmer

Reynolds

FOWLER'S FORD

Van Cleve

Brannan

POE FIELD

Stewart

Hood

McLaws

Cheatham (POLK)

LAMBERT'S FORD

Wood

Davis

Sheridan

WITHER'S

WIDOW GLENN'S

VINIARD'S

B.R. Johnson

Wilder

Hindman

LONGSTREET

Alexander's Bridge

Preston

TIMING OF CONFEDERATE ATTACKS
9:30 A.M. — Breckinridge
10:00 A.M. — Cleburne
10:00 A.M. — Stewart WALKER
11:30 A.M. — LONGSTREET

LEE and GORDON'S MILLS

TEDFORD'S FORD

DALTON'S FORD

CRAWFISH SPRINGS

GLASS'S MILL

Chickamauga Creek

West Chickamauga

CHICKAMAUGA CAMPAIGN

Situation at Dawn, 20 September 1863, and Movement Up to 10:00 A.M.

SCALE 3/4 1/2 1/4 0 1 Mile

Bragg had obviously abandoned his plan of turning the Union left, and now, somewhat desperately, was throwing everything into frontal assaults. Longstreet, the last in the sequence, moved forward at about 11:30 A.M. with his entire wing, except for Preston's division, which he kept in reserve.

On the Union side, Thomas, under heavy attack, and with an exposed left flank, persistently asked for reinforcements, and finally Rosencrans ordered Crittenden and McCook to move up in his support. So, between 10:00 and 11:30 A.M., there was much shifting of the Union forces. The remainder of Negley's division and most of Van Cleve's division had moved north by 11:30 A.M. Wood pulled out of his right flank position to combine with Reynolds, a move that, unbeknownst to Rosencrans, opened up Brannan's right flank. It was at this time of flux on the Union right that Longstreet struck, and he hit into the right flank of Wood, Sheridan, and Davis, all of whom were in the delicate process of repositioning. The result was a resounding success for Longstreet. Sheridan and David were forced off the field, and Rosencrans, swept up in the retreat, was convinced the battle was lost; McCook and Crittenden soon followed, leaving Thomas in sole command.

Meanwhile, Granger, at McAfee's Church, heard firing to the south and, on his own initiative, sent Brig. Gen. James B. Steedman to Thomas's support. Steedman arrived about 2:30 P.M., just in time to stop Longstreet's attempt to envelop Brannan's right. About 4:00 P.M. Longstreet made another attempt, spearheaded by Preston's division, but could not break through the stubborn Union defense. Likewise, Thomas threw back Bragg's final effort with Gen. Benjamin Cheatham's division on the north flank.

That night, Thomas withdrew to Rossville, aided by Sheridan and Davis who had returned to the battlefield by the Rossville road. The Confederates failed to pursue, an error perceived only by Forrest at that time. The Confederate casualties totaled 18,454; the Union, 16,170. Thomas, the "Rock of Chickamauga," had been the decisive factor in preventing a disastrous Union defeat.

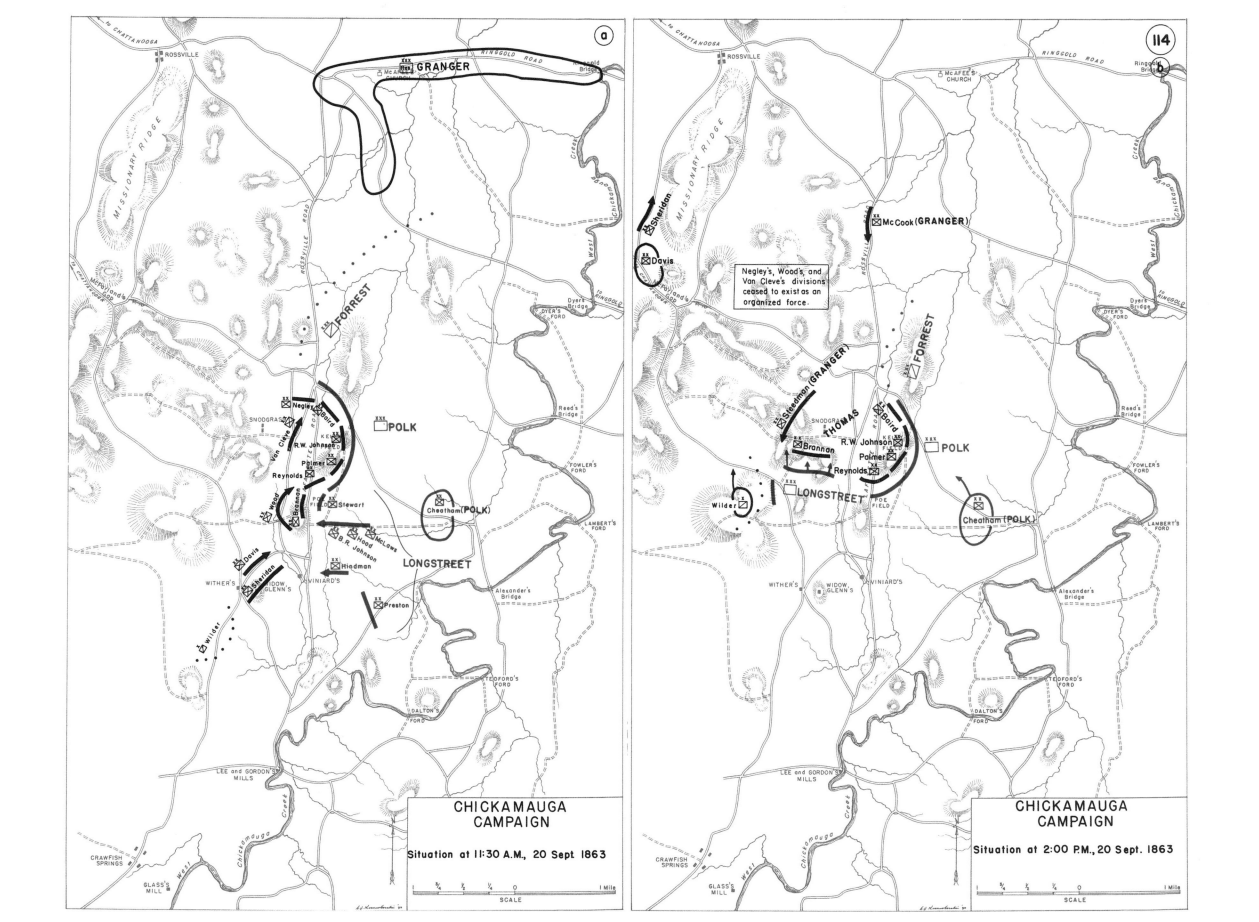

Map a (left):

To CHATTANOOGA

ROSSVILLE

RINGGOLD ROAD

McAfee's CHURCH

XXX GRANGER

Ringgold Bridge

MISSIONARY RIDGE

ROSSVILLE ROAD

FORREST

West Chickamauga Creek

Dyer's Bridge

To RINGGOLD

Dyer's Ford

Reed's Bridge

Negley

Baird

SNODGRASS

XXX POLK

Van Cleve

R.W. Johnson

KELLY FIELD

Palmer

Reynolds

Wood

Brannan

POE FIELD

Stewart

Cheatham (POLK)

Fowler's Ford

McLaws

Hood

B.R. Johnson

Davis

Sheridan

WIDOW GLENN'S

VINIARD'S

Hindman

LONGSTREET

Alexander's Bridge

Lambert's Ford

Preston

Wilder

WITHER'S

TEDFORD'S FORD

DALTON'S FORD

LEE and GORDON'S MILLS

West Chickamauga Creek

CRAWFISH SPRINGS

GLASS'S MILL

CHICKAMAUGA CAMPAIGN

Situation at 11:30 A.M., 20 Sept. 1863

SCALE

1   ¾   ½   ¼   0   1 Mile

Map b (right):

To CHATTANOOGA

ROSSVILLE

RINGGOLD ROAD

McAfee's CHURCH

Ringgold Bridge

Sheridan

McCook (GRANGER)

Davis

MISSIONARY RIDGE

Negley's, Wood's, and Van Cleve's divisions ceased to exist as an organized force.

ROSSVILLE ROAD

West Chickamauga Creek

Dyer's Bridge

To RINGGOLD

Dyer's Ford

FORREST

Reed's Bridge

Steedman (GRANGER)

SNODGRASS

THOMAS

Baird

Brannan

R.W. Johnson

KELLY FIELD

XXX POLK

Palmer

Reynolds

LONGSTREET

POE FIELD

Fowler's Ford

Wilder

Cheatham (POLK)

Lambert's Ford

WITHER'S

WIDOW GLENN'S

VINIARD'S

Alexander's Bridge

TEDFORD'S FORD

DALTON'S FORD

LEE and GORDON'S MILLS

West Chickamauga Creek

CRAWFISH SPRINGS

GLASS'S MILL

CHICKAMAUGA CAMPAIGN

Situation at 2:00 P.M., 20 Sept. 1863

SCALE

1   ¾   ½   ¼   0   1 Mile

BATTLES AROUND CHATTANOOGA

By the night of 21 September, Rosencrans had withdrawn into Chattanooga and succumbed to a defeatist attitude, accepted being invested (Bragg laid siege on the night of the 21st), and thus surrendered his ability to maneuver. The authorities in Washington meanwhile dispatched reinforcements. Hooker, with the XI and XII Corps from Meade's army, arrived at Nashville, and Grant was instructed to send troops from Vicksburg. By early October Lincoln established a unified command in the west, making Grant overall commander between the Mississippi and the Alleghenies, except for Banks at New Orleans. Grant immediately replaced Rosencrans with Thomas, and Grant himself arrived in Chattanooga on 23 October.

During October there was little action, but Thomas was about to change all that. The long supply route through Anderson's having proved unsatisfactory, Thomas decided to open a short route between Bridgeport and Chattanooga by driving away the Confederate troops and artillery that now controlled it. On the night of 26 October, under cover of a heavy fog, Hazen, with 1,500 men, moved downstream on bridge pontoons to Brown's Ferry and established a bridgehead. Meanwhile Hooker, leaving most of XII Corps to guard the railroad, advanced as shown with the remainder of his force and, by the evening of the 28 October, the short route to Bridgeport was open. Bragg, failing to appreciate the importance of this Union coup, felt secure enough to send Longstreet to attack Burnside at Knoxville.

Sherman, with XV and XVII Corps, arrived at Bridgeport on 15 November and was immediately ordered northeast to cross the river and seize Tunnel Hill. Meanwhile, Thomas was to advance, and together they would drive south along Missionary Ridge. Hooker would guard Lookout Valley, and Howard would act as a reserve. Meanwhile, Longstreet's move against Burnside had caused consternation in Washington. In response, Grant decided to send Thomas on a limited attack. As it happened, the attack was surprisingly successful, and Thomas occupied the line through Orchard Knob and Indian Hill.

Early on 24 November, Sherman and Hooker attacked as planned, and by noon Hooker had driven the Confederates from the defile between Lookout Mountain and the river. To the north, Sherman's crossing was successful, but he was not ready to advance on Tunnel Hill until the afternoon, by which time Cleburne had been rushed up and entrenched on the hill. Sherman halted for the night.

Grant now changed his plan for 25 November to a double envelopment by Sherman and Hooker; Thomas was to advance when Hooker reached Missionary Ridge. But Sherman's attack could not break Cleburne's lines, and Hooker's approach was agonizingly slow. Thomas was ordered to take the lowest Confederate trenches along Missionary Ridge, and again he excelled himself by advancing up the hill, to the amazement of the Union commanders, and carried it. By 4:30 P.M., Bragg's troops had broken and fled in panic.

Grant erred in failing to pursue, but he showed great flexibility in modifying his plans to meet changing conditions and, above all, had provided forceful leadership, something that was sorely lacking in Bragg. Union losses were 5,824; Confederate, 6,667.

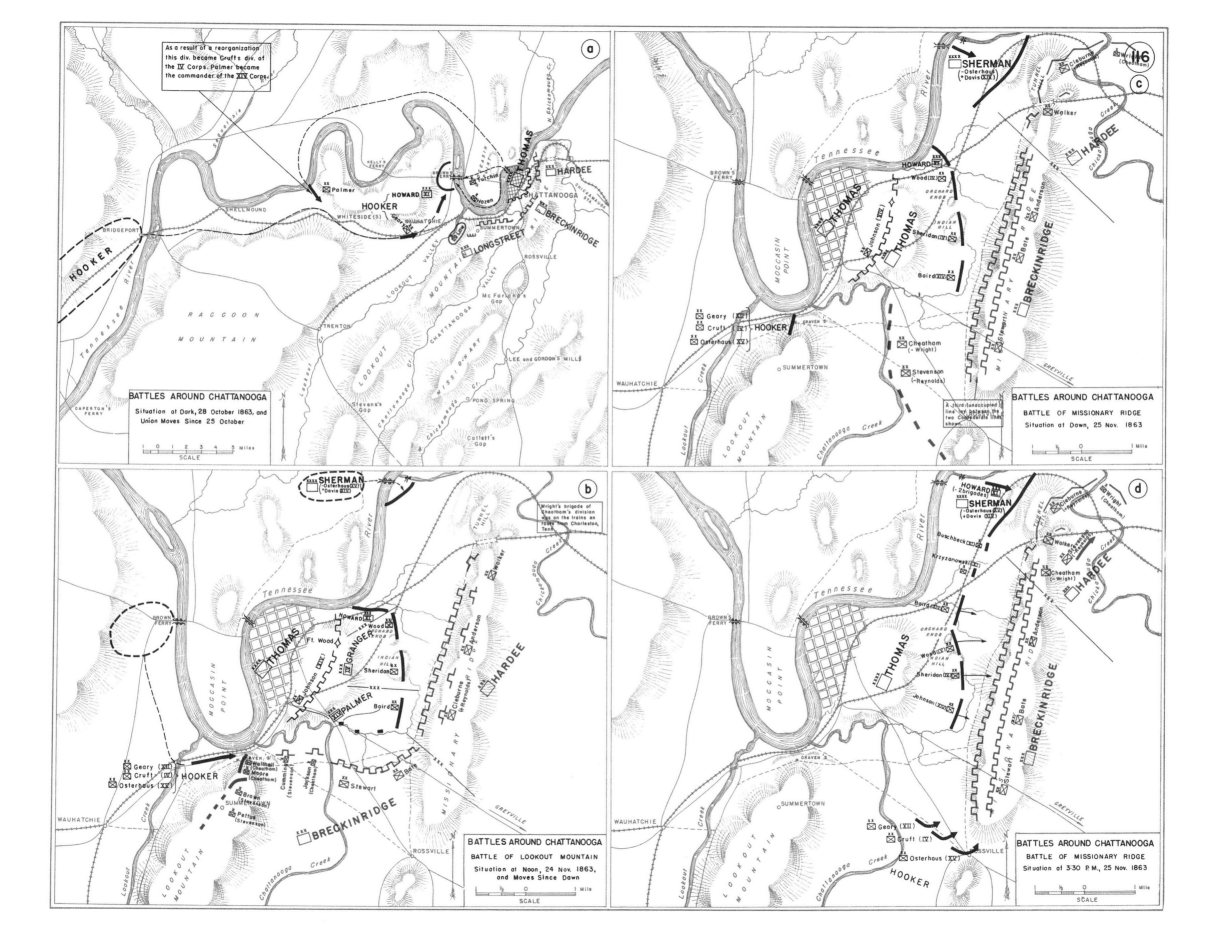

a

As a result of a reorganization this div. became Cruft's div. of the IV Corps. Palmer became the commander of the XIV Corps.

BATTLES AROUND CHATTANOOGA

Situation at Dark, 28 October 1863, and Union Moves Since 25 October

1 0 1 2 3 4 5 Miles
SCALE

b

SHERMAN
(Osterhaus)
+Davis (XIV)

Wright's brigade of Cheatham's division was on the trains en route from Charleston, Tenn.

Geary (XII)
Cruft (IV)   HOOKER
Osterhaus (XV)

BATTLES AROUND CHATTANOOGA

BATTLE OF LOOKOUT MOUNTAIN

Situation at Noon, 24 Nov. 1863, and Moves Since Dawn

½   0   1 Mile
SCALE

c

116

SHERMAN
(Osterhaus)
+Davis (XIV)

Geary (XII)
Cruft (IV)   HOOKER
Osterhaus (XV)

A third (unoccupied) line lay between the two Confederate lines shown.

BATTLES AROUND CHATTANOOGA

BATTLE OF MISSIONARY RIDGE

Situation at Dawn, 25 Nov. 1863

½   0   1 Mile
SCALE

d

HOWARD (XI)
(- 2 brigades)

SHERMAN
(Osterhaus)
+Davis (XIV)

Geary (XII)
Cruft (IV)
Osterhaus (XV)   HOOKER

BATTLES AROUND CHATTANOOGA

BATTLE OF MISSIONARY RIDGE

Situation at 3:30 P.M., 25 Nov. 1863

½   0   1 Mile
SCALE

THE WILDERNESS CAMPAIGN: 1

Following Gettysburg, the Army of Northern Virginia limped slowly up the Shenandoah Valley. Too many irreplaceable officers had been killed or disabled; morale was low in many regiments, and desertion rates soared. On 17 July, Meade began crossing the Potomac farther downstream, grumbling that Lee's army was stronger than his own. But once across the Potomac, he came rapidly down the eastern slope of the Blue Ridge Mountains and, on the 22nd, was opposite Manassas Gap while Lee was still moving past it on the western side. On the 24th, Meade planned to attack Lee's main body at Front Royal, but Lee again managed to slip away during the night and took up position at Culpeper, while Meade watched him from across the Rappahannock. Both armies now rested and reorganized.

Aware that Lee had been weakened by the detachment of Longstreet to reinforce Bragg in the western theater, Meade advanced and, on 13 September, the Union cavalry crossed the Rappahannock, drove Stuart south, and Meade occupied Culpeper, while Lee fell back behind the Rapidan. Meade now planned a turning movement, but the tables were turned and it was Meade who had to sacrifice XI and XII Corps to shore up Rosencrans after his defeat at Chickamauga. Now it was Lee's turn to try and turn the Federal right, and Meade chose to retreat. On 14 October, A. P. Hill finally overtook the Union rear guard near Bristoe Station, just south of Manassas Junction, and attacked with headlong fury, only to thrust his leading division into a clever trap, where it was shattered. This check

took the steam out of Lee's pursuit, and he returned to his old positions behind the Rappahannock, while maintaining a bridgehead on the north bank at the Rappahannock bridge. On 7 November, Meade began crossing at Kelly's Ford, where Sedgwick made a skillful surprise attack that captured almost the entire bridgehead garrison. These twin defeats sent Lee back below the Rapidan, his officers embittered by their lack of success. After some parrying, both armies went into winter quarters, and early in March 1864, Lincoln called on Grant to take overall command of all Union forces.

Grant's overall plan was to destroy the two largest remaining Confederate armies: Lee's in Virginia, and Johnston's in Georgia. Meade was to operate against Lee—"Wherever Lee goes, there you will go also"—and Sherman was to tackle Johnston.

Lee's position along the Rapidan was too strong to be taken by frontal attack. An envelopment of his left flank would have the advantage of moving across favorable terrain, but it would expose the Union line of communications, whereas an envelopment of his right flank would cover the Union communications and threaten Lee's. It would also place the Army of the Potomac and Butler's Army of the James in better positions for mutual support. Its major drawback would be advancing through the same Wilderness that had blinded Hooker at Chancellorsville, but Grant chose to take that risk and, on the night of 3 May, Union forces crossed the Rapidan and, on the 4th, Lee moved to counter them.

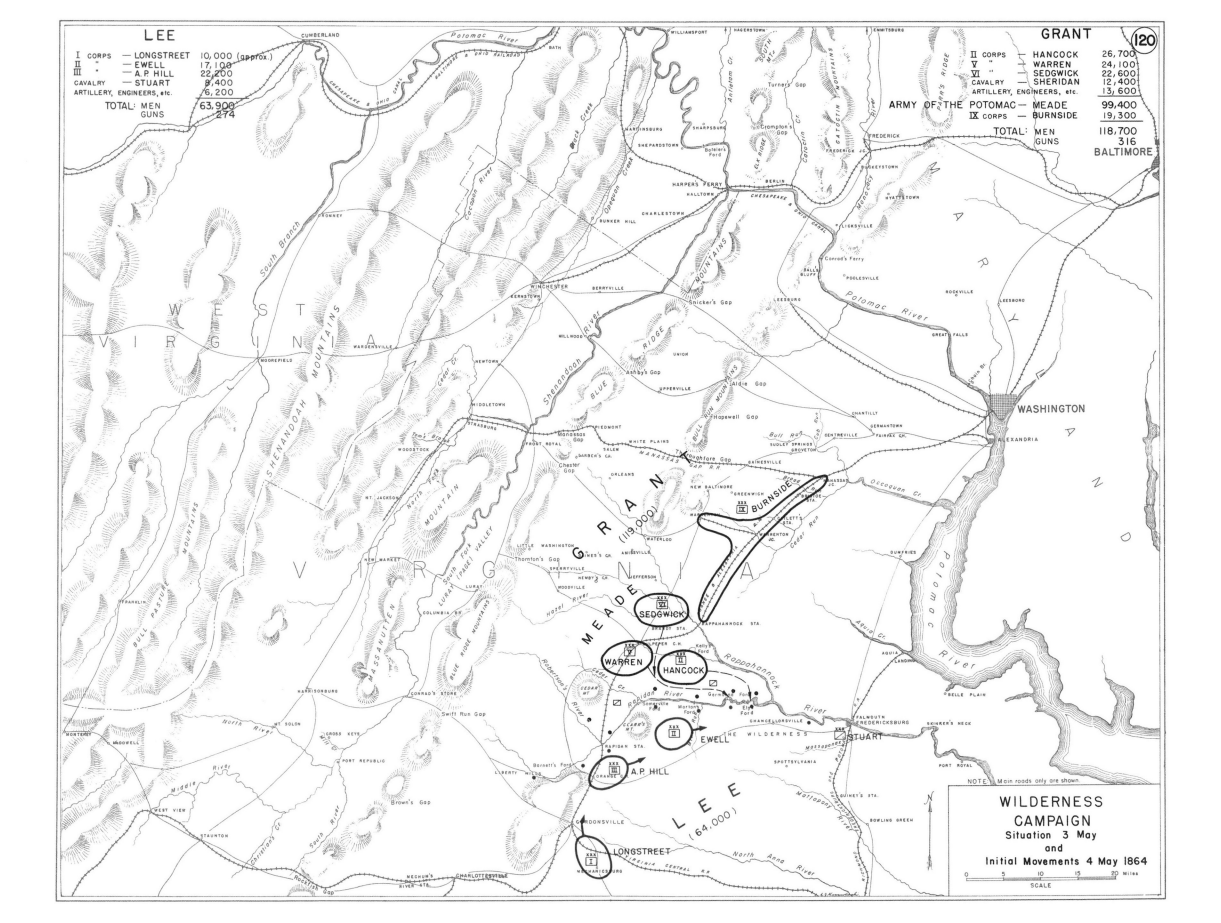

LEE

I CORPS	— LONGSTREET	10,000 (approx.)
II "	— EWELL	17,100
III "	— A. P. HILL	22,200
CAVALRY	— STUART	8,400
ARTILLERY, ENGINEERS, etc.		6,200

TOTAL: MEN 63,900
GUNS 274

GRANT

II CORPS	— HANCOCK	26,700
V "	— WARREN	24,100
VI "	— SEDGWICK	22,600
CAVALRY	— SHERIDAN	12,400
ARTILLERY, ENGINEERS, etc.		13,600

ARMY OF THE POTOMAC — MEADE 99,400
IX CORPS — BURNSIDE 19,300

TOTAL: MEN 118,700
GUNS 316

120

WEST VIRGINIA

MARYLAND

VIRGINIA

GRANT (119,000)

MEADE

LEE (64,000)

WASHINGTON

BALTIMORE

NOTE: Main roads only are shown.

WILDERNESS
CAMPAIGN
Situation 3 May
and
Initial Movements 4 May 1864

0   5   10   15   20 Miles
SCALE

THE WILDERNESS CAMPAIGN: 2

Grant began his advance at midnight on 3 May in two columns, hoping to pass through the Wilderness quickly enough to forestall an attack by Lee. He traveled light, but even so his wagon trains spread out over seventy miles or so. The cavalry corps was again divided, with Meade sending one division ahead of each cavalry column ahead of each infantry column, so there was no effective screening of the exposed Federal right flank during the move through the Wilderness; in hindsight, it might have been better to use the cavalry to seize the southern and western exits. Also, Grant should have started earlier, to get through in one day: as it happened his trains soon lagged, and the II and V Corps were halted in the Wilderness early in the afternoon of 4 May to let them close up. Here, the two corps provided Lee with an excellent target.

Lee had been seeking an opportunity to launch another major offensive against the Army of the Potomac. Now, with that army on the march, his hopes were fulfilled that it would move through the Wilderness, where the superior numbers of Union troops and their splendid artillery would be nullified by the tangled, unfamiliar terrain; he planned to strike the flank of the marching column with the whole of his army. His initial dispersions, however, were poor. During the winter of 1863/64, it had been necessary to disperse his army, to make feeding them a little easier (even so, many starved), and it was hard to get

them back into a concentrated force. Stuart, wayward as ever, should have been scouting the line of the Rapidan, but was still near Fredericksburg; Longstreet was at Gordonsville, some forty-two miles away, and thus out of supporting range. Had Lee had the whole of his army available on 5 May, it is quite possible he could have overwhelmed Warren's and Hancock's corps.

The first clash, on the morning of 5 May 1864, was a chance encounter. Ewell, advancing eastward along the Orange-Fredericksburg Turnpike at about 7:00 A.M., collided with Warren, who was marching toward Parker's Store. The surprise was mutual.

Lee had not wanted to bring on a general engagement until Longstreet arrived. Meade was only anxious to get out of the green maze of the Wilderness. So poorly had the cavalry of both armies done their work that neither commander had any conception of the other's location and strength. Meade apparently thought that Warren had met a division-size delaying force, left behind by Lee to cover the Confederate concentration further south along the North Anna River. He ordered Warren to attack those Confederates and determine their actual strength. Hancock was to halt at Todd's Tavern until this matter was settled, one way or the other. Sedgwick was to cover Warren's right flank.

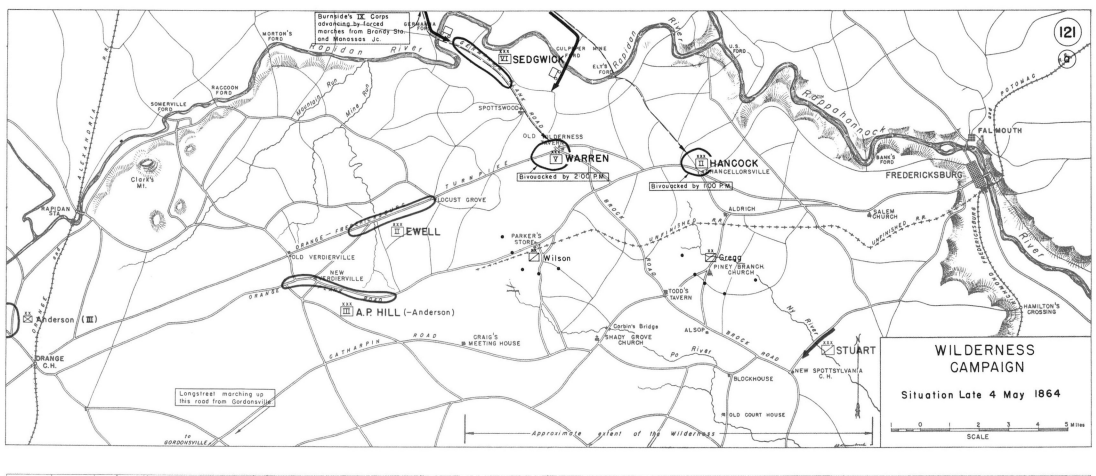

Burnside's IX Corps
advancing by forced
marches from Brandy Sta.
and Manassas Jc.

XXX
VI SEDGWICK

XXX
V WARREN
Bivouacked by 2:00 P.M.

XXX
II HANCOCK
Bivouacked by 1:00 P.M.

XXX
II EWELL

Wilson

XX
Gregg

XXX
III A.P. HILL (–Anderson)

XX
Anderson (III)

XXX
STUART

Longstreet marching up
this road from Gordonsville

Approximate extent of the Wilderness

WILDERNESS
CAMPAIGN

Situation Late 4 May 1864

SCALE

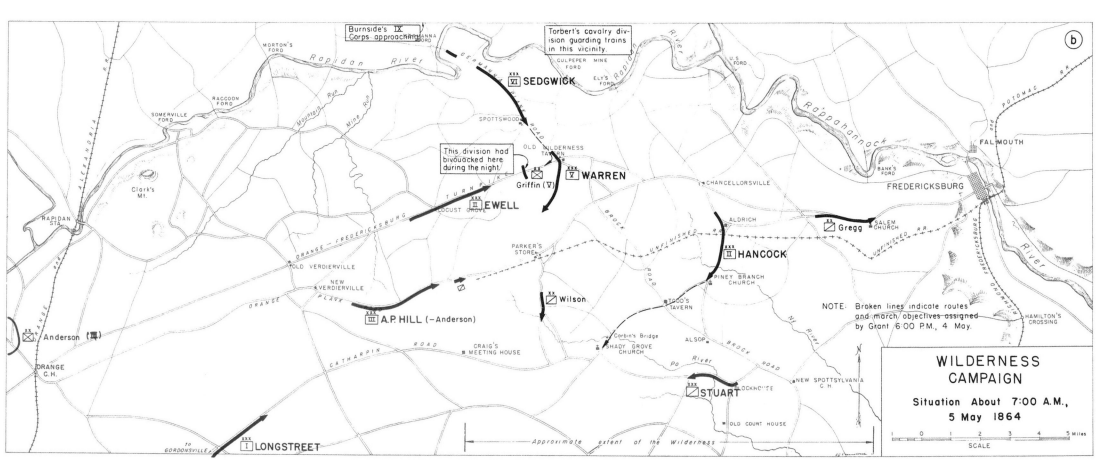

(b)

Burnside's IX
Corps approaching

Torbert's cavalry div-
ision guarding trains
in this vicinity.

XXX
VI SEDGWICK

This division had
bivouacked here
during the night.

XX
Griffin (V)

XXX
V WARREN

XXX
II EWELL

Gregg

XXX
II HANCOCK

Wilson

XXX
III A.P. HILL (–Anderson)

XX
Anderson (III)

XXX
STUART

NOTE: Broken lines indicate routes
and march objectives assigned
by Grant 6:00 P.M., 4 May.

I LONGSTREET

Approximate extent of the Wilderness

WILDERNESS
CAMPAIGN

Situation About 7:00 A.M.,
5 May 1864

SCALE

THE WILDERNESS CAMPAIGN: 3

In accordance with Meade's orders, Warren sent Griffin west along the turnpike. Wads-worth moved off the road to prolong Griffin's left flank, while Brig. Gen. Horatio G. Wright (VI Corps) advanced from Spottswood to support his right. Attacking vigorously, Griffin hustled Johnson's division back in some disorder, until Ewell put in his reserves. Wright, meanwhile, found his "road" so overgrown that it was almost impassable. Wadsworth lost his direction in the dense undergrowth and advanced to the northeast instead of the southwest, thus exposing his left flank to Ewell's fire. Ewell counterattacked and recovered the ground originally held by Johnson. Then, having received orders to avoid bringing on a general engagement until Longstreet arrived, he entrenched.

A. P. Hill's advance up the Orange Plank Road encountered a detachment from Brig. Gen. James H. Wilson's cavalry division. This detachment fell back slowly, using its repeating carbines effectively to check Hill's march. Mead at once realized the importance of holding the Brock Road, the loss of which would separate Hancock and Wilson from the rest of the army. He therefore ordered Getty (VI Corps) to move to the Orange Plank Road junction and, if possible, drive the Confederates back beyond Parker's Store. Hancock was ordered to countermarch to the Brock Road–Orange Plank Road junction and support Getty.

Getty reached the junction about 11:00 A.M. and sent a skirmish line forward to establish contact with A. P. Hill's leading troops. From prisoners captured in his first clash, Getty learned that two Confederate divisions were in front of him. He therefore constructed some light entrenchments and prepared to hold the crossroads until Hancock arrived.

In the meantime, the fight on the turnpike road died down, and both sides gradually reorganized and fortified their lines. On the Orange Plank Road, Hill (also under orders to wait for Longstreet) took up the best available position and awaited orders. About 2:00 P.M. Hancock's corps began coming into line on Getty's left flank. Getty said he expected an attack, and so Hancock ordered his lead companies to throw up light breastworks.

Already, the fighting had taken on the frustrating characteristics that would mark it to the end. Numbers meant little; in fact, they were an active disadvantage on the narrow trails. Visibility was limited, making it extremely difficult for officers to exercise effective control. Attackers could only thrash noisily through the undergrowth, perfect targets for the concealed defenders. In attack or retreat, formations could rarely be maintained, and in this junglelike environment the better woodsman skills of the Confederates and their relative familiarity with the terrain gave them a decided advantage. Union officers, on the other hand, were forced to rely on maps that proved thoroughly unreliable.

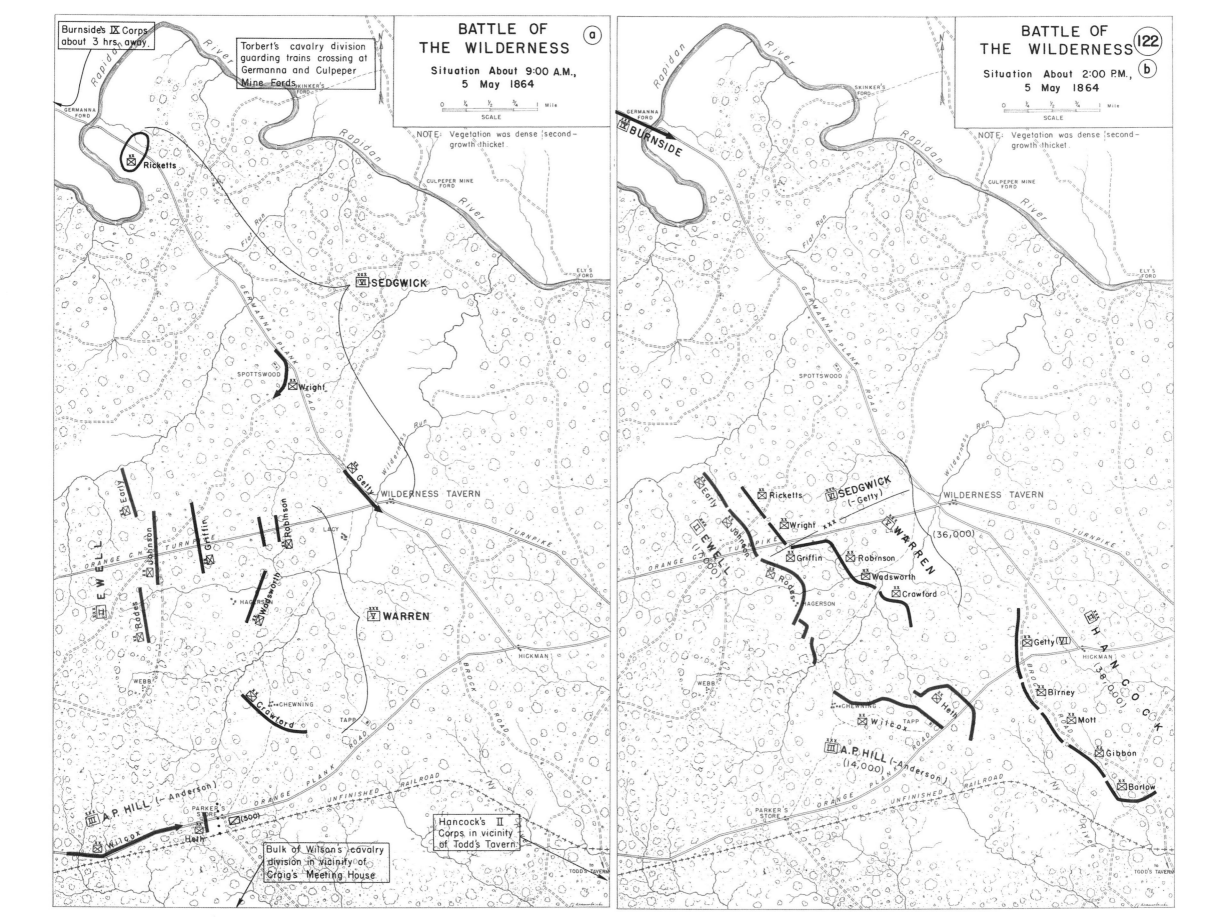

BATTLE OF THE WILDERNESS (a)

Situation About 9:00 A.M., 5 May 1864

SCALE
0 ¼ ½ ¾ 1 Mile

NOTE: Vegetation was dense (second-growth thicket).

Burnside's IX Corps about 3 hrs. away.

Torbert's cavalry division guarding trains crossing at Germanna and Culpeper Mine Fords.

Bulk of Wilson's cavalry division in vicinity of Craig's Meeting House.

Hancock's II Corps in vicinity of Todd's Tavern.

BATTLE OF THE WILDERNESS 122 (b)

Situation About 2:00 P.M., 5 May 1864

SCALE
0 ¼ ½ ¾ 1 Mile

NOTE: Vegetation was dense (second-growth thicket).

By 3:30 P.M. Lee was debating the possibility of seizing the Brock Road without bringing on a general engagement. Heth was dubious but willing to try if so ordered. But before Lee could reach a decision, the Federals attacked.

Sometime after 3:15 P.M. Getty received orders to attack at once. Hancock's divisions were to support him. Meade wanted the attack to be made immediately, to take advantage of Longstreet's absence. Hancock, however, delayed in order to complete his breastworks, which gave Hill time to strengthen his position; and so when Getty went into the attack at about 4:15 P.M., he met savage resistance. He was reinforced by Hancock, while Wilcox moved in support of Heth. The fighting raged desperately until dark, with the Confederates barely managing to hold their line. Despite their valiant defense, night found Hill's men shaken and somewhat scattered, their ammunition almost exhausted. With Hill too sick to exercise effective command, his position was not properly reorganized.

During the late afternoon, Meade sent Wadsworth across country to reinforce Hancock's right flank, and also ordered renewed attacks, which turned out to be futile and costly, on Ewell's line. Wadsworth found the woods almost impassable and was unable to get into the action before dark.

Both armies planned to attack the next day (6 May), and Lee sent word to Longstreet to hurry forward because he wanted to use his corps and Anderson's division to turn the Federal left flank and drive them back against the Rapidan. Meanwhile, Grant ordered Hancock, Warren, Sedgwick, and Burnside to resume the attack at 5:00 A.M.

At the appointed hour, the Federal attack jumped off—except for Burnside, who was still trying to find his way forward through the roadless tangle of undergrowth between the Turnpike and the Orange Plank Road. On the north, Ewell repulsed Sedgwick and Warren with heavy loss, while on the south, Hill's men, struck in front and flank by Hancock's massive assault, broke and fled to the rear. Confederate artillery, firing across the open fields of the Tapp farm in Hill's rear, slowed the Union rush but could not stop it. If it had not been for those guns, Lee's entire right flank would have crumbled.

But, shouldering through the rearbound wreckage of Heth's and Wilcox's divisions, came Longstreet—his men remarking that the spectacle reminded them of Bragg's army. Lee, at this stage of the battle, was unusually excited, and his subordinates had considerable trouble getting him to move farther to the rear.

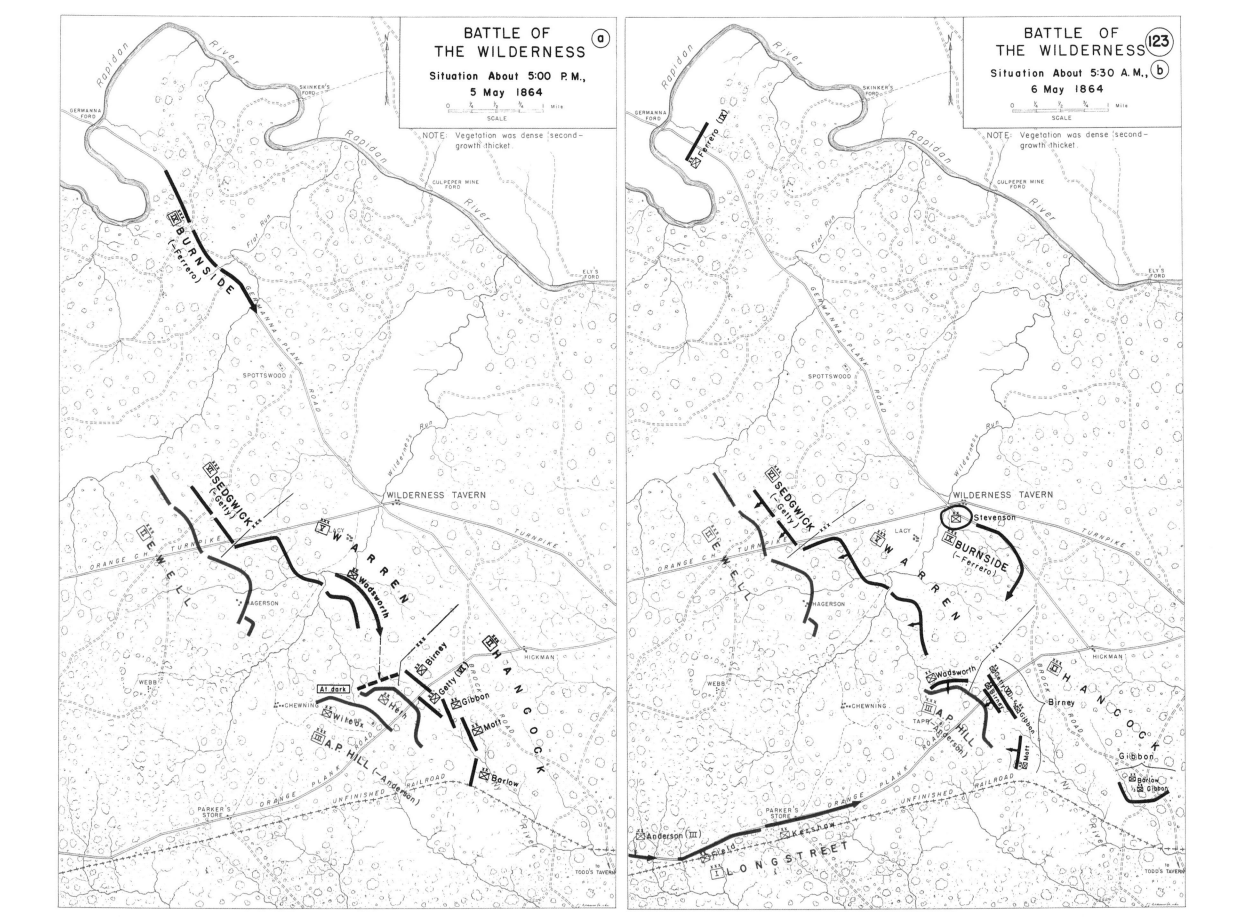

BATTLE OF
THE WILDERNESS ⓐ

Situation About 5:00 P.M.,
5 May 1864

SCALE

NOTE: Vegetation was dense second-
growth thicket.

BATTLE OF
THE WILDERNESS ⑫③

Situation About 5:30 A.M.,
6 May 1864 ⓑ

SCALE

NOTE: Vegetation was dense second-
growth thicket.

Longstreet went directly into action, stopping Maj. Gen. David Bell Birney, but also meeting stubborn resistance. A succession of assaults by both armies surged back and forth between the Brock Road and the Tapp farm. About 8:00 A.M., Meade sent Brig. Gen. Thomas G. Stevenson (IX Corps), who had been held in reserve at Wilderness Tavern, to reinforce Hancock; Warren and Sedgwick were ordered to renew their offensive, and Sheridan's cavalry was sent against Longstreet's right rear.

At 7:00 A.M., Hancock had ordered Gibbon to send Barlow's divisions against the Confederate right flank, but only one brigade was ever dispatched because of a series of apparent threats to the Federal left (there was a mistaken notion that Pickett was with Longstreet, whereas he was, in fact, on garrison duty in the Richmond area). The result was that Barlow was held out of the action at a critical period.

By 11:00 A.M., both sides were temporarily fought out, but the lull was deceptive. Longstreet, with Lee's approval, had prepared a Chancellorsville-style flank attack to roll up the Union line. A reconnaissance by Maj. Gen. Martin L. Smith, Lee's chief engineer, had discovered that Birney's south flank was unprotected and could be easily turned by an advance along the bed of an unfinished railroad that ran parallel to the Orange Plank Road.

Longstreet directed one of his staff officers, Lt. Col. G. Moxley Sorrel, to assemble four brigades and carry out this attack, while he himself led an advance along the Orange Plank Road. Sorrel's flank attack was immediately successful and Birney's line collapsed from left to right. Only Hancock's dominating leadership rallied it behind the entrenchments he had ordered dug the day before along the Brock Road. Longstreet, pushing the Confederate drive forward, was accidentally wounded by his own men, and Lee took on the direction of the attack, but found the troops too disordered by their advance through the underbrush to continue. It was 4:15 P.M. before they could be reorganized, but even so, their attack collapsed in front of Hancock's defenses.

To the north, Gordon had spent a thwarted day. During the day, his scouts discovered that the Union right flank was unprotected and, in addition, it was overlapped by the Confederate left, but he was denied permission by Early and Ewell to attack. It was only through an appeal directly to Lee that an attack was sanctioned, but by then it was too late in the day, even though his assault was quite successful and was only halted by Sedgwick's calm leadership.

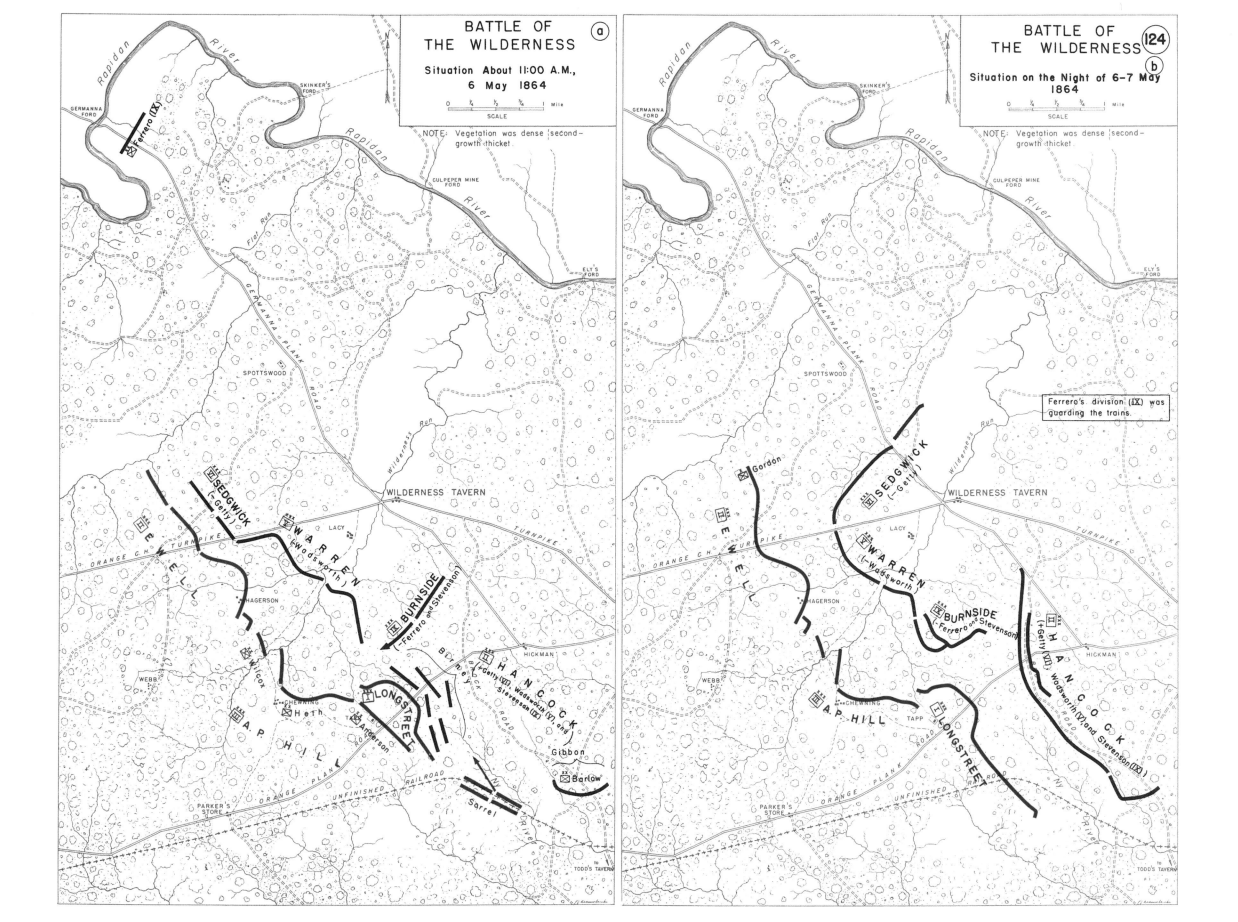

BATTLE OF
THE WILDERNESS (a)

Situation About 11:00 A.M.,
6 May 1864

SCALE

NOTE: Vegetation was dense second-
growth thicket.

BATTLE OF
THE WILDERNESS (124)
(b)

Situation on the Night of 6-7 May
1864

SCALE

NOTE: Vegetation was dense second-
growth thicket.

Ferrero's division (IX) was
guarding the trains.

SPOTSYLVANIA*: 1

During the 7 May, both armies lay behind their breastworks, separated by three-quarters of a mile of smoldering Wilderness. It had been a blind, blundering battle in which even the casualties remained in doubt. Union losses had been between 15,000 and 18,000, while Confederate estimates (although records are fragmentary) vary from 7,750 to 11,400. Both Grant and Lee had shown great determination but no particular skill. Grant especially seems to have ignored the limitations which the terrain would impose on his attacks, and neither he, Meade, nor Sheridan had employed the strong Union cavalry corps effectively. Lee, too, had failed to use his cavalry properly and so had created a situation in which he had to commit his forces piecemeal as they came on to the field. He had failed in his attempt to seize the Brock Road, but had succeeded in turning both flanks of the Union army.

Unlike Hooker a year before, Grant chose not to fall back across the Rapidan, and as the days passed it became evident that he intended to shift to the southeast instead of retiring. To Lee, that meant that it would be necessary to hold the important road junction at New Spotsylvania Court House.

At 8:30 P.M. on 7 May, the Army of the Potomac began to move as shown. Grant had studied the Confederate positions and concluded that they were too strong for a frontal attack. Warren and Sedgwick pulled out of the line and marched for Spotsylvania; Burnside started for Aldrich, while Hancock remained in position until the rest of the army had passed behind him, and then moved to Todd's Tavern. It was a black night; the roads were poor and hard to follow, and the march of some units was not particularly well handled.

Around 8:30 A.M. on 8 May, Warren's leading infantry came out into the open ground near Alsop, pushing Fitzhugh Lee's cavalry slowly before them. Here, they were suddenly checked by infantry and artillery of Longstreet's corps that, following its commander's wounding, was now under Anderson; even their presence here was due to a combination of hard marching and good luck. Lee had ordered Anderson to withdraw from his position on the Orange Plank Road as soon as possible after dark, assemble in some quiet area where they could rest, and to start before 3:00 A.M. the next morning for Spotsylvania, where he arrived just in time to block Warren.

Wilson had held Spotsylvania for two hours, and now the Confederate cavalry concentrated against him, until Sheridan ordered him to withdraw. At 1:00 P.M., Meade ordered Sedgwick to support an attack by Warren, but time was needed to get the tired troops into position on strange ground and coordinate their efforts. As a result, the attack was not launched until late in the afternoon, and even then it was half-hearted.

* Note: Unlike Spottswood, the correct spelling of Spotsylvania has one t.

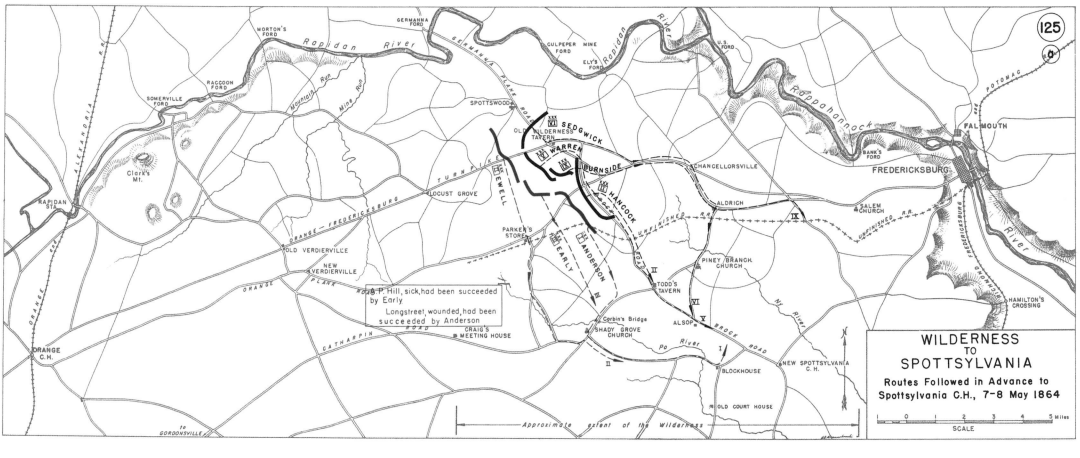

P. Hill, sick, had been succeeded by Early

Longstreet, wounded, had been succeeded by Anderson

WILDERNESS TO SPOTTSYLVANIA

Routes Followed in Advance to Spottsylvania C.H., 7-8 May 1864

0 1 2 3 4 5 Miles

SCALE

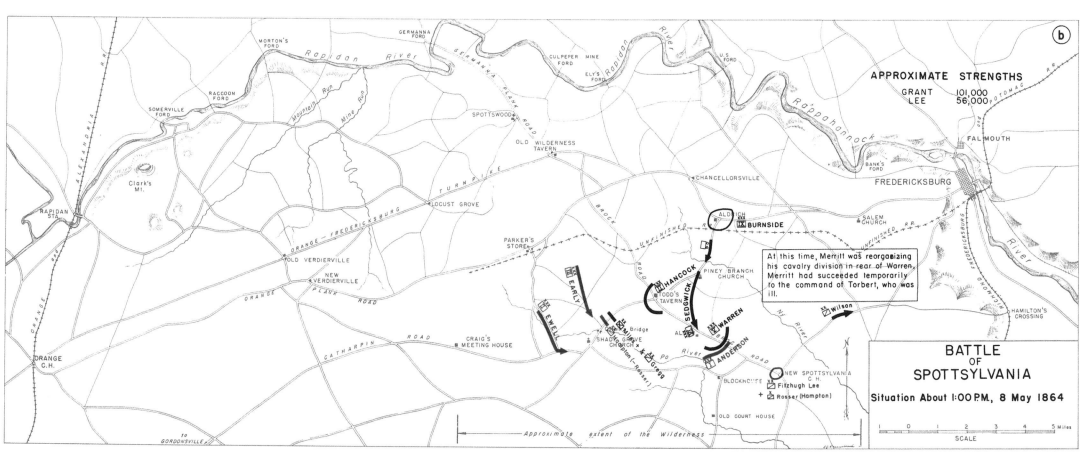

APPROXIMATE STRENGTHS

GRANT 101,000
LEE 56,000

At this time, Merritt was reorganizing his cavalry division in rear of Warren. Merritt had succeeded temporarily to the command of Torbert, who was ill.

BATTLE OF SPOTTSYLVANIA

Situation About 1:00 P.M., 8 May 1864

1 0 1 2 3 4 5 Miles

SCALE

SPOTSYLVANIA: 2

On 9 May, both armies continued to close up. Lee carefully organized and entrenched his lines, emplacing artillery all along them so as to be able to place enfilading fire on any attacking column. It was extremely difficult for the Union forces to determine the actual extent, strength, and location of Lee's position since much of it was concealed by trees and undergrowth. In addition, the Confederate skirmish line had been pushed well forward to keep Union scouts and staff officers from reconnoitering; and, in fact, it was a sharpshooter who picked off Sedgwick.

Grant, perhaps a little unnerved by the Wilderness, became concerned that Lee's entire army was preparing an offensive against the new Union supply base at Fredericksburg, so he ordered Hancock to cross the Po River to his front, advance down its west bank, and recross it at Blockhouse Bridge, and so turn Lee's left flank. At dawn on 10 May, Hancock's scouts found the Confederates strongly entrenched on the east bank of the Po at Blockhouse, so he shifted further along the river and got Col. John R. Brooke's brigade across to establish a bridgehead in the Confederate rear. Lee's left flank was turned and his communications threatened. A rapid reinforcement of Hancock's advance was all that was required, but Grant, not appreciating his opportunity, decided on a frontal attack, and told Meade to recall Hancock with two of his divisions and send him to Warren's position, where they were to prepare for a vigorous attack on Lee's fortified line at 5:30 P.M. It should be noted that senior officers of both armies still had not learned the futility of assaulting strongly held fortifications. The artillery of this period was devastating against troops caught in the open, but was relatively ineffective against even crude breastworks and trenches. The explosive charges of its shells lacked necessary power, and the fuses were too erratic for accurate fire. It became abundantly clear that one man well entrenched equaled three in the open.

The reason Grant gave up this promising maneuver in order to impose a Fredericksburg-type direct assault has never been explained. Neither has it ever been positively decided whether it was Grant or Meade who was the architect of the decision; but Grant, as the senior commander, had to take the final responsibility. This was the first serious failure of the anomalous system of command under which the Army of the Potomac had to finish the war. In effect, the army was commanded by two generals, each with his own, occasionally jealous, staff; their respective responsibilities were never clearly defined; and the result was frequently confusion.

On the 9th, Lee, alert to the danger of the Union offensive at the Po, ordered Heth's division across the river to deal with this unidentified Federal force. Advancing by a circuitous route, Heth encountered Hancock's flank guards, and some skirmishing ensued that, when reported to Meade, resulted in Barlow being recalled, because Meade did not want the distraction of a battle in the west of the Po while he was preparing to launch his grand attack in the east. But it was an opportunity missed.

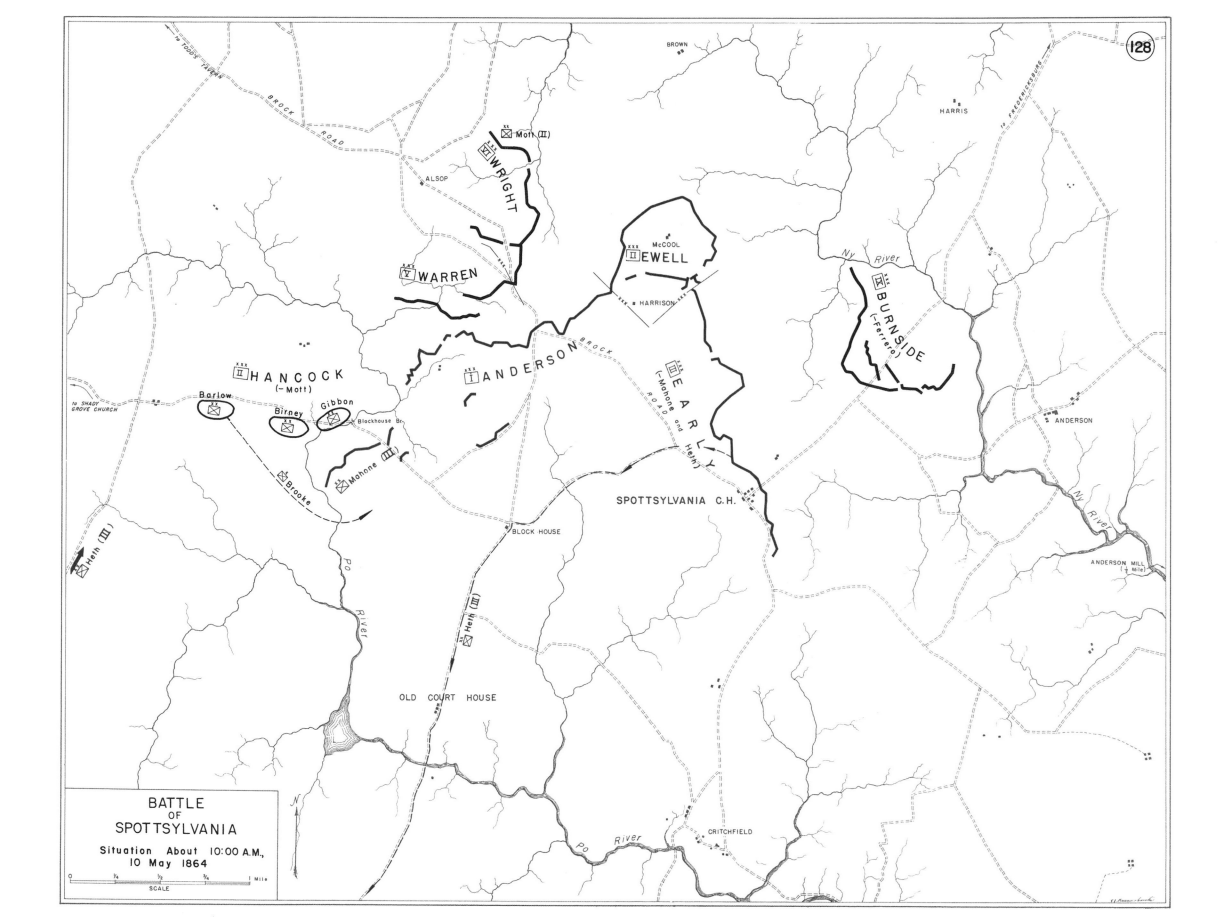

BATTLE
OF
SPOTTSYLVANIA

Situation About 10:00 A.M.,
10 May 1864

0   ¼   ½   ¾   1 Mile
SCALE

128

SPOTSYLVANIA: 3

West of the Po River, Heth pushed his attack, but the two brigades of Barlow's rear guard that faced him beat him off twice and successfully recrossed the river. Some time before 3:30 P.M., Warren reported that he was of the opinion that an immediate attack on his front would have an excellent chance of success. Meade therefore authorized it, and Warren advanced at about 4:00 P.M. with Wright's VI Corps on his left and Gibbon's division of II Corps on his right. Warren led the attack in full dress uniform, but his courage proved better than his judgment. Some of his men broke through the tangles of underbrush and felled trees in front of the Confederate lines, and a few even got into the first line of entrenchments, but they were either killed or driven out. Raked by carefully planned crossfires, the whole attacking force streamed back to its start line.

Farther to the east there was more intelligent planning. Wright, after careful reconnaissance of the Confederate position to his front, had decided that its weakest point was the west face of the salient (called the "Mule Shoe" by the Confederates) enclosing the McCool house. The entrenchments here were strong and backed up by a partially completed second line, but the position could be enfiladed by Union artillery. Also, there was a belt of timber, which would conceal Union troops forming for the attack, some two hundred yards in front of the Confederate works. Col. Emory Upton was to lead the attack, with Mott's II Corps in support.

Upton was a born soldier and a keen student of his profession, and his plans were careful and detailed. He formed his troops in four lines of three regiments each. When the first line reached the Confederate works, it was split right and left to widen the penetration. The second line was to carry the second Confederate position, while the last two were to form the reserve and lie down just outside the breastworks until they were needed.

At 6:10 P.M. Upton charged. Although the Confederate fire was heavy and accurate, the yelling Union advance went through it and over both lines of entrenchments, beating down determined opposition and taking about 1,000 prisoners. Mott, however, had formed his men in the open; they were an unreliable lot and artillery fire soon scattered them. Upton was left isolated, with a large part of the Confederate army concentrated against him. To give some support, Hancock renewed the attack of the Federal right, but it was repulsed. Upton hung on until dark when he withdrew. Meanwhile, Burnside got his IX Corps up near the Confederate right flank and entrenched.

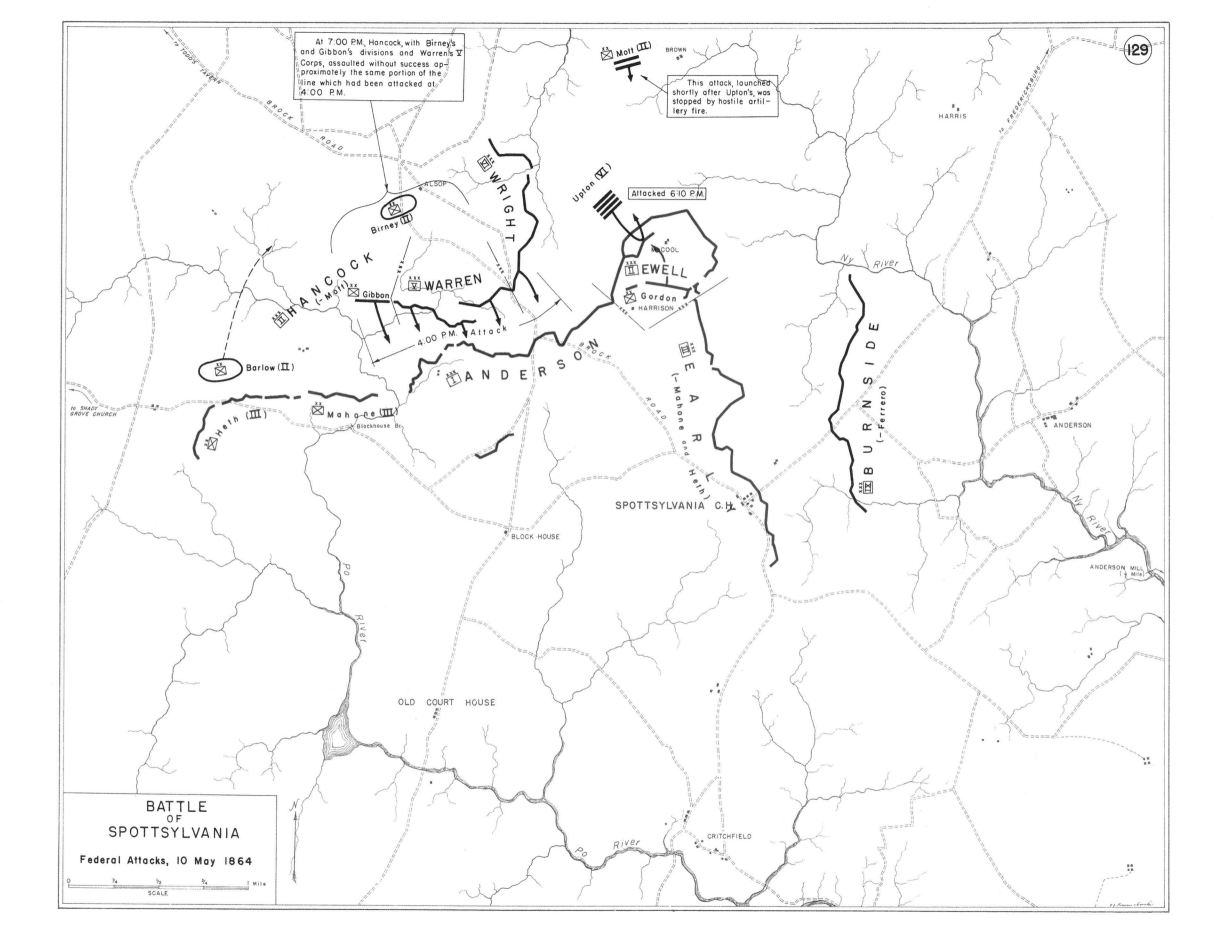

At 7:00 P.M., Hancock, with Birney's and Gibbon's divisions and Warren's V Corps, assaulted without success approximately the same portion of the line which had been attacked at 4:00 P.M.

This attack, launched shortly after Upton's, was stopped by hostile artillery fire.

Attacked 6:10 P.M.

Upton (VI)

4:00 P.M. Attack

BATTLE
OF
SPOTTSYLVANIA

Federal Attacks, 10 May 1864

SCALE

SPOTSYLVANIA: 4

There was no fighting on 11 May, but Lee was still convinced that the only chance of a Confederate victory lay in a successful battle. If Grant retreated, Lee intended to attack him. In fact, Grant was indeed carrying out a major repositioning, and had instructed Meade to organize a strong attack, by Hancock and Burnside with the II and IX Corps, on Ewell at the Mule Shoe at 4:00 A.M. on 12 May; V and VI Corps were to be ready to exploit any successes gained by the main effort. It was to be a repeat of Upton's attack, but on a decisive scale. Hancock moved from his position on the right after dark in a steady rain and began forming for his attack. Then a heavy fog set in around 4:35 A.M., before it was light enough to advance. Then out of the fog came a great cheer and masses of Federals swamped the Mule Shoe, capturing its garrison along with much artillery. They swept on until checked by an incomplete line of breastworks about half way down the salient. Here, the capable Gordon was rapidly organizing a counterattack that Lee wanted to lead personally, until restrained by his staff.

Gordon's audacious counterattack, supported by part of Early's corps, forced the Federals out of the Mule Shoe, but it could not completely restore the original positions. Even where driven out of the recently captured fortifications, the Federals clung to their outer edge. The fighting raged savagely through the day and into the night, especially at the so-called Bloody Angle, where Wright struck the Confederate defenses.

Both exhausted armies were relatively quiet during 13 May. Looking at the situation, Grant discounted further frontal assaults as too costly, and a movement against Lee's left would probably result in a Confederate withdrawal to the North Anna River, so he decided to make his next effort against Lee's right flank, hoping to envelop it before Lee could shift men over from the left or extend his fortifications further south from Spotsylvania Court House. Accordingly, Warren and Wright were to circle round behind Hancock and Burnside to attack Early on the right wing.

The weather that night favored the Confederates; heavy rains and fog blinded the Union columns as they struggled through knee-deep mud and underbrush. Not until 6:00 A.M. did the head of V Corps come on to the Fredericksburg Road, and it took the rest of the day to collect and organize its exhausted men. The attack had to be called off.

Confederate reaction had been comparatively slow, the complete withdrawal of the V Corps from the Union right not being definitely established until the afternoon of the 14th. Lee now began shifting troops from his left to right flank as well as extending his trenches southward. Probably only the weather had saved him from surprise and serious trouble.

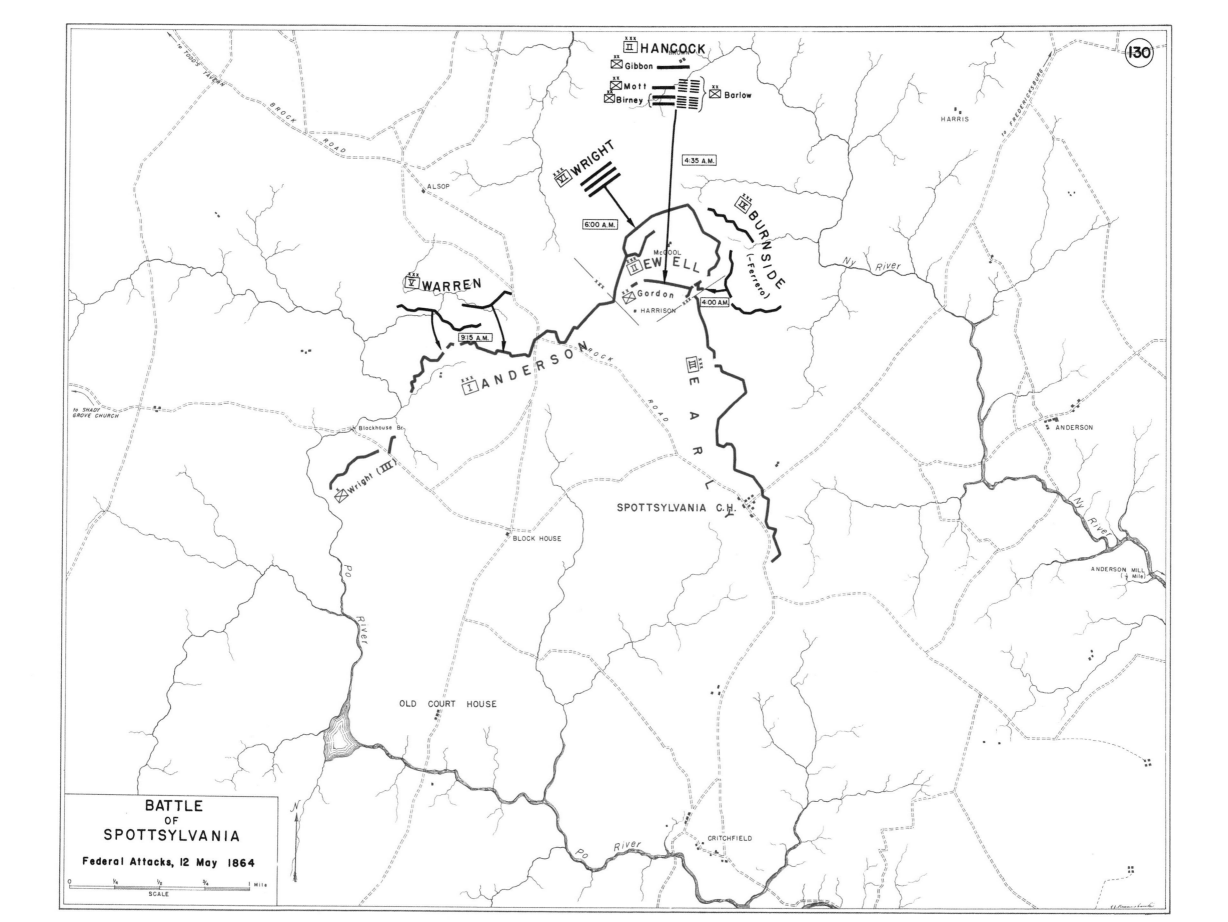

130

BATTLE
OF
SPOTTSYLVANIA

Federal Attacks, 12 May 1864

SCALE
0 ¼ ½ ¾ 1 Mile

XXX
II HANCOCK

XX
Gibbon

XX
Mott

XX
Birney

XX
Barlow

4:35 A.M.

XXX
VI WRIGHT

XXX
IX BURNSIDE
(~Ferrero)

6:00 A.M.

McCOOL

XXX
II EWELL

XX
Gordon

HARRISON

4:00 A.M.

XXX
V WARREN

9:15 A.M.

XXX
I ANDERSON

XXX
III EARLY

Ny River

ALSOP

HARRIS

to TODD'S TAVERN

BROCK ROAD

to FREDERICKSBURG

to SHADY GROVE CHURCH

Blockhouse Br.

XX
Wright (III

BLOCK HOUSE

SPOTTSYLVANIA C.H.

ANDERSON

ANDERSON MILL
(¼ Mile)

Po River

OLD COURT HOUSE

CRITCHFIELD

Po River

N

SPOTSYLVANIA: 5

Grant had disappointments in addition to the one that the weather had just inflicted on him. Two minor operations he had intended would assist the advance of the Army of the Potomac had been complete failures. In the Shenandoah Valley, the patriotic but inept Sigel had managed to get himself defeated on 15 May at New Market, where the cadets of the Virginia Military Institute formed part of the Confederate force. On the James River front, the energetic but incompetent Butler had brought on another fiasco. After failing to seize Petersburg in early May, when it was weakly garrisoned, he then delayed until Beauregard could scrape together enough troops to defeat him on 10 May at Drewry's Bluff. Now he was bottled up in the Bermuda Hundred—the neck of land just north of Petersburg between the converging James and Appomattox Rivers—where he possessed little but nuisance value.

Grant could no longer hope that these operations would weaken Lee by forcing him to detach troops from his army in order to defend Richmond and Petersburg, or to hold the Shenandoah. In fact, it was Lee who received reinforcements from the victorious Confederates in both those areas. If the war was to be won in the east, the Army of the Potomac would have to do it alone.

During 14–17 May, the two armies improved their positions as shown below. Though there were no actual engagements of any size during this period, the opposing troops were in close and constant contact. Continual skirmishing, sniping, and artillery exchanges resulted in steady losses. Grant pulled most of Hancock's II Corps out of the line to rest them for the next offensive.

Wright suggested that his corps might suddenly be shifted back to the right of the Union line for an attack on the Confederate left flank, which might have been weakened as men were taken out to extend Lee's right to the Po River. Grant accepted and expanded the idea: Hancock and Wright were to shift their troops into the former Mule Shoe area for an assault at daylight on the 18th; Burnside was to attack in conjunction with them; and Warren was to support the attack with his artillery and to stand ready to advance.

Apparently, Confederate scouts and patrols detected the movement. At any rate, no surprise was achieved and the advancing Federals found their opponents ready and waiting. The Union attacks were made with gallantry and energy, but were rapidly shot to pieces by Confederate artillery; only in a few cases did the attackers get close to the Confederate line and, by about 10:00 A.M., even Grant was willing to call a halt.

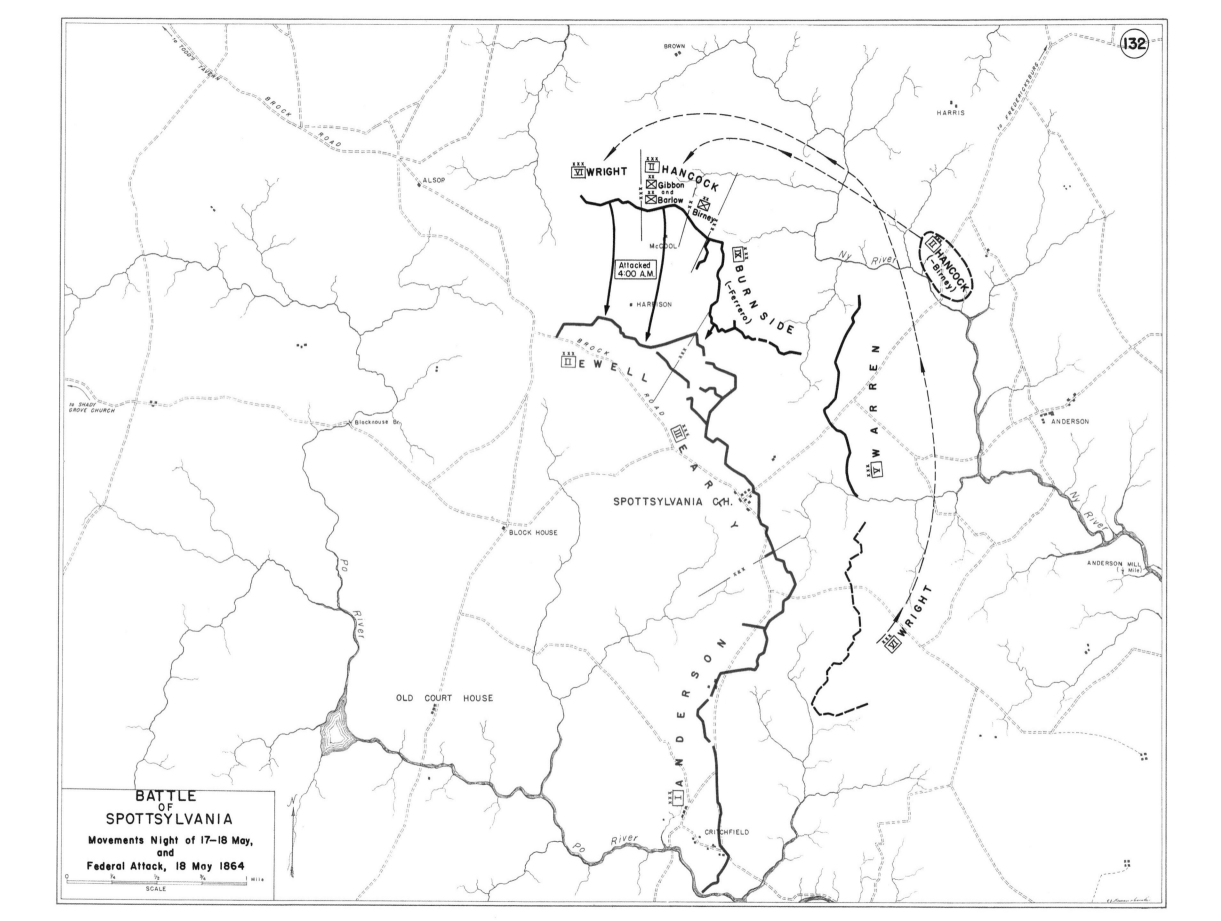

BROWN

HARRIS

to FREDERICKSBURG

to TODD'S TAVERN

BROCK ROAD

ALSOP

XXX
VI WRIGHT

XXX
II HANCOCK

Gibbon

Barlow
and

Birney

Ny River

XXX
II HANCOCK
(Birney)

McCOOL

Attacked
4:00 A.M.

IX BURNSIDE
(-Ferrero)

HARRISON

to SHADY GROVE CHURCH

XXX
II EWELL

BROCK ROAD

XXX
III EARLY

Blocknouse Br.

WARREN

XXX
V

ANDERSON

SPOTTSYLVANIA C.H.

BLOCK HOUSE

Po River

XXX
VI WRIGHT

OLD COURT HOUSE

Ny River

ANDERSON MILL
(⅓ Mile)

ANDERSON

XXX
I ANDERSON

CRITCHFIELD

Po River

N

BATTLE
OF
SPOTTSYLVANIA

Movements Night of 17–18 May,
and
Federal Attack, 18 May 1864

0   ¼   ½   ¾   1 Mile
SCALE

SPOTSYLVANIA: 6

Following the repulse of the 18 May attack, Grant moved Wright back to his former position and again placed Hancock in reserve. During the night of the 18th he shifted Burnside to his extreme left, and Warren extended the right flank of his V Corps across the Ny River. Grant now formed a plan that, he hoped, would lure Lee out from behind his earthworks. Hancock was ordered to advance rapidly southward on the night of the 19th along the line of the Fredericksburg & Potomac Railroad, five miles to the east. The rest of the army would remain in its present position, ready to follow after Hancock had gotten about a twenty-mile head start. It was intended to be a trap for Lee, and Hancock was to be the bait. Grant expected Lee to overtake and attempt to destroy Hancock, and this would give Grant a chance to pounce with the rest of the army and destroy Lee in the open before he had time to entrench. If Lee did not take the bait, the operation would still be useful as another effort to envelop Lee's right flank. It was a daring plan but, as we shall see, Grant would eventually lose his nerve and compromise its chance of success

Some indication of these shifts reached Lee, who knew that a rapid, undetected Federal advance south might cut in between his army and Richmond. Suspicious that this was Grant's intention, he ordered Ewell to advance on his front on the 19th and determine whether troops had been withdrawn from the Union right.

By now, Ewell's corps had been reduced to approximately 6,000 men, and he felt his force was too weak to risk in front of the Union fortifications; he requested and got Lee's approval to move around the Union flank. The countryside had been sodden from recent downpours and Ewell was forced to leave all his artillery behind. So, his infantry advanced unsupported and, at about 3:00 P.M., established contact with Federal units covering the Fredericksburg Road. They were raw troops and had never before seen action; they should have had little chance against Ewell's veterans but they met the Confederates straight on, if with more courage than skill, and fought them to a standstill. Both Hancock and Warren sent reinforcements, and in the end it was Ewell who was lucky to get away, thanks to the arrival of Hampton's cavalry and some horse artillery to cover his retreat. However, he had discovered that the Union right was indeed strong, and as a bonus his adventure caused Grant to postpone Hancock's advance until the night of the 20th.

Union losses during the fighting around Spotsylvania Court House are variously reported but appear to be in the 17,000–18,000 range. Confederate casualty figures are unknown, but since they fought behind fortifications during most of the engagements their losses would have been considerably less: perhaps between 9,000 and 10,000.

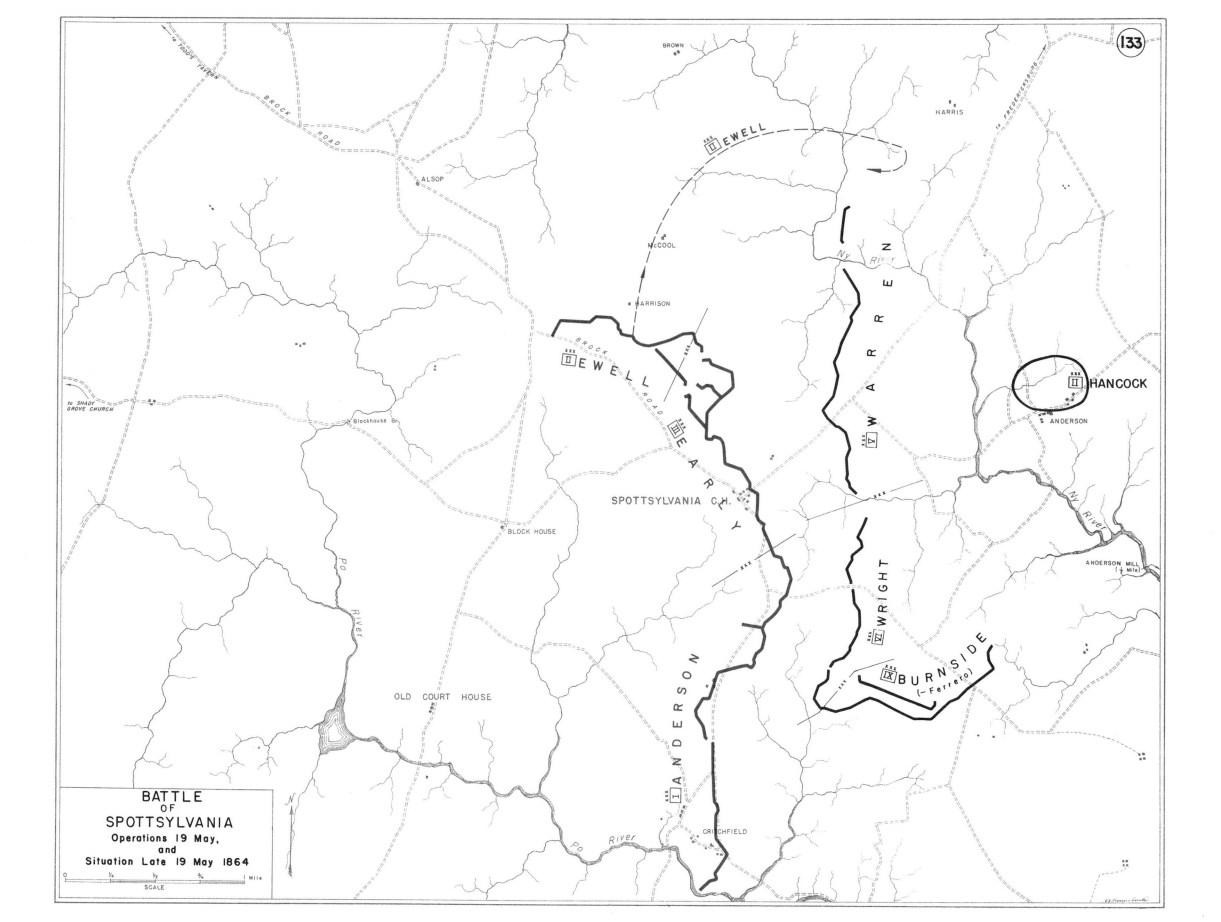

133

BROWN

HARRIS

to FREDERICKSBURG

to TODDS TAVERN

BROCK ROAD

ALSOP

EWELL

McCOOL

Ny River

HARRISON

WARREN

BROCK ROAD

EWELL

EWELL

V

HANCOCK

to SHADY GROVE CHURCH

EARLY

Blockhouse Br.

Ny River

SPOTTSYLVANIA C.H.

ANDERSON

BLOCK HOUSE

ANDERSON MILL (¾ Mile)

WRIGHT

Po River

OLD COURT HOUSE

VI

BURNSIDE
(-Ferrero)

IX

ANDERSON

N

BATTLE
OF
SPOTTSYLVANIA
Operations 19 May,
and
Situation Late 19 May 1864

Po River

CRITCHFIELD

SCALE
0   ¼   ½   ¾   1 Mile

WILDERNESS TO COLD HARBOR

The map below shows the progressive movements of the opposing forces from their first engagement in the Wilderness in early May 1864 to their meeting at Cold Harbor in early June.

During the night of 20 May, Hancock began his march from Spotsylvania to Milford Station, on the west bank of the Mattapony, by way of Guiney's Station. His orders were simple: to attack the Confederates wherever he found them and to keep Grant fully appraised of their whereabouts; all available cavalry was to scout for him. When he reached Guiney's Station at dawn, he pushed out a detachment of Brig. Gen. Wade Hampton's cavalry and moved on to Milford Station, where again he ejected a small Confederate detachment as well as set up a bridgehead on the west bank so he could bring the rest of his II Corps across.

Lee, warned of this development by Hampton's cavalry, thought it was yet another attempt to turn his right flank and get between his army and Richmond. He therefore began shifting his troops to the south bank of the Po and, when Warren, Burnside, and Wright successfully withdrew from Spotsylvania during the 21st, ordered a retreat to the North Anna River. It would appear that Grant, having pushed Hancock out as bait, suddenly became apprehensive and hurried the rest of the army forward prematurely without giving Lee time to strike at the isolated II Corps. The two armies collided at the North Anna on the 23rd.

The Union army left the North Anna area immediately after dark on 26 May and once more moved south, crossing the Pamunkey River at Hanover Town. By the 28th, Lee had his army in a naturally strong position behind the Totopotomoy Creek where it covered all the direct approaches to Richmond from the Pamunkey River crossings. To find out whether Federal infantry had already crossed that stream in strength, Lee sent Hampton east to Haw's Shop near the river, where he collided with Sheridan. After a hard, daylong fight, Hampton was defeated, but not before discovering the presence of the Union infantry around Hanover Town.

On the 29th, Grant came up to Lee's new position, but after some skirmishing decided an attack would be futile. The next day, Early attacked Warren but was roughly dealt with. Five miles eastward, Union cavalry under Brig. Gen. Alfred Torbert drove Maj. Gen. Fitzhugh Lee back to Cold Harbor.

On 22 May, Grant ordered Butler to group all his troops, except for a small garrison at Bermuda Hundred under Maj. Gen. W. F. Smith, and send them to the Army of the Potomac. Smith's force, about 12,500, went by boat to White House. Lee also beefed up his force by literally wringing 7,000 men of Maj. Gen. Robert F. Hoke's division from Beauregard, who was south of Richmond.

When Smith arrived at White House he was dismayed to find practically no facilities for disembarking his troops. His isolated and vulnerable force was protected by Sheridan, who drove Fitzhugh Lee out of Cold Harbor. However, seeing a sizable buildup of Confederate infantry threatening him, Sheridan decided to withdraw—until stopped by Meade, who ordered him to hold Cold Harbor at all costs.

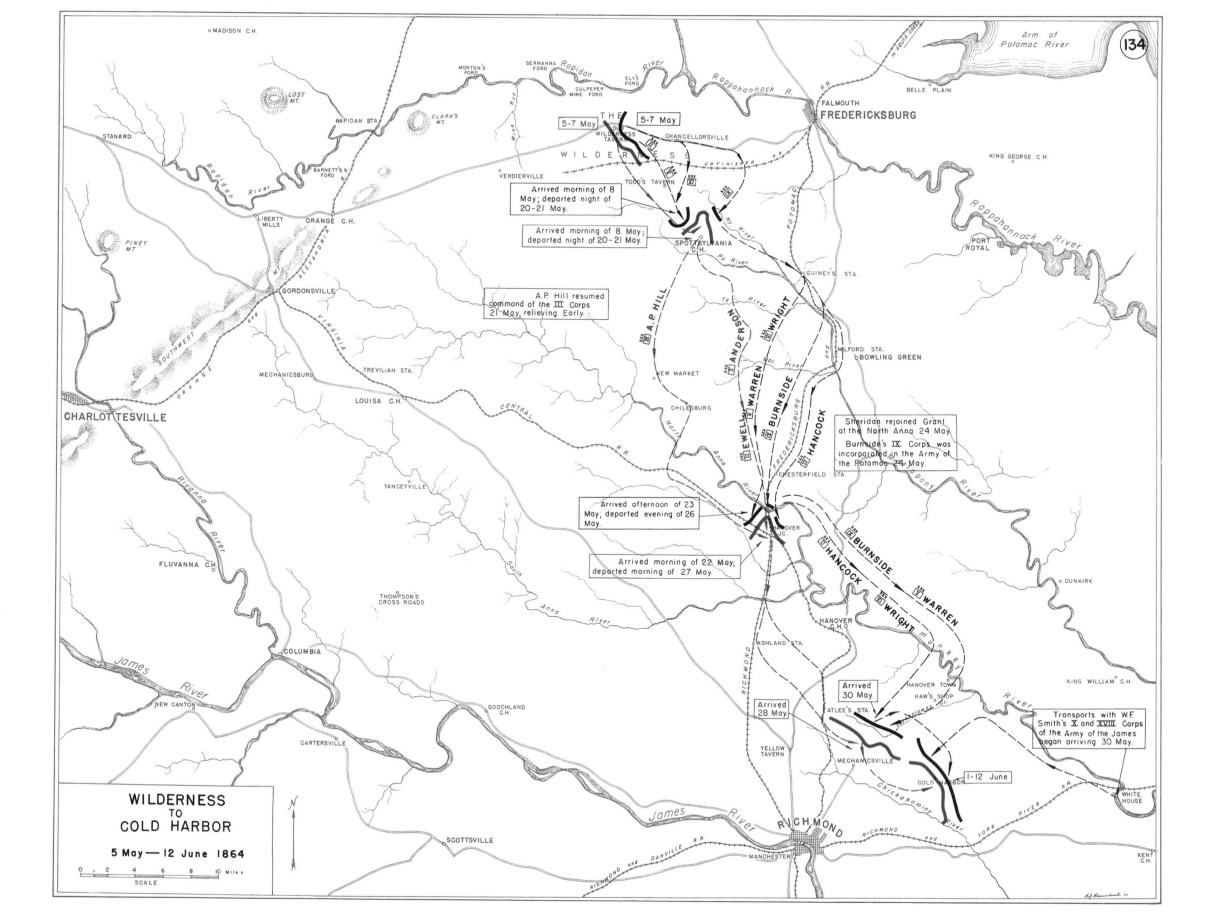

134

MADISON C.H.

Arm of
Potomac River

MORTON'S
FORD

GERMANNA
FORD

Rapidan River

Ely's
FORD

Rappahannock R.

to AQUIA CREEK

R.R.

BELLE PLAIN

FALMOUTH

FREDERICKSBURG

LOST
MT.

RAPIDAN STA.

CLARK'S
MT.

Mine Run

CULPEPER
MINE FORD

5-7 May

5-7 May

THE
WILDERNESS
TAVERN

CHANCELLORSVILLE

UNFINISHED R.R.

KING GEORGE C.H.

STANARD

VERDIERVILLE

THE   WILDERNESS

TODD'S TAVERN

VI

Rappahannock River

Arrived morning of 8
May; departed night of
20-21 May.

Po River

PORT
ROYAL

LIBERTY
MILLS

ORANGE C.H.

PINEY
MT.

Rapidan River

SPOTSYLVANIA
C.H.

Ni River

Arrived morning of 8 May;
departed night of 20-21 May.

GUINEY'S STA.

GORDONSVILLE

A.P. Hill resumed
command of the III Corps
21 May, relieving Early.

A.P. HILL

To River

Mat River

MILFORD STA.

BOWLING GREEN

SOUTHWEST   MT.   ORANGE   and   ALEXANDRIA   R.R.

VIRGINIA   CENTRAL

MECHANICSBURG

TREVILIAN STA.

LOUISA C.H.

NEW MARKET

CHILESBURG

ANDERSON

WRIGHT

EWELL

WARREN

BURNSIDE

HANCOCK

North Anna River

Sheridan rejoined Grant
at the North Anna 24 May.

Burnside's IX Corps was
incorporated in the Army of
the Potomac 24 May.

CHARLOTTESVILLE

Rivanna River

YANCEYVILLE

South Anna River

CHESTERFIELD STA.

Arrived afternoon of 23
May; departed evening of 26
May.

HANOVER
JC.

FLUVANNA C.H.

THOMPSON'S
CROSS ROADS

Anna River

Arrived morning of 22 May;
departed morning of 27 May.

HANCOCK

BURNSIDE

WRIGHT

WARREN

Pamunkey River

DUNKIRK

NEW CANTON

COLUMBIA

James River

CARTERSVILLE

GOOCHLAND
C.H.

RICHMOND

ASHLAND STA.

HANOVER
C.H.

KING WILLIAM C.H.

Arrived
30 May.

HANOVER TOWN

HAW'S SHOP

Pamunkey River

Transports with W.F.
Smith's X and XVIII Corps
of the Army of the James
began arriving 30 May.

Arrived
28 May.

ATLEE'S STA.

YELLOW
TAVERN

MECHANICSVILLE

COLD HARBOR

1-12 June

WHITE
HOUSE

Chickahominy River

YORK RIVER R.R.

SCOTTSVILLE

James River

RICHMOND

MANCHESTER

RICHMOND and DANVILLE R.R.

RICHMOND and

KENT
C.H.

WILDERNESS
TO
COLD HARBOR

5 May — 12 June 1864

0 2 4 6 8 10 Miles
SCALE

N

BATTLE OF THE NORTH ANNA

Robert E. Lee's army had reached the North Anna on 22 May, and here it received its first sizable reinforcements since the campaign opened, including Pickett's division from the James River front and Breckinridge's command from the Shenandoah: in all between 8,000 and 9,000 men. Unfortunately, though, this increase in combat strength was offset by a decrease in the command capabilities of the Army of Northern Virginia. A. P. Hill, although returned to duty, was still sick; Ewell was physically exhausted; Anderson was the only corps commander who was fit, but he was relatively inexperienced. Then, Lee was crippled with dysentery, leaving his army almost leaderless.

The Confederate position, though, had been established with great skill behind the steep-banked North Anna and carefully fortified. The V shape would enable troops to move quickly from one flank to another, either to repel attack or mass for counterattack.

The Army of the Potomac arrived at the line of the North Anna on the 23rd, and Warren found the ford at Jericho Mill undefended. At 6:00 P.M., just as his corps had crossed, he was ferociously attacked by A. P. Hill, but Hill was beaten off and Warren was able to entrench.

Early on the 24th, Hancock found that the Confederates on his front had withdrawn to their main line, and so he moved the rest of his corps to the west bank. To the west, Wright joined Warren. Grant now, for the first time, realized the shape of Lee's position, and the awkward implications it had for his own. His aggressiveness had split his army into three widely separated parts, so that troops moving from one flank to the other would have to cross the North Anna twice. Had Lee not been too sick to direct an attack, it is possible he would have thrown his whole weight against Hancock (although Hancock was well dug in and might have proved difficult to defeat).

There was only light skirmishing during the 25th and 26th, and Grant decided against attacking. Stretches of the railroads were destroyed, and after having made a cavalry feint against Lee's left flank, Grant withdrew southeast to Cold Harbor.

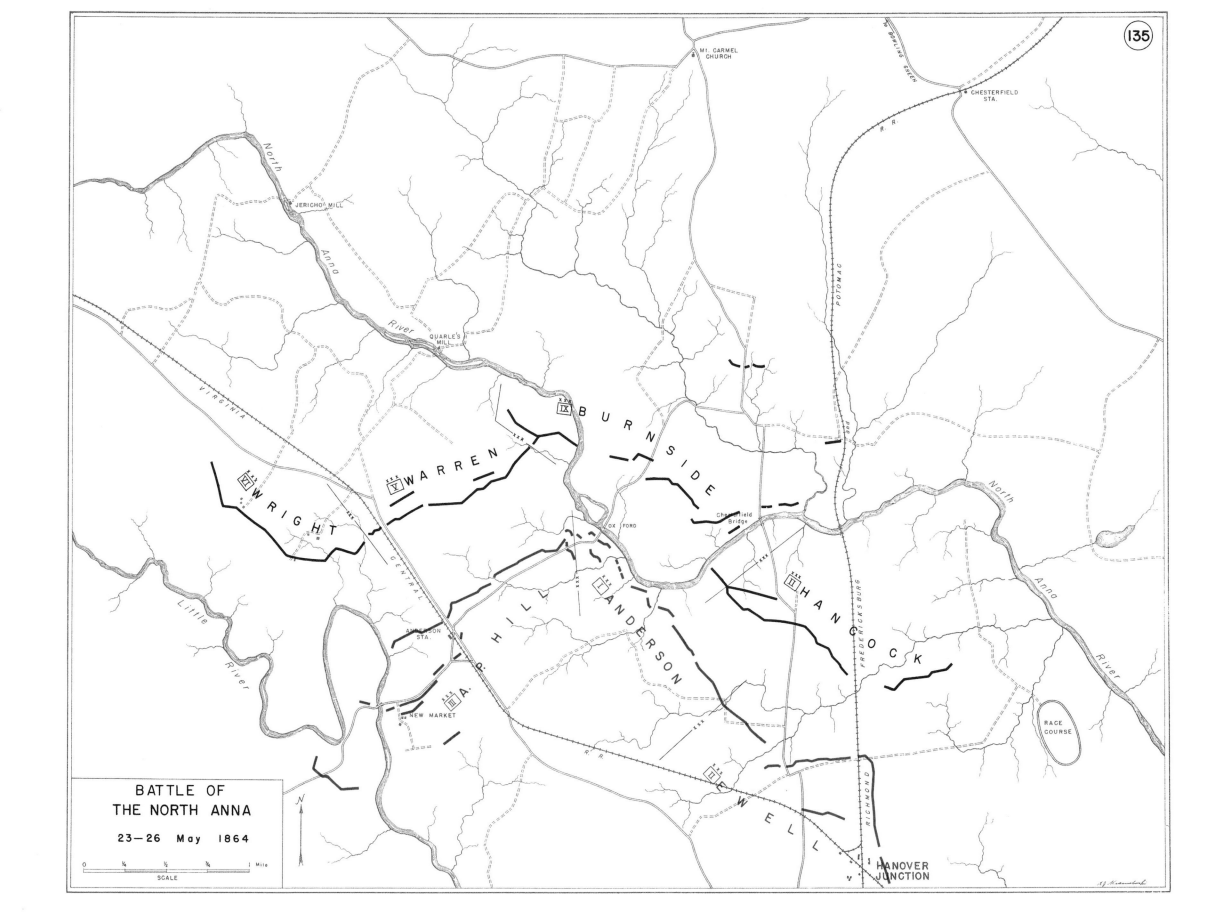

MT. CARMEL
CHURCH

CHESTERFIELD
STA.

JERICHO MILL

QUARLE'S
MILL

IX

BURNSIDE

WARREN

V

WRIGHT

XXX
VI

OX FORD

Chesterfield
Bridge

North

Anna

River

II

HANCOCK

H I L L

ANDERSON

XXX
III

ANDERSON
STA.

A. P.

III

NEW MARKET

E W E L L

XXX
II

RACE
COURSE

HANOVER
JUNCTION

Little

River

VIRGINIA

CENTRAL

R. R.

POTOMAC

to BOWLING GREEN

FREDERICKSBURG

RICHMOND

BATTLE OF
THE NORTH ANNA

23—26 May 1864

0   ¼   ½   ¾   1 Mile
SCALE

N

BATTLE OF COLD HARBOR

During the night of 31 May/1 June, Sheridan reorganized his position at the little crossroads town of Old Cold Harbor. In accordance with Meade's order to hold the place at all costs, he threw up hasty field fortifications and waited for infantry support to arrive. Grant had urged Wright to make every effort to get to Old Cold Harbor by daylight on the 1st, but this involved an exhausting fifteen-hour march over strange, backcountry roads. Further east, the frustrated Smith had finally disembarked his command at White House at 3:00 A.M. and immediately set off without waiting for his reserve wagons or reserve ammunition but, due to misdirections from Grant's headquarters, he was sent north to Pamunkey instead of west to Old Cold Harbor.

Lee now planned to recover the initiative, and sent Anderson (with Hoke's command attached) hurrying down toward Old Cold Harbor with orders to take the town preparatory to a general attack to roll up Grant's left. In the early morning of 1 June, Anderson and Hoke came rolling down on Sheridan's two small dismounted cavalry divisions behind their makeshift defenses.

Once more, as at Gettysburg where Buford's cavalry had held back a much bigger Confederate force, breech-loading and repeating carbines, backed by horse artillery, gained fire superiority over infantry muskets. Hoke's men displayed little ferocity and, when the commander of Anderson's leading brigade was shot down, his men suddenly broke and ran. A Federal counterattack at this point might well have wrecked Lee's entire right flank, but Wright was still working his way to Cold Harbor and Smith was still trying to find the place; it was 6:00 P.M. before they were in line, but by that time Anderson had entrenched and was able to repel the Federal attacks.

Both armies now shifted toward Cold Harbor and, on 2 June, Early tried unsuccessfully to overrun the Federal right. As Lee's new position, between Totopotomoy Creek and the Chickahominy River, was almost impossible to outflank, Grant decided to try a head-on attack in the hope that he might drive Lee back on to the Chickahominy. At 4:30 A.M. on 3 June, the II, VI, and XVIII Corps went into the attack. Within an hour, they had taken 7,000 casualties (the Confederates suffered about 1,500). Neither Grant nor Meade had taken the precaution of reconnoitering Lee's lines or had paid particular attention to organizing the assault. But the decimated Union units, instead of retreating, dug in where they had been halted near the Confederate breastworks, and so a terrible and costly trench warfare set in until 12 June.

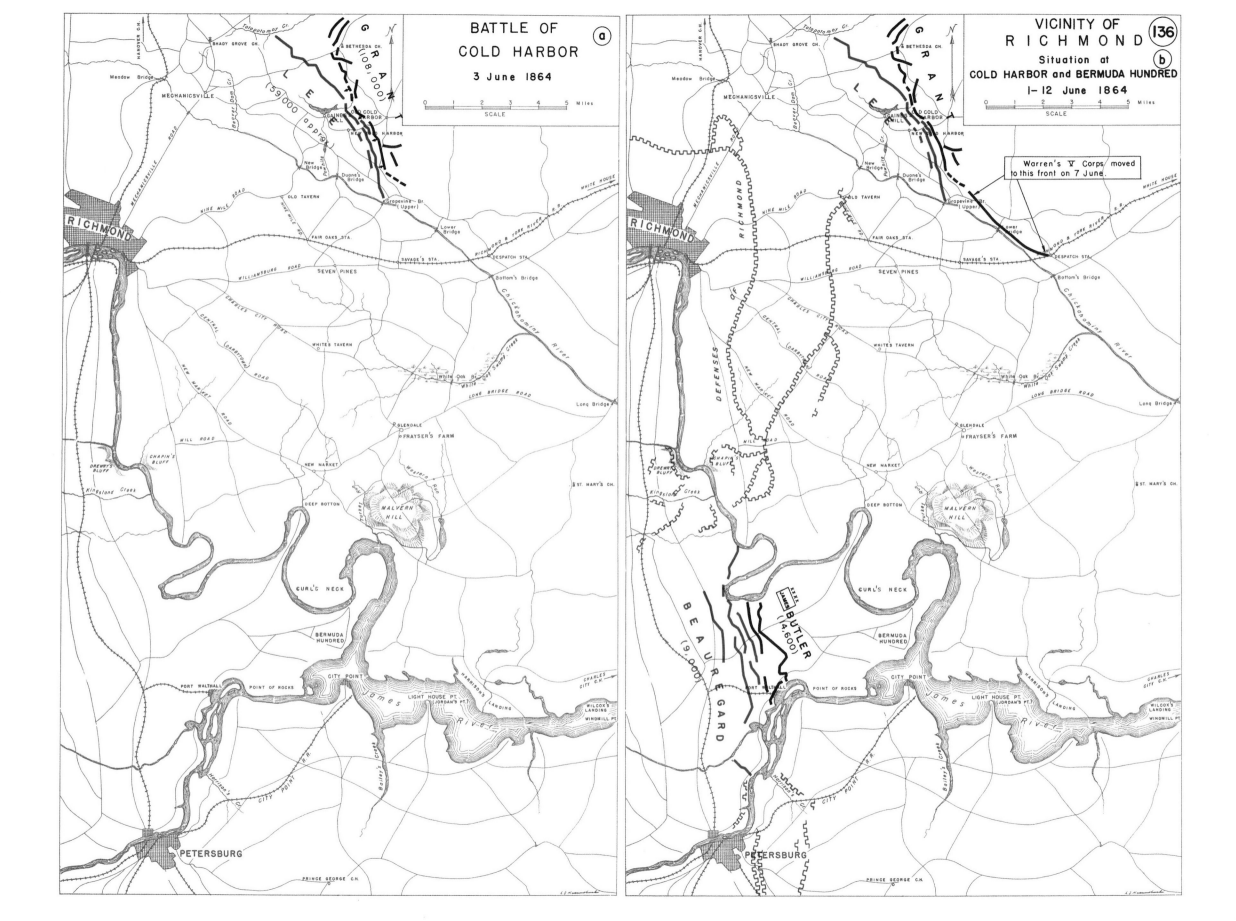

BATTLE OF
COLD HARBOR

3 June 1864

SCALE

VICINITY OF
RICHMOND

Situation at
COLD HARBOR and BERMUDA HUNDRED
1-12 June 1864

SCALE

Warren's V Corps moved
to this front on 7 June.

MOVEMENT TO THE JAMES RIVER

So far, Grant's campaign had been remarkable for persistence and the 55,000 casualties it had cost. (Lee's losses during the same period were somewhere between 20,000 and 40,000.) Now, however, out of the stubborn and cold-blooded Grant of Cold Harbor emerged the far-sighted and imaginative commander that had been so brilliant at Vicksburg. All but one of the major railroads supplying both Richmond and the Army of Northern Virginia passed through Petersburg, and Grant determined to have it. He would transfer his army to the south bank of the James, seize Petersburg, outflank Beauregard (thus releasing Butler), then turn north and operate against the remaining rail line into Richmond. Success here would force Lee to either stand siege in the Confederate capital or abandon it and move westward. The whole Union army had to be silently extricated from its trenches under Lee's nose and then taken across both the Chickahominy and James. If Lee got wind of this and decided to strike Grant's columns on the march, it would have been hard to avoid a disastrous defeat. And just to compound the risk, there was a strong Confederate flotilla, including several ironclads, on the upper reaches of the James.

On 12 June, as soon as it was dark, the movement began. Hancock and Wright occupied the rearward line, ready to meet any sudden attack, until the roads behind their corps were clear. Smith moved off first, heading back to White House. Wilson rode south across the Chickahominy, then turned and pushed boldly westward. Warren followed him and took up a good position just east of Riddell's Shop, which he held until the rest of the army passed behind him. Hancock formed the advance guard and was ferried across the James on the 14th and 15th. While he crossed, engineers, in one of the great feats of military engineering, began building a pontoon bridge (2,100 feet long, built to resist strong tidal currents and to adjust to a four-foot tidal rise and fall), which they completed by midnight.

On the morning of 13 June, Lee found the trenches opposite him empty, but presumed Grant's movement was just another of his short-range attempts to envelop his right flank. Lee promptly shifted southward and dug in from Malvern Hill to White Oak Swamp Creek. But by that time there was nothing in front of him except Wilson's single cavalry division, which reconnoitered aggressively all along his front and blocked Lee's every effort to discover the Union infantry's dispositions.

Grant had done the near-impossible and had completely outwitted Lee. It had been a very risky business, but it had been planned and executed to perfection.

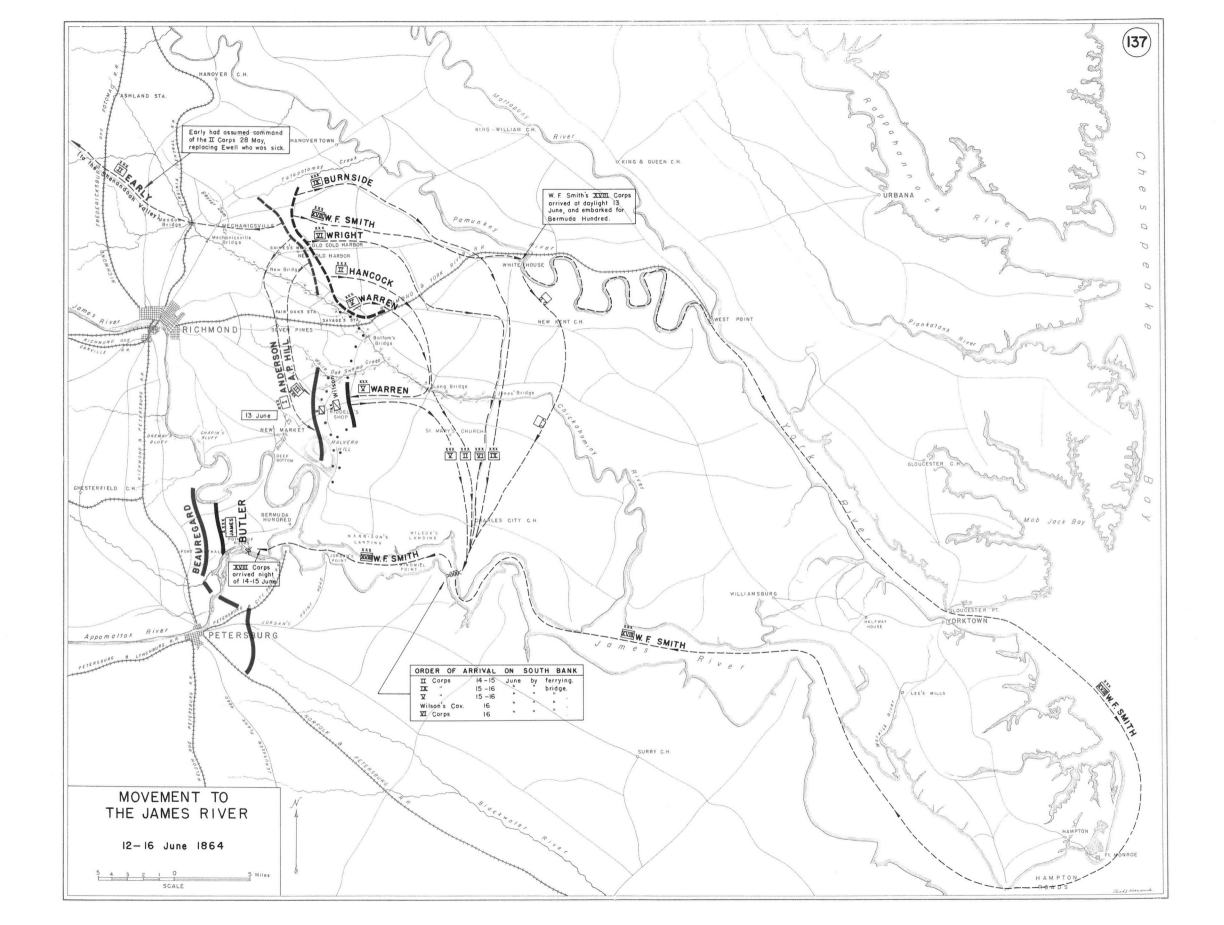

HANOVER C.H.

ASHLAND STA.

Early had assumed command
of the II Corps 28 May,
replacing Ewell who was sick.

HANOVER TOWN

KING WILLIAM C.H.

King & Queen C.H.

URBANA

IX BURNSIDE

XVIII W. F. SMITH

VI WRIGHT
OLD COLD HARBOR

NEW COLD HARBOR

II HANCOCK

W. F. Smith's XVIII Corps
arrived at daylight 13
June, and embarked for
Bermuda Hundred.

WEST POINT

WHITE HOUSE

V WARREN

RICHMOND

FAIR OAKS STA.

SEVEN PINES

SAVAGE'S STA.

Bottom's Bridge

NEW KENT C.H.

A.P. HILL

ANDERSON

V WARREN

Long Bridge

James' Bridge

GLOUCESTER C.H.

13 June

NEW MARKET

RIDDELL'S SHOP

St. Mary's Church

V II VI IX

CHARLES CITY C.H.

MALVERN HILL

DEEP BOTTOM

CHESTERFIELD C.H.

BUTLER
JAMES

BEAUREGARD

BERMUDA HUNDRED

HARRISON'S LANDING

WILCOX'S LANDING

Mob Jack Bay

XVIII Corps
arrived night
of 14-15 June

JORDAN'S POINT

WINDMILL POINT

XVIII W. F. SMITH

WILLIAMSBURG

GLOUCESTER PT.

YORKTOWN

HALFWAY HOUSE

PETERSBURG

XVIII W. F. SMITH

James River

Appomattox River

ORDER OF ARRIVAL ON SOUTH BANK

II Corps	14-15	June	by ferrying.
IX "	15-16	"	" bridge.
V "	15-16	"	" "
Wilson's Cav.	16	"	" "
VI Corps	16	"	" "

LEE'S MILLS

SURRY C.H.

Blackwater River

XVIII W. F. SMITH

MOVEMENT TO
THE JAMES RIVER

12-16 June 1864

HAMPTON

FT. MONROE

HAMPTON ROADS

5 4 3 2 1 0   5 Miles
SCALE

SIEGE OF PETERSBURG: 1

For his attack on Petersburg, Smith had been reinforced with Brig. Gen. Edward W. Hinks's division of black troops and Brig. Gen. August V. Kautz's cavalry division. Nevertheless, he advanced cautiously, delayed along his march by Beauregard's outposts.

The Petersburg defenses consisted of a chain of strong redans (artillery positions designed for both flanking and frontal fire) connected by entrenchments; all the approaches were obstructed by ditches and tangles of felled trees. And although Beauregard had plenty of cannon, he had insufficient troops to man them.

Smith, remembering the hastily conceived, badly planned, and disastrous attack at Cold Harbor, took great care to make exhaustive reconnaissances, and about 7:00 P.M. on 15 June, his attack jumped off against Redans 5 and 6, both of which fell quickly. Hinks's division swarmed down the Confederate line as far as Redan 11 and opened a mile-wide gap in the fortifications. Petersburg lay open. But Smith had picked up a rumor that Lee was arriving, and so decided to stand on his laurels and wait for Hancock to join him. And so the initiative passed, and Hancock's troops relieved Smith's exhausted men.

The next day, Grant and Meade arrived with IX Corps and, at 6:00 P.M., all three corps attacked. But by now Beauregard had moved most of his men from the Bermuda Hundred to Petersburg. Union advances captured more redans, but they also suffered heavily, both in the attacks and in Beauregard's counterattacks. A surprise assault by Burnside at dawn on the 17th captured the Shand house ridge, but other attacks failed. At 4:00 A.M. on the 18th, Grant launched a major assault only to discover that Beauregard had already pulled back to a new line of defenses. Grant needed time to regroup, but in the meantime, Lee's troops were finally arriving and subsequent Union attacks gained little at great cost.

Grant's strategy had been brilliant, but his earlier tactics had left his officers and men reluctant to attack fortifications, and this, together with poor staff work, lost him a golden opportunity to win the war here at Petersburg. Grant now suspended all attacks and entrenched his line, extending it south of the city.

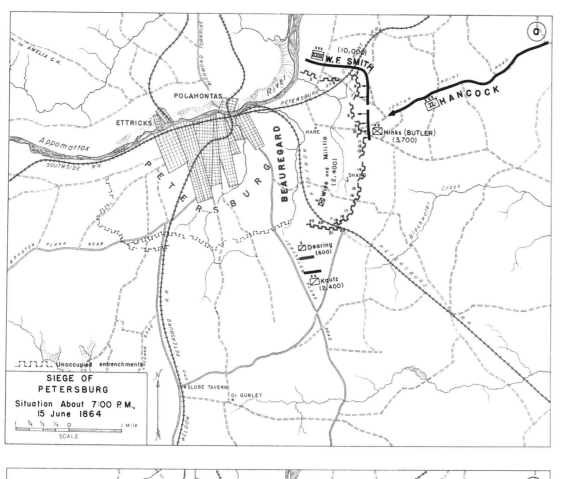

Unoccupied entrenchments

SIEGE OF
PETERSBURG

Situation About 7:00 P.M.,
15 June 1864

SCALE

(10,000)
XVIII W. F. SMITH

II HANCOCK

Hinks (BUTLER)
(3,700)

Wise and Militia
(2,400)

Dearing
(600)

Kautz
(2,400)

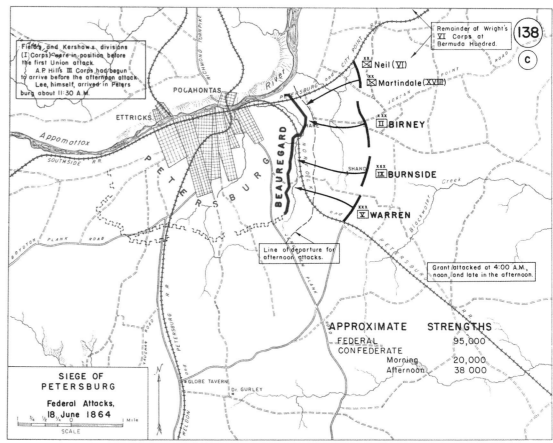

138

Remainder of Wright's
VI Corps at
Bermuda Hundred.

Field's and Kershaw's divisions
(I Corps) were in position before
the first Union attack.
A.P. Hill's III Corps had begun
to arrive before the afternoon attack.
Lee, himself, arrived in Petersburg about 11:30 A.M.

Neil (VI)
Martindale (XVIII)

II BIRNEY

IX BURNSIDE

V WARREN

Line of departure for
afternoon attacks.

Grant attacked at 4:00 A.M.,
noon, and late in the afternoon.

APPROXIMATE STRENGTHS
FEDERAL   95,000
CONFEDERATE
   Morning   20,000
   Afternoon   38,000

SIEGE OF
PETERSBURG

Federal Attacks,
18 June 1864

SCALE

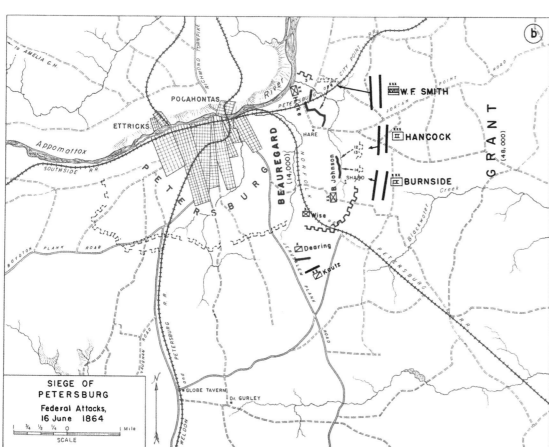

XVIII W. F. SMITH

II HANCOCK

IX BURNSIDE

GRANT
(48,000)

B. Johnson

Wise

Dearing

Kautz

SIEGE OF
PETERSBURG

Federal Attacks,
16 June 1864

SCALE

BEAUREGARD
(14,000)

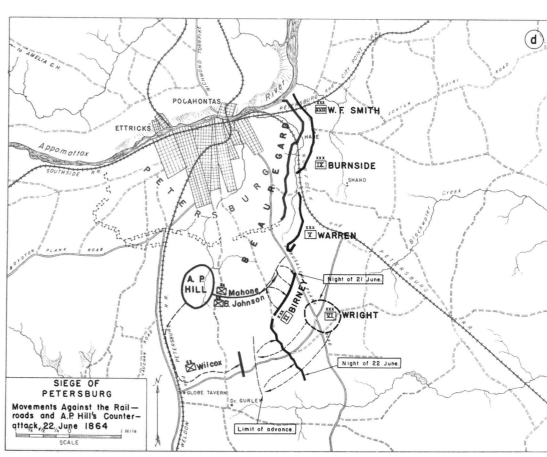

XVIII W. F. SMITH

IX BURNSIDE

V WARREN

A. P.
HILL

Mahone
B. Johnson

II BIRNEY

VI WRIGHT

Night of 21 June.

Night of 22 June.

Wilcox

Limit of advance.

SIEGE OF
PETERSBURG

Movements Against the Railroads and A.P. Hill's Counterattack, 22 June 1864

SCALE

SIEGE OF PETERSBURG: 2

The Petersburg front now subsided into static trench warfare. Both sides were exhausted, but especially Grant's.

In an attempt to break the deadlock, Lt. Col. Henry Pleasants, commander of the 48th Pennsylvania Infantry Regiment, a unit with a lot of coalminers, proposed mining the redan opposite IX Corps. The plan was approved and Pleasants's men tunneled 511 feet and planted 8,000 pounds of powder underneath the earthworks. Burnside selected Brig. Gen. Edward Ferrero's division of black troops, his only fresh unit, to spearhead the assault after the explosion. Before the attack (scheduled for 30 July), Ferrero's men were to be given specialized training.

Meade and Grant had some misgivings but nevertheless approved the scheme and, to increase its chances of success, had Hancock and Sheridan make a feint against Richmond, which succeeded in drawing all but three Confederate divisions north of the James. But barely twelve hours before the attack, Meade, with Grant's approval, modified the plan: a white division must lead the attack, and it would move against the high ground without trying to widen the gap. Burnside was stunned. The commanders of the three white divisions drew lots, like condemned men, to see who would go first. Brig. Gen. James H. Ledlie drew the short straw. Only a few hours of daylight remained with no time to train the new troops. Meade issued detailed orders that gaps were to be opened in the Union parapets and abatis so that men could move forward unhindered (in the event, it was not done), and the maze of trenches that had to be navigated proved a huge problem.

At 4:40 A.M., the mine exploded, and bodies, dirt, and guns, soared upward; the defenders fled in terror, leaving 500 yards of earthworks abandoned. Ledlie, in a blue funk, hid in a dugout and sought refuge in a bottle of rum. Ferrero joined him.

Unable to leave their trenches easily, the troops came out in small groups, without effective leadership, and moved down in the crater, only to find that they could not climb the thirty-foot slope at the far side. Others followed, until there was a jammed mass milling around at the bottom. It took two hours to start another piecemeal advance, but by then it was too late; Confederates lined the rim and poured fire into the Federals below; mortar shells rained in, and Meade called off the attack that ended up costing him 4,400 casualties.

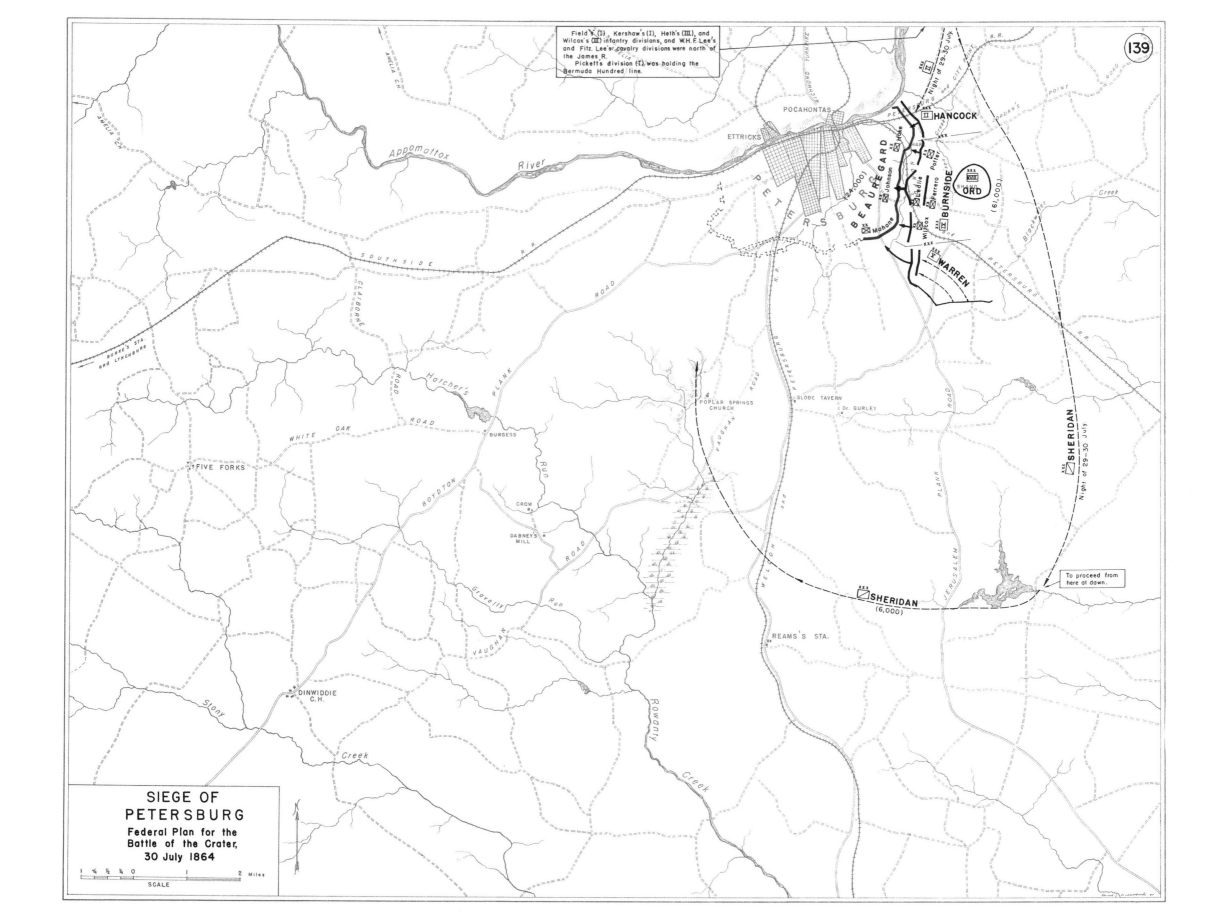

Field's (I), Kershaw's (I), Heth's (III), and
Wilcox's (III) infantry divisions, and W.H.F. Lee's
and Fitz. Lee's cavalry divisions were north of
the James R.
Pickett's division (I) was holding the
Bermuda Hundred line.

POCAHONTAS

ETTRICKS

Appomattox River

HANCOCK

BEAUREGARD (24,000)

Hoke

Johnson

Elliott

Potter

Ferrero

BURNSIDE

ORD (16,000)

Mahone

Wilcox

WARREN

SOUTHSIDE R.R.

Night of 29-30 July

SHERIDAN

POPLAR SPRINGS
CHURCH

BURGESS

WHITE OAK ROAD

HATCHER'S

PLANK ROAD

SLOBE TAVERN

Dr. GURLEY

CLAIBORNE ROAD

BOYDTON

CROW

DABNEY'S MILL

FIVE FORKS

Run

Gravelly Run

Vaughan Run

VAUGHAN ROAD

WELDON R.R.

JERUSALEM PLANK ROAD

SHERIDAN (6,000)

To proceed from
here at dawn.

Night of 29-30 July

REAMS'S STA.

DINWIDDIE
C.H.

BURKE'S STA.
and LYNCHBURG

Stony Creek

Rowanty Creek

SIEGE OF
PETERSBURG

Federal Plan for the
Battle of the Crater,
30 July 1864

SCALE
1 ¾ ½ ¼ 0   1   2 Miles

SIEGE OF PETERSBURG: 3

Grant knew that if he were to strangle the supply route to Petersburg, and thus to Lee, and thus to the Confederate cause, he had to cut the railroad links coming up from the south and in from the west. Warren managed to cut the Weldon & Petersburg Railroad on 18 August, at Globe Tavern, but Confederate supplies were still brought up further south and then transferred to wagons. Hancock tried, unsuccessfully, to cut the connection further south, and Grant kept hammering away at Lee's line, north of the James and then south. Such was the pressure that Anderson was recalled from the Shenandoah, and this gave Sheridan the opportunity he needed. He defeated Early four times in a month and devastated the entire Valley.

For Lee's army, the winter of 1864/65 was another one of hardship and discontent. The war was being lost, and many men drifted away back to their homes. Lee was forced to send Hoke's division to help defend Wilmington, North Carolina, the Confederacy's last seaport, and Hampton took one division of cavalry into South Carolina. Grant, on the other hand, was enjoying a flow of reinforcements when men from VI Corps returned from the Valley in December.

On 23 January, popular resentment against Jefferson Davis's conduct of the war resulted in the establishment of an overall commander of the forces of the South; and, of course, Robert E. Lee was elected by the Confederate Congress. The situation that faced him was daunting, if not hopeless. Thomas had smashed Hood at Nashville; Sher-

man was in Savannah; there was a strong Federal beachhead at Wilmington; and Sheridan had all but cleared out the Shenandoah Valley. In desperation, the Confederate high command concocted a plan. If a surprise attack could cripple Grant at Petersburg, Lee could then move south, join Johnston, and crush Sherman; that done, the united Confederate forces would return and deal with Grant. It was a fantasy, but that was all they had to cling to. At 4:00 P.M. on 25 March 1865, Gordon made a surprise attack at the northern end of the Union's Petersburg line. It stalled, and counterattacks drove it back, with 5,000 casualties.

Two days later Sheridan came down from the Shenandoah to join Grant; Lee, foreseeing an attack on his key supply route, the Southside Railroad, concentrated most of his remaining cavalry on his right flank and prepared to reinforce it with infantry.

The attack Lee expected came swiftly, because Grant wanted to engage decisively before Lee had a chance to evacuate Petersburg. Sheridan, Warren, and Humphreys advanced on the 29th, and for three days made steady progress. By the 31st, they had extended their line as far west as White Oak Road, repulsing a counterattack on the same day.

Sheridan pushed on to Dinwiddie Court House, where he was held by fierce opposition. Gen. George E. Pickett was entrenched at Five Forks, but Sheridan found him there and, by combining with Warren and Mackenzie, hit Pickett from almost every angle. Pickett's resistance collapsed, as 4,500 of his men were captured.

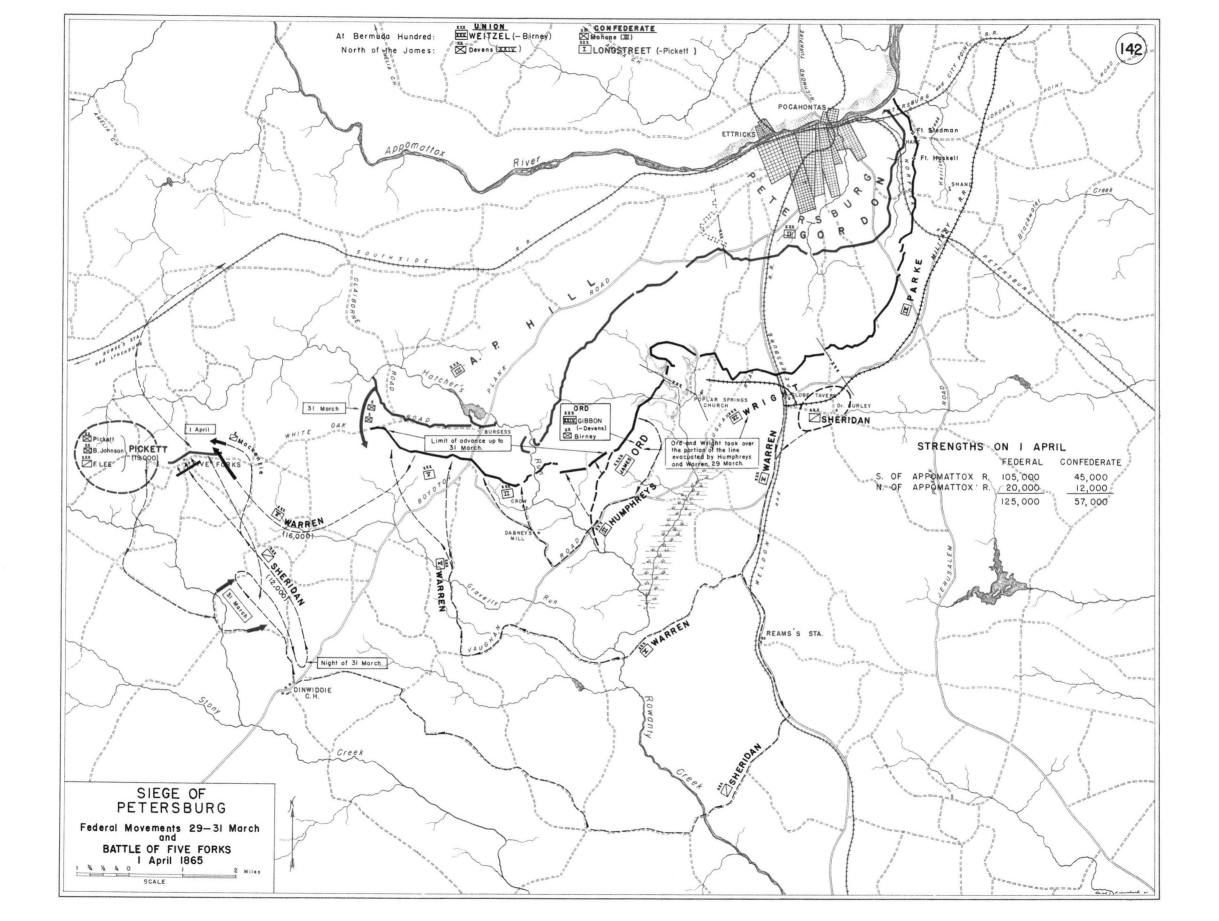

At Bermuda Hundred:
North of the James:

UNION
WEITZEL (-Birney)
Devens (XXIV)

CONFEDERATE
Mahone (III)
LONGSTREET (-Pickett)

POCAHONTAS
ETTRICKS
PETERSBURG
GORDON
Ft. Stedman
Ft. Haskell

Appomattox River

SOUTHSIDE R.R.

A. P. HILL

PARKE

31 March

Hatcher's

BURGESS

ORD
GIBBON (-Devens)
Birney

Limit of advance up to 31 March.

Ord and Wright took over the portion of the line evacuated by Humphreys and Warren, 29 March.

WRIGHT

POPLAR SPRINGS CHURCH

GLOBE TAVERN
Dr. GURLEY
SHERIDAN

WHITE OAK ROAD

Pickett
B. Johnson
F. LEE

PICKETT (19,000)

FIVE FORKS

1 April

Mackenzie

WARREN (16,000)

BOYDTON

WARREN

JAMES

ORD

HUMPHREYS

WARREN

CROW

DABNEY'S MILL

STRENGTHS ON 1 APRIL

	FEDERAL	CONFEDERATE
S. OF APPOMATTOX R.	105,000	45,000
N. OF APPOMATTOX R.	20,000	12,000
	125,000	57,000

SHERIDAN (12,000)

31 March

Gravelly Run

VAUGHAN ROAD

WARREN

REAMS'S STA.

WELDON R.R.

Rowanty Creek

Night of 31 March.

DINWIDDIE C.H.

Stony Creek

SHERIDAN

JERUSALEM

SIEGE OF PETERSBURG

Federal Movements 29–31 March
and
BATTLE OF FIVE FORKS
1 April 1865

SCALE
2 Miles

SIEGE OF PETERSBURG: 4

The defeat at Five Forks cost Lee the use of Southside Railroad (crucial for supplies) and most of his meager reserves. At 4:00 A.M. on 2 April, the Federals renewed their attack against his right flank, having softened it up throughout the previous night. Wright had carefully reconnoitered to his front and noticed several gaps in the abatis. Although Lee was short of troops to man the lines, these defenses were tremendously strong, built mainly by slave labor, and Wright's assault was fantastically costly (although the Confederacy also suffered a grievous loss when A. P. Hill was killed as he inadvertently rode into the Federal lines). He lost 1,100 in the first fifteen minutes (among the deadliest fifteen minutes of the war) before he could make the breakthrough. On his left, Gen. Edward O. C. Ord and Humphreys also overran the fortifications, and Maj. Gen. John G. Parke took the second line of defenses.

Humphreys' left flank division encountered Heth's division below the Southside Railroad and, after being rebuffed twice, pushed it out. And so the main Federal attack swept ahead up to the line or earthworks protecting the western face of Petersburg, but it was now late and the Whitworth and Gregg forts stalled the advance, giving Longstreet time to bring up troops across the James. Grant prepared to attack both Petersburg and Richmond early on the morning of the 3rd.

Lee realized the situation was hopeless, but all he could do was to wait for dark and try to get his troops out west and south, where perhaps he might be able to link up with Johnston in North Carolina. Shortly after 3:00 P.M. on 2 April, the various scattered units of Lee's army were instructed to withdraw and assemble at Amelia Court House and, at 8:00 P.M., the retreat began.

The evacuation was excellently handled, but the Richmond mob soon formed and began wholesale looting. Fires started and spread through the tinder boxes that were the city's tobacco warehouses. Grant realized Lee had gone, and quickly occupied the city. Richmond was formally surrendered by its mayor at 8:15 A.M. on 2 April 1865, and Union troops set to work putting out the fires and putting down the mobs.

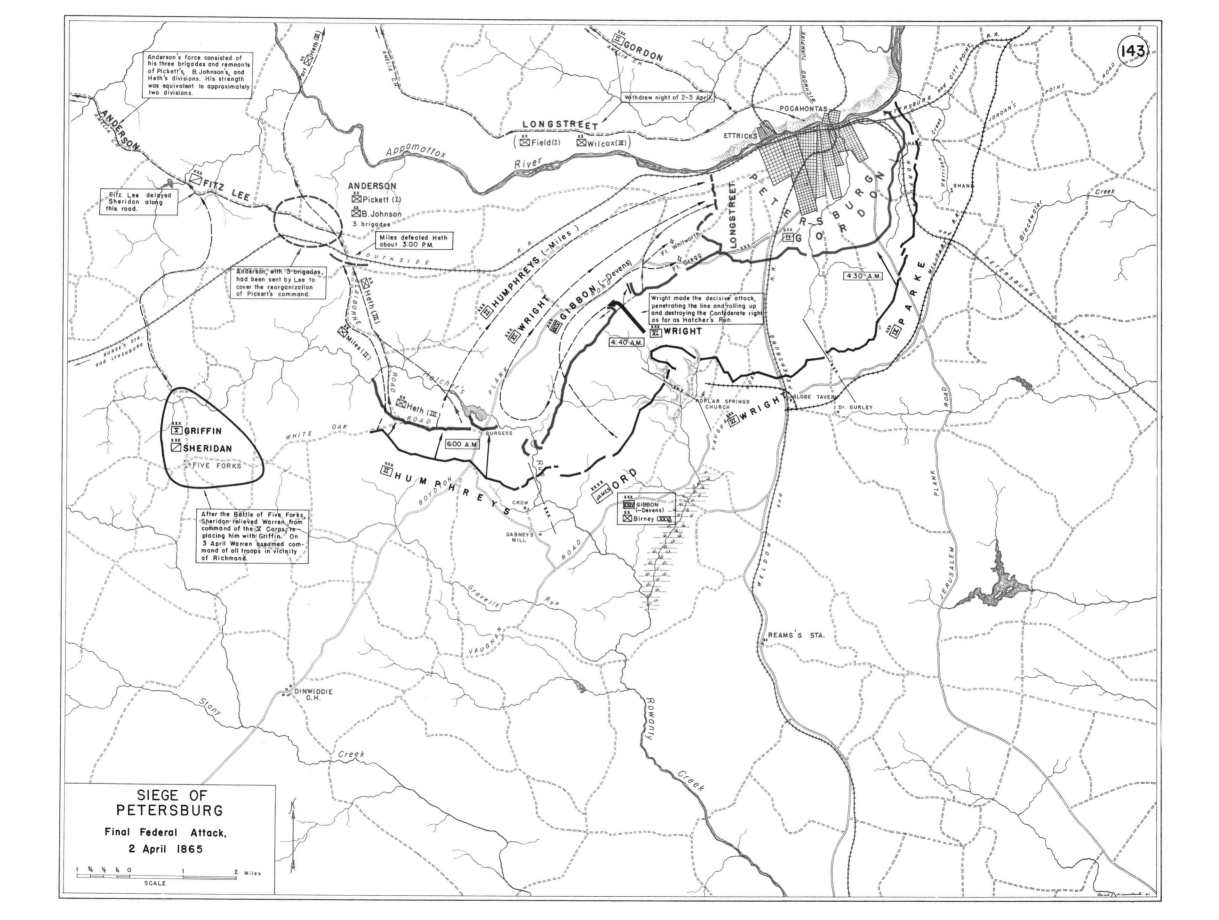

143

Anderson's force consisted of his three brigades and remnants of Pickett's, B. Johnson's, and Heth's divisions. His strength was equivalent to approximately two divisions.

Withdrew night of 2-3 April.

GORDON

LONGSTREET
(Field (I))   (Wilcox (III))

POCAHONTAS

ETTRICKS

PETERSBURG

ANDERSON
Pickett (I)
B. Johnson
3 brigades

FITZ LEE

Fitz Lee delayed Sheridan along this road.

Miles defeated Heth about 3:00 P.M.

Anderson, with 3 brigades, had been sent by Lee to cover the reorganization of Pickett's command.

4:30 A.M.

HUMPHREYS (-Miles)

WRIGHT

GIBBON (-Devens)

Ft. Whitworth

Ft. Gregg

LONGSTREET

Wright made the decisive attack, penetrating the line and rolling up and destroying the Confederate right as far as Hatcher's Run.

4:40 A.M.   WRIGHT

Heth (III)

Miles (I)

GRIFFIN

SHERIDAN

FIVE FORKS

POPLAR SPRINGS CHURCH

WRIGHT

Globe Tavern

Dr. Gurley

After the Battle of Five Forks, Sheridan relieved Warren from command of the V Corps, replacing him with Griffin. On 3 April Warren assumed command of all troops in vicinity of Richmond.

6:00 A.M.

BURGESS

HUMPHREYS

FORD

JAMES

GIBBON (-Devens)

Birney

DABNEY'S MILL

CROW

REAMS'S STA.

DINWIDDIE C.H.

SIEGE OF
PETERSBURG

Final Federal Attack,
2 April 1865

SCALE
1 ¾ ½ ¼ 0   1   2 Miles

GRANT'S PURSUIT OF LEE

Lee's last hope was to withdraw either southwest to Danville or west to Lynchburg, where he could connect with Johnston. That this would accomplish nothing but a futile extension of the war, as Lee must have known, but his sense of duty kept him from capitulating. His army was just a shadow of its former self—approximately 30,000 infantrymen and 20,000 cavalry, artillery, engineers, and other assorted troops—and they were weak from short rations and lack of sleep.

Amelia Court House had been designated as the rallying point, and Lee had ordered rations sent there from Richmond; but when he arrived there was nothing. Under tremendous pressure, the Confederate supply system had completely broken down. Everything depended on supplies coming down the railroad from Danville to Burke's Station, but the line had been cut. Lee's hopes were dashed. Grant, aware of the routes Lee could take, took steps to intercept him, and by the afternoon of 4 April, Union cavalry were nipping at Lee's heels.

At 1:00 P.M. on the 5th, Lee marched south from Amelia Court House, only to find Union cavalry across his path. He could not risk an assault, so instead urged his troops westward toward Farmville where there was a hope of receiving rations from Lynchburg.

It was a killing night march, and in some units discipline broke down, and starving men fell by the wayside. Union cavalry harried the Confederate left flank and rear, repeatedly delaying the retreat.

At Sailor's Creek, the Federal caught up and II Corps overwhelmed Gordon, who was trying to cover the Confederate supply trains. Further south, along the same creek, Wright's VI Corps and the cavalry trapped Ewell's corps and about half of Anderson's.

Early on 7 April, the remaining Confederates reached Farmville, where some were issued rations for the first time since the retreat had begun. II Corps again struck Lee's rear, and Lee formed up to try to protect his supply trains and hold Humphreys at bay; but while he was engaged with Humphreys, Ord's and Sheridan's corps came up on his south flank.

On the morning of the 9th, Lee sent Brig. Gen. John B. Gordon and Fitzhugh Lee to break through Sheridan's cordon; and at first they were successful, but only briefly, for they soon ran into the massed infantry of Ord's two corps. At the same time, II Corps closed against the Confederate rear.

At 4:00 P.M. on 9 April 1865, the formalities of Lee's surrender were completed.

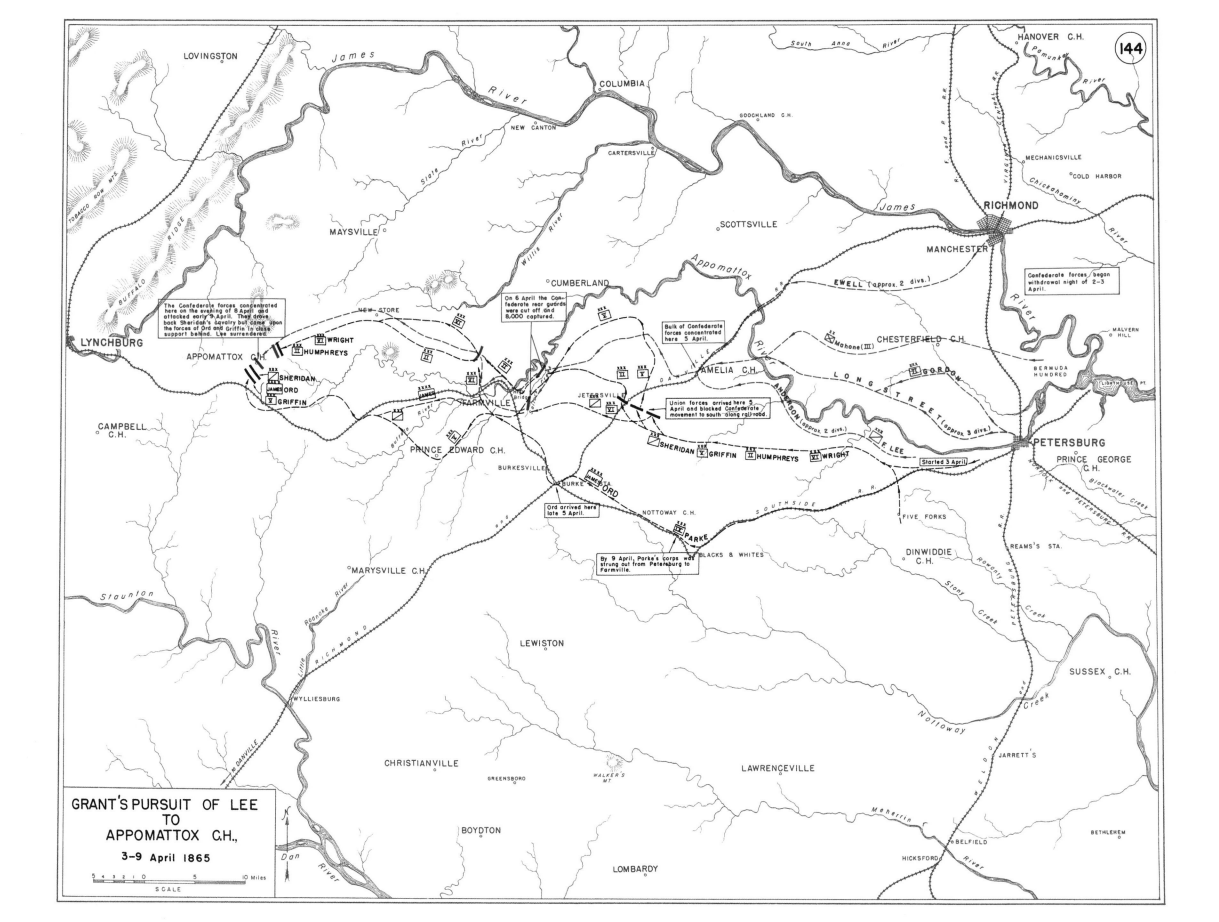

LOVINGSTON

HANOVER C.H.

South Anna River

Pamunkey River

James River

COLUMBIA

NEW CANTON

GOOCHLAND C.H.

CARTERSVILLE

MECHANICSVILLE

COLD HARBOR

Chickahominy River

SCOTTSVILLE

James River

RICHMOND

MAYSVILLE

MANCHESTER

Confederate forces began withdrawal night of 2-3 April.

MALVERN HILL

Appomattox River

CUMBERLAND

EWELL (approx. 2 divs.)

The Confederate forces concentrated here on the evening of 8 April and attacked early 9 April. They drove back Sheridan's cavalry but came upon the forces of Ord and Griffin in close support behind. Lee surrendered.

On 6 April the Confederate rear guards were cut off and 8,000 captured.

CHESTERFIELD C.H.

Mahone (III)

LYNCHBURG

NEW STORE

Bulk of Confederate forces concentrated here 5 April.

BERMUDA HUNDRED

APPOMATTOX C.H.

VI WRIGHT
II HUMPHREYS

SHERIDAN
ORD
GRIFFIN

JAMES

AMELIA C.H.

LONGSTREET (approx. 3 divs.)

GORDON

CAMPBELL C.H.

FARMVILLE

JETERSVILLE

ANDERSON (approx. 2 divs.)

PETERSBURG

PRINCE GEORGE C.H.

Union forces arrived here 5 April and blocked Confederate movement to south along rail road.

PRINCE EDWARD C.H.

SHERIDAN GRIFFIN HUMPHREYS WRIGHT

F. LEE

Started 3 April

BURKESVILLE

BURKE FORD

Ord arrived here late 5 April.

NOTTOWAY C.H.

SOUTHSIDE R.R.

FIVE FORKS

REAMS'S STA.

MARYSVILLE C.H.

PARKE

BLACKS & WHITES

DINWIDDIE C.H.

By 9 April, Parke's corps was strung out from Petersburg to Farmville.

Staunton River

Roanoke River

Little River

LEWISTON

SUSSEX C.H.

WYLLIESBURG

Nottoway River

Meherrin River

JARRETT'S

CHRISTIANVILLE

GREENSBORO

WALKER'S MT.

LAWRENCEVILLE

BOYDTON

HICKSFORD

BETHLEHEM

Dan River

LOMBARDY

BELFIELD

GRANT'S PURSUIT OF LEE
TO
APPOMATTOX C.H.,
3-9 April 1865

5 4 3 2 1 0   5   10 Miles
SCALE

144

ATLANTA CAMPAIGN: 1

Following the Chattanooga campaign of late November 1863, nothing much happened in that theater until May 1864. By then, Johnston had taken over Bragg's command, and Sherman had succeeded Grant as commander of the Military Division of the Mississippi. His forces consisted of the Army of the Tennessee (Sherman's old command, now under McPherson), the Army of the Cumberland (under Thomas), and the Army of the Ohio (Burnside's former command in the Knoxville area, now under Gen. John McAllister Schofield).

Sherman's advance on Atlanta was part of Grant's overall design for winning the war. He had instructed Sherman "to move against Johnston's army, break it up, and get into the interior as far as you can, inflicting all the damage you can against their war resources. . . ." As will be seen, Sherman gradually became so obsessed with the final provision of this mission (which, to him, meant the capture of Atlanta) that Johnston's army was not destroyed, but survived to create further trouble.

On 7 May 1864, Sherman began his advance as shown. McPherson was to move along the route Lafayette–Villanow–Snake Creek Gap to sever Johnston's rail communications, while Thomas demonstrated on Johnston's front and Schofield moved south against the Confederate right flank. McPherson passed through the Gap on the 9th and drove the Confederate brigade at Resaca into its defenses. But then he withdrew to the Gap (sanctioned by his discretionary orders) because he felt he was not strong enough to cut the Confederate supply line. So, through overcaution, an excellent chance to destroy Johnston's army was lost. On 13 May, Johnston withdrew to Resaca and, after some ineffectual skirmishing by Sheridan, he moved just north of Cassville on the 18th, where he hoped to destroy Schofield before he could be supported by Thomas or McPherson. While Hardee blocked the approach from Kingston and Polk held the valley, Hood, from his position on the hill, was to strike Schofield's flank. But Hood, under the impression that McCook had gotten in his rear, faced north, which gave enough time for Sherman's columns to close up, and so the opportunity to crush Schofield passed. Johnston now fell back south of Cassville and then on to Allatoona Pass.

Sherman rested at Kingston for three days, repairing the railroad and filling his wagons with twenty days' supplies. Then, having no intention of assaulting Johnston's strong position at Allatoona, he cut loose from his railroad (as Grant had done at Vicksburg) and marched toward Dallas. Johnston moved to block him at New Hope Church.

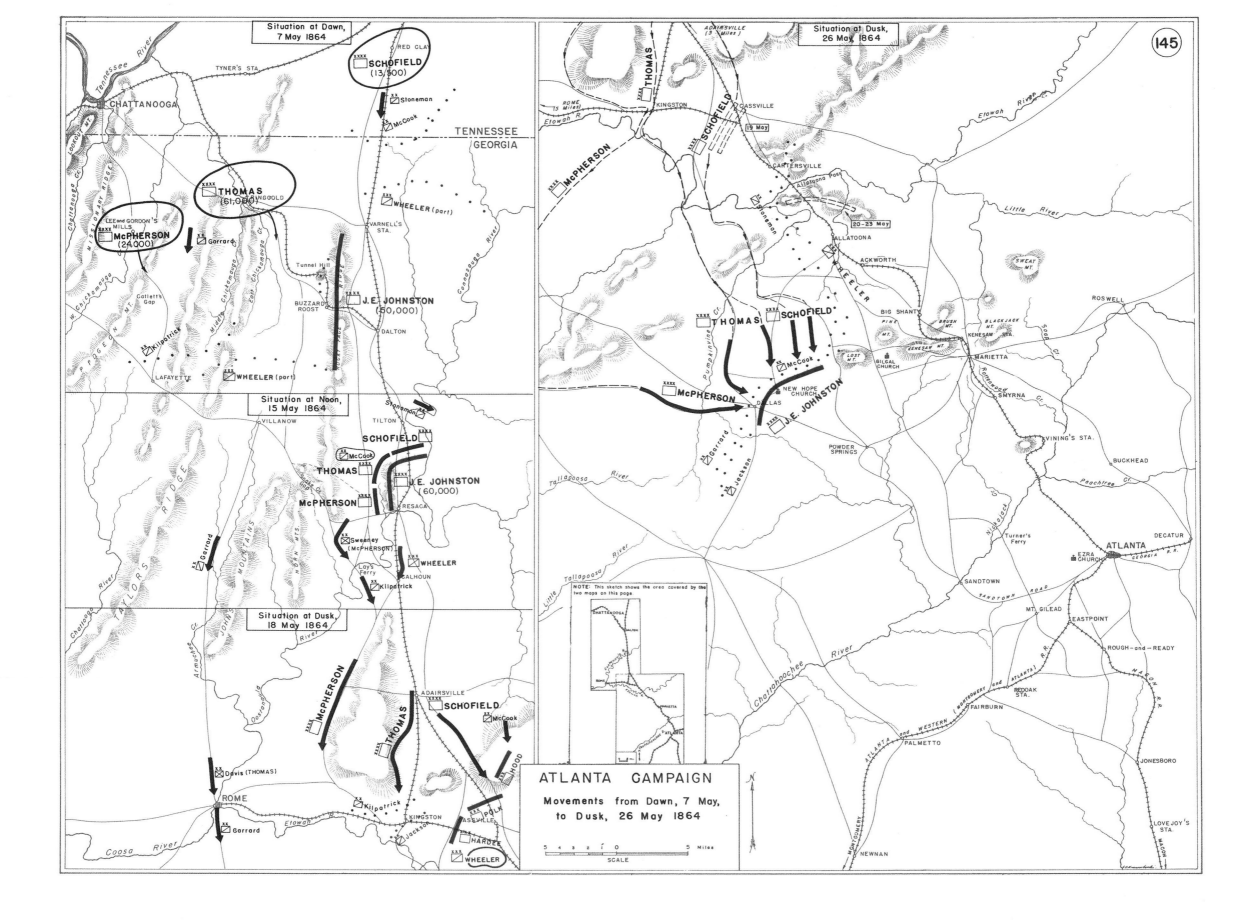

Situation at Dawn, 7 May 1864

XXXX SCHOFIELD (13,500)

RED CLAY

TYNER'S STA.

Tennessee River

CHATTANOOGA

XX Stoneman

XX McCook

TENNESSEE
GEORGIA

LOOKOUT MT.

MISSIONARY RIDGE

Chattanooga Cr.

XXXX THOMAS (61,000)

RINGGOLD

XX WHEELER (part)

Conasauga River

VARNELL'S STA.

LEE and GORDON'S MILLS

XXXX McPHERSON (24,000)

XX Garrard

W. Chickamauga Cr.

PIGEON MT.

Catlett's Gap

Middle Chickamauga Cr.

East Chickamauga Cr.

Tunnel Hill

BUZZARD ROOST

XXXX J. E. JOHNSTON (50,000)

DALTON

XX Kilpatrick

LAFAYETTE

XX WHEELER (part)

Situation at Noon, 15 May 1864

Stoneman XX

VILLANOW

TILTON

XXXX SCHOFIELD

XX McCook

XXXX THOMAS

XXXX J. E. JOHNSTON (60,000)

Snake Cr. Gap

XXXX McPHERSON

RESACA

XX Sweeny (McPHERSON)

XX Garrard

Lay's Ferry

CALHOUN

XX WHEELER

XX Kilpatrick

TAYLORS RIDGE

JOHNS MOUNTAINS

JOHN MTS.

Chattooga River

Armuchee Cr.

Oostanaula River

Situation at Dusk, 18 May 1864

ADAIRSVILLE

XXXX SCHOFIELD

XX McCook

XXXX McPHERSON

XXXX THOMAS

XX HOOD

XX Davis (THOMAS)

ROME

XX Garrard

XX Kilpatrick

KINGSTON

Jackson

CASSVILLE

POLK

HARDEE

XXX WHEELER

Etowah R.

Coosa River

Situation at Dusk, 26 May 1864

ADAIRSVILLE (3 Miles)

XXXX THOMAS

ROME (15 Miles)

Etowah R.

KINGSTON

CASSVILLE

XXXX SCHOFIELD

19 May

Little River

XXXX McPHERSON

CARTERSVILLE

Allatoona Pass

Stoneman

20-23 May

ALLATOONA

WHEELER

ACKWORTH

SWEAT MT.

XXXX THOMAS

XXXX SCHOFIELD

BIG SHANTY

PINE MT.

BRUSH MT.

BLACKJACK MT.

ROSWELL

Pumpkinvine Cr.

XX McCook

LOST MT.

KENESAW MT.

KENESAW MT.

GILGAL CHURCH

MARIETTA

XXXX McPHERSON

NEW HOPE CHURCH

DALLAS

XXXX J. E. JOHNSTON

POWDER SPRINGS

SMYRNA

Rottenwood Cr.

VINING'S STA.

BUCKHEAD

XX Garrard

XX Jackson

Tallapoosa River

Turner's Ferry

Peachtree Cr.

Nickajack Cr.

DECATUR

ATLANTA

EZRA CHURCH

GEORGIA R.R.

Little Tallapoosa River

NOTE: This sketch shows the area covered by the two maps on this page.

CHATTANOOGA

DALTON

ROME

ATLANTA

E. SANDTOWN

SANDTOWN ROAD

MT. GILEAD

EASTPOINT

Chattahoochee River

ROUGH-and-READY

REDOAK STA.

FAIRBURN

MONTGOMERY and ATLANTA R.R.

PALMETTO

ATLANTA and WESTERN R.R.

MACON R.R.

JONESBORO

NEWNAN

LOVEJOY'S STA.

ATLANTA CAMPAIGN

Movements from Dawn, 7 May, to Dusk, 26 May 1864

5 4 3 2 1 0   5 Miles
SCALE

N

ATLANTA CAMPAIGN: 2

Again Sherman refused battle on Johnston's terms. He bypassed New Hope Church and leapfrogged his troops toward the railroad, forcing Johnston to abandon his defenses and seek to confront Sherman in the new position. The Federals were now being reinforced, building up their supplies and exerting pressure on Johnston's line. Both sides had been using field fortifications extensively since their initial contact; every time a new position was taken, fortifications were in place within hours, which was a characteristic of this late stage of the war and in sharp contrast to, say, the battle of Shiloh two years earlier. Under constant pressure, Johnston began to contract his line, dropping his right wing back to Kennesaw Mountain, and his left toward Marietta. It was during this period that Polk was killed by carefully aimed artillery fire, and Loring assumed temporary command of his corps. By 25 June, the Union line had been extended far to the south, and Schofield's supply connection to the railroad had become impracticable (supply dumps could not be moved further south because it would expose them to Johnston's artillery on the mountain).

Fearing that Johnston might strike a blow at the main supply depot at Big Shanty, Sherman decided to preempt the threat and directly attack Kennesaw Mountain. But the assault, which went in at 9:00 A.M. on 27 June, was poorly planned. There was no attempt at deception or softening up, and Thomas and McPherson were sent in headlong frontal assaults against the strongest Confederate positions. The result, inevitably, was a slaughter that cost the attackers 3,000 casualties.

Sherman now reverted to a campaign of maneuver: Gen. George Stoneman Jr. and Schofield edged along the Sandtown Road, and McPherson was withdrawn from the line and also directed down the same road. Johnston, undoubtedly discouraged by the regularity with which his left flank was being turned, withdrew on 4 July and took up the strongly fortified position shown on the far right map below. Surprised to find Johnston defending the west bank of the Chattahoochee River, Sherman sent Stoneman and McPherson to operate against the Confederate southern flank while Schofield stealthily moved upstream to find a likely crossing site. On 9 July, Schofield crossed the Chattahoochee at the mouth of Soap Creek, taking the small cavalry security force completely by surprise. Johnston withdrew his army to the east bank and prepared to oppose Sherman's latest turning movement.

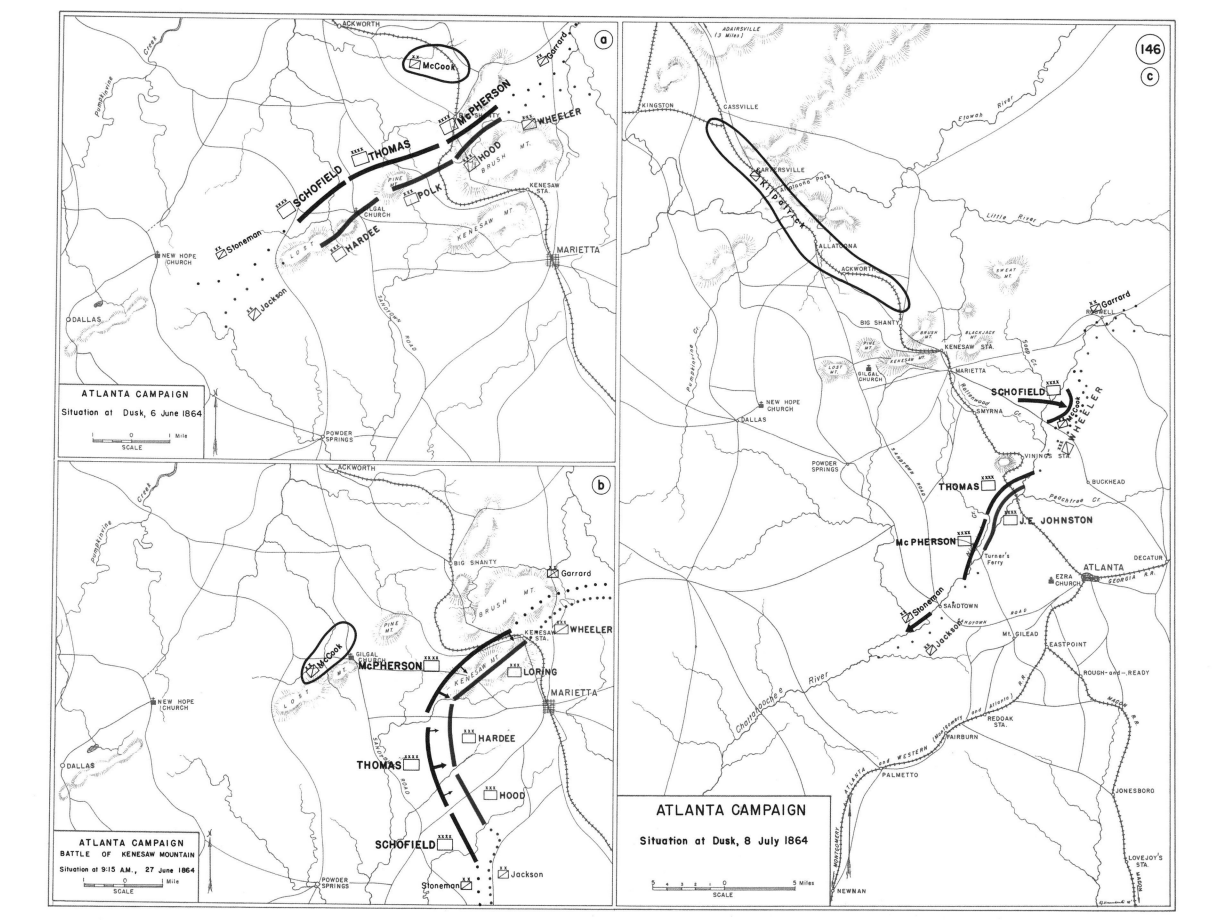

a

McCook

Garrard

McPHERSON

THOMAS

WHEELER

SCHOFIELD

PINE MT.

Hood

BRUSH MT.

POLK

GILGAL CHURCH

KENESAW MT.

KENESAW STA.

Stoneman

LOST MT.

HARDEE

MARIETTA

NEW HOPE CHURCH

Jackson

DALLAS

SANDTOWN ROAD

ATLANTA CAMPAIGN

Situation at Dusk, 6 June 1864

1   0   1 Mile
SCALE

POWDER SPRINGS

ACKWORTH

Pumpkinvine Creek

---

b

ACKWORTH

Pumpkinvine Creek

BIG SHANTY

Garrard

BRUSH MT.

PINE MT.

WHEELER

McCook

GILGAL CHURCH

KENESAW STA.

McPHERSON

LOST MT.

KENESAW MT.

LORING

MARIETTA

NEW HOPE CHURCH

HARDEE

SANDTOWN ROAD

THOMAS

HOOD

DALLAS

SCHOFIELD

Jackson

Stoneman

POWDER SPRINGS

ATLANTA CAMPAIGN

BATTLE OF KENESAW MOUNTAIN

Situation at 9:15 A.M., 27 June 1864

1   0   1 Mile
SCALE

---

c

ADAIRSVILLE
[3 Miles]

KINGSTON

CASSVILLE

Etowah River

Little River

Allatoona Pass

CARTERSVILLE

Kilpatrick

SWEAT MT.

ALLATOONA

ACKWORTH

BIG SHANTY

Garrard

ROSWELL

BRUSH MT.

BLACKJACK MT.

KENESAW STA.

Soap Cr.

PINE MT.

LOST MT.

KENESAW MT.

MARIETTA

GILGAL CHURCH

SCHOFIELD

McCook

WHEELER

Rottenwood Cr.

VINING'S STA.

SMYRNA

Pumpkinvine Cr.

NEW HOPE CHURCH

THOMAS

BUCKHEAD

Peachtree Cr.

DALLAS

J.E. JOHNSTON

SANDTOWN ROAD

McPHERSON

Turner's Ferry

DECATUR

ATLANTA

EZRA CHURCH

GEORGIA R.R.

POWDER SPRINGS

Stoneman

SANDTOWN

Jackson

Chattahoochee River

MT. GILEAD

SANDTOWN ROAD

EASTPOINT

ROUGH-and-READY

ATLANTA and WESTERN (Montgomery and Atlanta) R.R.

REDOAK STA.

FAIRBURN

MACON R.R.

PALMETTO

Montgomery R.R.

JONESBORO

NEWNAN

LOVEJOY'S STA.

ATLANTA CAMPAIGN

Situation at Dusk, 8 July 1864

5 4 3 2 1 0   5 Miles
SCALE

ATLANTA CAMPAIGN: 3

From 10 to 17 July, Sherman busied himself moving supplies forward in preparation for crossing the Chattahoochee in force. Meanwhile, Jefferson Davis pressured Bragg to replace Johnston with a more aggressive general and, on 17 July, Hood took over, a change Sherman considered to be in the Union's favor, because although Hood was indeed aggressive, he was also considered rash and reckless.

By 18 July, Sherman was across the Chattahoochee and began to wheel clockwise on Thomas as a pivot; by the 20th, they had reached the positions shown on the upper left-hand map. That morning, Hood launched an unsuccessful offensive, and then withdrew into the defenses of Atlanta. Sherman following on the 21st, was under the impression that the city had been evacuated, but Hardee's attack on McPherson's left flank persuaded him otherwise. In this action, McPherson, one of the outstanding Union commanders, was killed.

On 27 July, Howard (McPherson's replacement) moved toward Ezra Church in furtherance of Sherman's plan to cut the railroads below Atlanta, which were Hood's last link with the Confederacy. Hood sent Gen. S. D. Lee to attack him, but again the Confederates were foiled by hastily erected Union field fortifications. Finally, on 26 August, Sherman set all his forces in motion and reached the Macon Railroad south of Atlanta on the 31st.

Hardee was sent to try and block the advance, but when his attack was repulsed, Hood evacuated Atlanta and joined Hardee at Lovejoy's Station. Sherman telegraphed Lincoln: "Atlanta is ours and fairly won."

The city might have been won, but Hood was still at large and preparing to attack Union supply lines and force them out of Atlanta. On his arrival in Atlanta on 2 September, Sherman seemed to sink into a victor's lethargy. On 21 September, Hood moved to Palmetto, where he was visited by Jefferson Davis. They agreed that Hood should move toward Chattanooga and operate against Sherman's lines of communication. It was all a bit vague. Sherman, in the meantime, had reinforced key points, but he in a constant flux of concern about that great cavalry scourge, Nathan Bedford Forrest, and whether Hood was preparing to come north. The Confederate strategy, it seemed, was working. Sherman was beginning to disperse his strength along his lines of communication. But the wily Union general had no intention of displacing his entire army to the rear. On 29 September, Hood began his advance over the Chattahoochee and, by 1 October, had 40,000 men across. As Hood moved north, Sherman trailed him looking for an opportunity to attack, but never dispersed his forces as to leave them exposed to the attack Hood's strategy envisioned. But weave and dodge as Hood might, a major battle was looming.

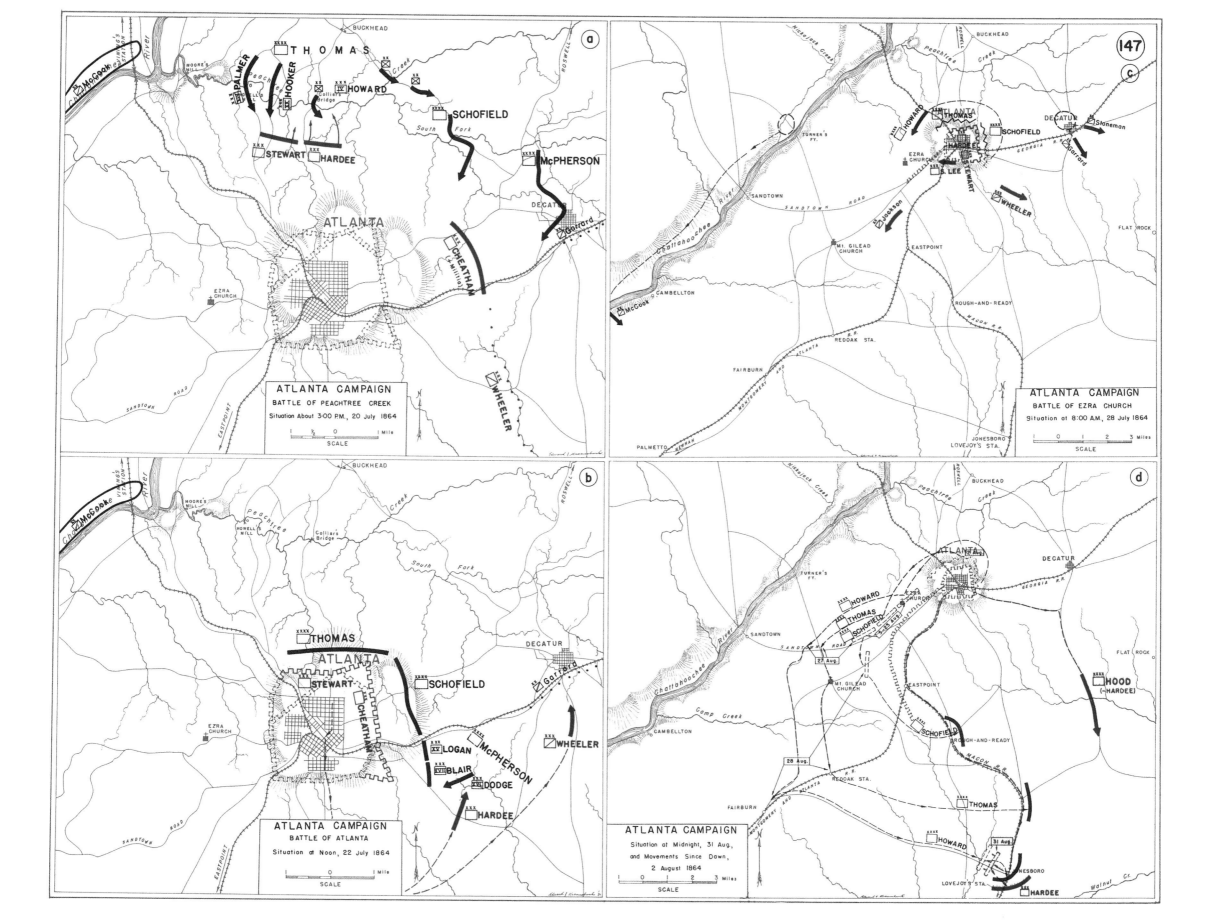

a

THOMAS

PALMER   HOOKER   HOWARD

SCHOFIELD

STEWART   HARDEE

South Fork

McPHERSON

DECATUR

Garrard

ATLANTA

EZRA CHURCH

CHEATHAM (+ Militia)

WHEELER

ATLANTA CAMPAIGN
BATTLE OF PEACHTREE CREEK
Situation About 3:00 P.M., 20 July 1864

SCALE

b

BUCKHEAD

McCook

Peachtree Creek

MOORE'S MILL

HOWELL MILL

Collier's Bridge

South Fork

THOMAS

ATLANTA

STEWART

SCHOFIELD

DECATUR

Garrard

CHEATHAM

LOGAN   McPHERSON

BLAIR

DODGE

HARDEE

WHEELER

EZRA CHURCH

ATLANTA CAMPAIGN
BATTLE OF ATLANTA
Situation at Noon, 22 July 1864

SCALE

147

c

Nickajack Creek

ROSWELL

BUCKHEAD

Peachtree Creek

TURNER'S FY.

HOWARD

ATLANTA
THOMAS

SCHOFIELD

DECATUR

Stoneman

Garrard

GEORGIA R.R.

HARDEE

EZRA CHURCH

STEWART

S. LEE

WHEELER

Jackson

Chattahoochee River

SANDTOWN

SANDTOWN ROAD

MT. GILEAD CHURCH

EASTPOINT

ROUGH-AND-READY

MACON R.R.

McCook

CAMBELLTON

FLAT ROCK

FAIRBURN

ATLANTA AND MONTGOMERY R.R.

REDOAK STA.

JONESBORO
LOVEJOY'S STA.

PALMETTO

ATLANTA CAMPAIGN
BATTLE OF EZRA CHURCH
Situation at 8:00 A.M., 28 July 1864

SCALE

d

Nickajack Creek

ROSWELL

BUCKHEAD

Peachtree Creek

TURNER'S FY.

2 Aug.

ATLANTA

DECATUR

GEORGIA R.R.

HOWARD

THOMAS

SCHOFIELD

EZRA CHURCH

HOOD (-HARDEE)

Chattahoochee River

SANDTOWN

SANDTOWN ROAD

27 Aug.

MT. GILEAD CHURCH

Camp Creek

CAMBELLTON

EASTPOINT

SCHOFIELD

ROUGH-AND-READY

MACON R.R.

28 Aug.

REDOAK STA.

THOMAS

FAIRBURN

ATLANTA AND MONTGOMERY R.R.

HOWARD

31 Aug.

JONESBORO

LOVEJOY'S STA.

HARDEE

Walnut Cr.

FLAT ROCK

ATLANTA CAMPAIGN
Situation at Midnight, 31 Aug,
and Movements Since Dawn,
2 August 1864

SCALE

FRANKLIN AND NASHVILLE CAMPAIGN: 1

At Resaca, Sherman found that Hood had withdrawn to the west, and he pushed on in pursuit. On 16 October, he learned that the Confederates had fallen back toward Gaylesville, and Sherman had Thomas send him two divisions to meet him at Gaylesville.

While resting at Cross Roads, en route to Gaylesville, Hood had concocted the strategy that would eventually lead to the battle of Nashville. Aware that time was on the side of the Union and that, given enough of it, Thomas would eventually reunite his whole force with Sherman's and overwhelm him, Hood reasoned that if he moved swiftly to Tennessee he might be able to defeat Thomas before that commander could assemble his scattered army. Once Thomas was eliminated, Hood proposed to move into central Kentucky, where he was convinced he could get a good supply of recruits before Sherman decided to follow him or march on Savannah (Sherman's preferred course of action). If Sherman followed him, they would fight in Kentucky; if not, he would go through the Cumberland Gap and join Lee. Beauregard blessed the plan, but insisted that Wheeler stay behind and watch Sherman. Forrest would accompany Hood as his cavalry screen.

Sherman learned of Hood's appearance near Decatur on 26 October and at once reinforced Thomas with Stanley's corps. Seeing how far west Hood had gone, Sherman decided to march on Savannah (though he did not receive permission from Grant until 2

November), again reinforcing Thomas, this time with Schofield's XXIII Corps, which he was sure was sufficient to parry Hood's thrust.

At Tuscumbia, Hood learned with dismay that his march would have to be delayed because Forrest had not yet arrived. He stayed at Tuscumbia for three weeks, slowly replenishing his supplies. Thomas, as slowly, gathered his scattered troops together. On the 17th, Forrest arrived, and Hood's advance resumed the next day. By the 24th, Schofield's entire force was at Columbia on the south bank of the Duck River and, by the 26th, Hood was also concentrated there. On the 27th, convinced that Hood would turn his position, Schofield pulled back to the north bank. Hood, leaving Lee's corps at Columbia, crossed Gen. Alexander P. Stewart and Cheatham further west and began moving north. Along with Forrest, who was also moving north, but on a wider arc, Hood hoped to cut off Schofield who was now moving north on the Columbia Pike to take up position at Spring Hill. There Schofield was attacked, ineffectually, by Cheatham, but a combination of Confederate tactical ineptitude and excellent Union artillery work secured the Union position. While the Confederates dithered and bumbled, Schofield took his opportunity to get out of his predicament. He needed to get back to Franklin and hurried his troops northward all night. By 6:00 A.M., all Union troops (except a rear guard) were north of Spring Hill. Hood, furious with Cheatham for letting the cat out of the bag, took up the pursuit.

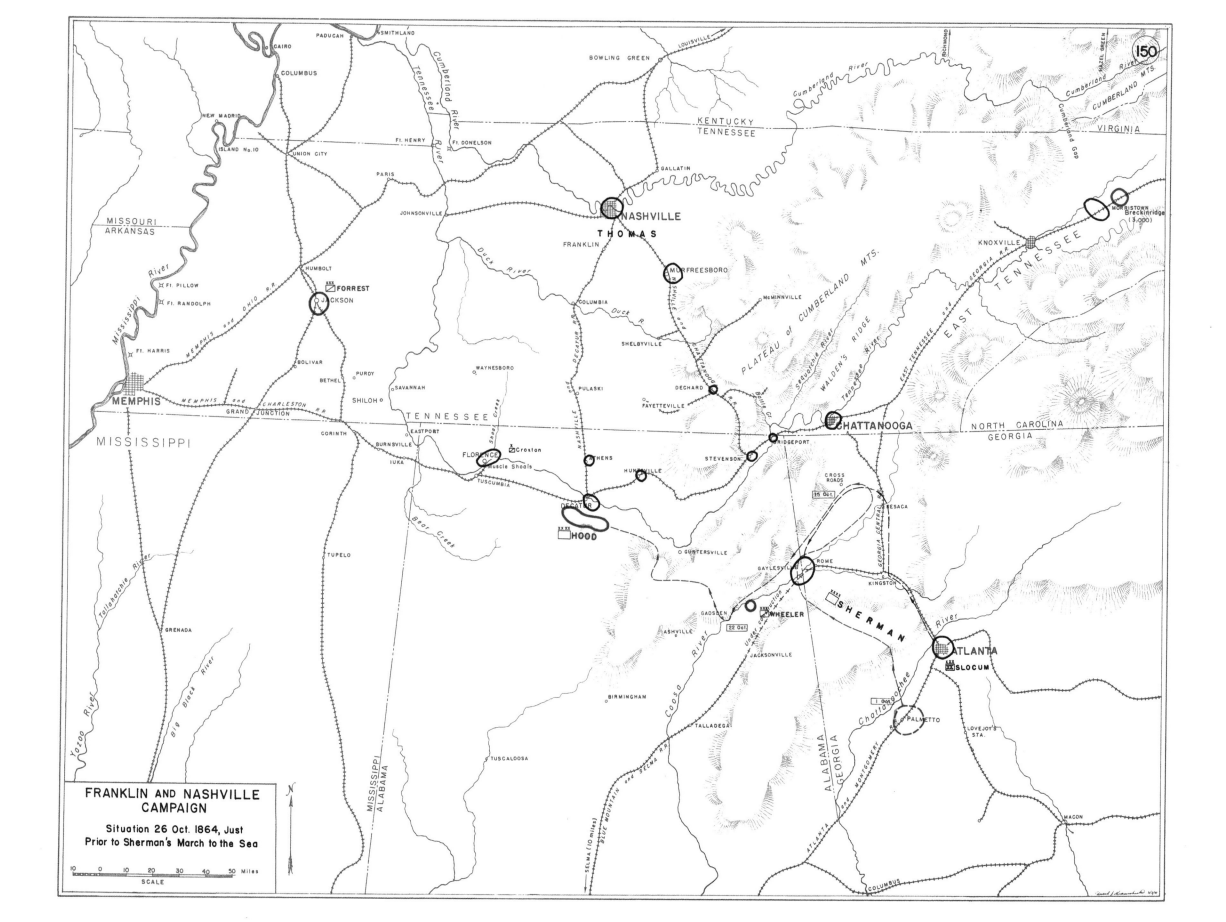

FRANKLIN AND NASHVILLE
CAMPAIGN

Situation 26 Oct. 1864, Just
Prior to Sherman's March to the Sea

FRANKLIN AND NASHVILLE CAMPAIGN: 2

Schofield's advance guard, exhausted from days of fighting and marching, reached Franklin about 6:00 A.M. on 30 November. They were immediately put to work throwing up earthworks south of the town, and by noon their line described a great cordon, with both flanks resting on the Harpeth River. Two brigades of Wagner's division were placed out front as a covering force. To the northeast of the city, Wood's division was sent on across the river to guard against any flanking approach.

Hood urged his men forward along the Columbia Pike toward Franklin. By 2:00 P.M., Stewart had reached Wagner's positions and had deployed for the attack and, by 3:00 P.M., he was determined to take the position by frontal attack. Nettled by their constant retreats since Atlanta and humiliated by their failure at Spring Hill, Hood's commanders were fired up to storm the Union fortifications.

Wagner, in his exposed position, was ordered back, but he waited too long and was engulfed by Maj. Gen. John C. Brown and Cheatham's assault force. His troops turned and fled and became intermingled with the enemy. The Union main line, reluctant to fire on their own, hesitated, and a gap opened up in Schofield's line that Cleburne, Brown, and French converged on. But just as they were about to roll out through the breach there was a Union counterattack (led by the courageous Col. Emerson Opdycke) that managed to seal it after thirty minutes of ferocious combat. Again and again, Hood's commanders hurled their troops at the Union line but they could not beak it. By 9:00 P.M. the fighting had died down, and Hood once again had to accept defeat. His casualties had been horrific: 6,252, compared with the Union's 2,326.

While the fighting raged around Franklin, Forrest had crossed the Harpeth and had attempted to turn Schofield's left flank. But he was opposed by the resolute Union cavalry under Wilson and so roughly handled that he was forced back across the river.

That night, Schofield began to move his troops north across the bridges en route to Nashville, which he reached, exhausted, on 1 December. Hood, trying to digest the magnitude of his defeat, remained in place.

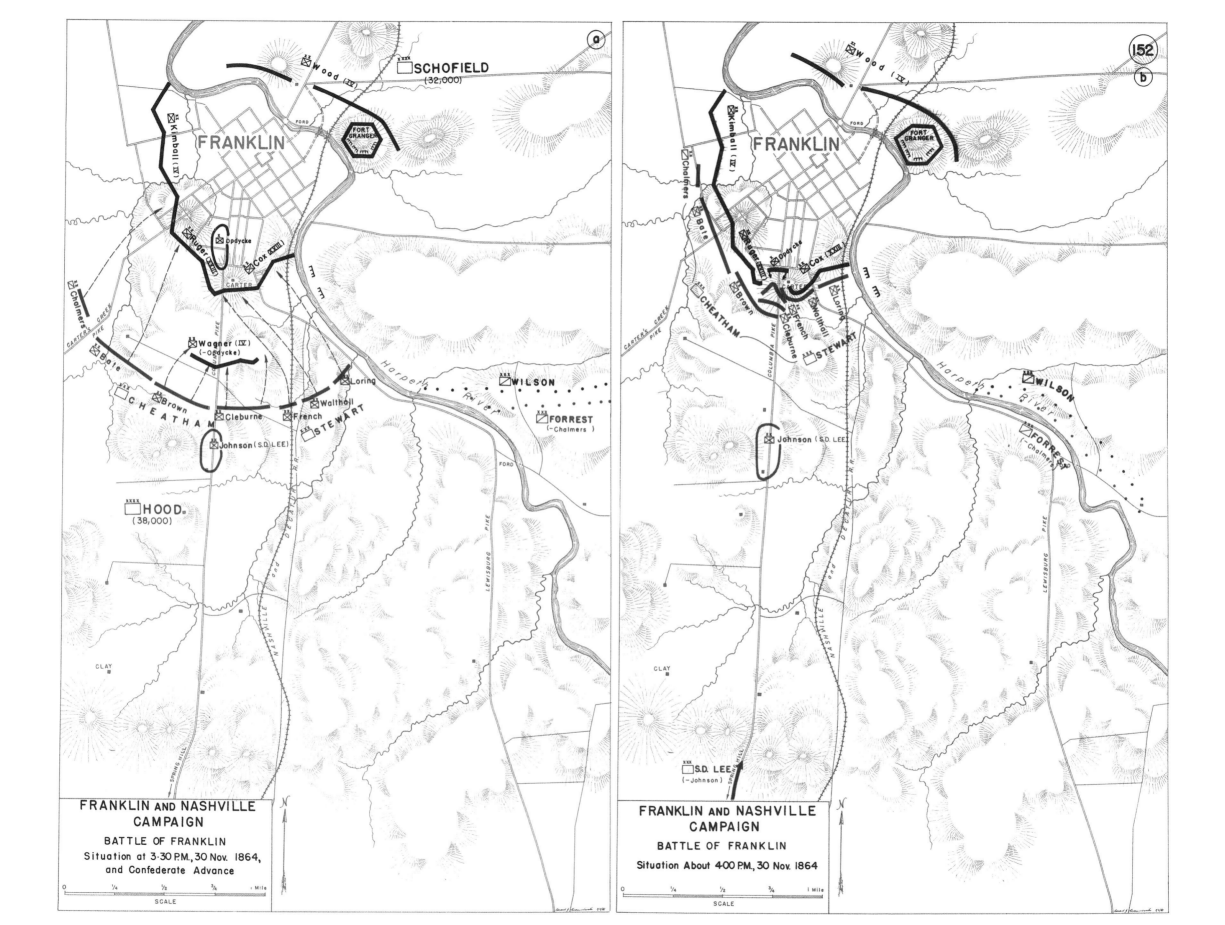

FRANKLIN AND NASHVILLE
CAMPAIGN

BATTLE OF FRANKLIN

Situation at 3·30 P.M., 30 Nov. 1864,
and Confederate Advance

0   ¼   ½   ¾   1 Mile
SCALE

FRANKLIN AND NASHVILLE
CAMPAIGN

BATTLE OF FRANKLIN

Situation About 4·00 P.M., 30 Nov. 1864

0   ¼   ½   ¾   1 Mile
SCALE

FRANKLIN AND NASHVILLE CAMPAIGN: 3

Hood was pugnacious, and seems not too have been too discouraged by the disaster at Franklin. On he moved to Nashville, where he found Thomas's army behind formidable entrenchments. Hood entrenched opposite.

Thomas had more men than Hood, so a direct assault stood little chance of success. Hood hoped Thomas might attack, and that once contained could be counterattacked with devastating impact. Hood's expectations were a little too optimistic, for his highly competent foe was about to plan and execute one of the classic battles of the war, and one that would leave the Confederate broken and driven from the field.

Thomas made his plans, but the authorities in Washington intervened. They were disconcerted by Hood's advance through Tennessee and Grant's current stalemate at Petersburg, and as a result, pressure was put on Thomas to attack; Grant himself sent orders to get moving. But the ever stoical Thomas would not be hurried. He wanted Wilson's cavalry to be properly mounted. The delay almost got him sacked (Logan was actually directed to Nashville to take over) but on 15 December 1864, Thomas struck Hood a shattering blow.

Early on the 15th, Steedman, making the secondary attack, advanced on Cheatham and kept the Confederate right occupied for the rest of the day. Meanwhile, Thomas's main attack—Smith, Wood, and Brig. Gen. John P. Hatch—had advanced at dawn, wheeling left to a line parallel with the Hillsboro Pike. Maj. Gen. James L. Donaldson, with a force consisting largely of armed quartermaster employees, took over the trenches on the Union right. By noon, Smith and Hatch had seized Hood's detached unit on a hill west of the Hillsboro Pike and had reached the pike itself; Wood was preparing to assault the Confederate outpost on Montgomery Hill in the center of Hood's line.

Hood, seeing the threat to his left, ordered Cheatham to send reinforcements to Stewart. Montgomery Hill was taken in a gallant and impetuous charge by Beatty's division. Now, at 1:00 P.M. Thomas ordered Wood to attack the angle in Stewart's line, Schofield was to come up to support Smith on his right, and Wilson was to reinforce Hatch and get astride the Granny White Turnpike.

By 1:30 P.M. Stewart's position along Hillsboro Pike became untenable, and shortly afterward his whole corps began to break up and stream back to the rear toward Granny White Turnpike. But it was not a complete rout, and by nightfall Hood had managed to pull together enough units to continue the battle the next day.

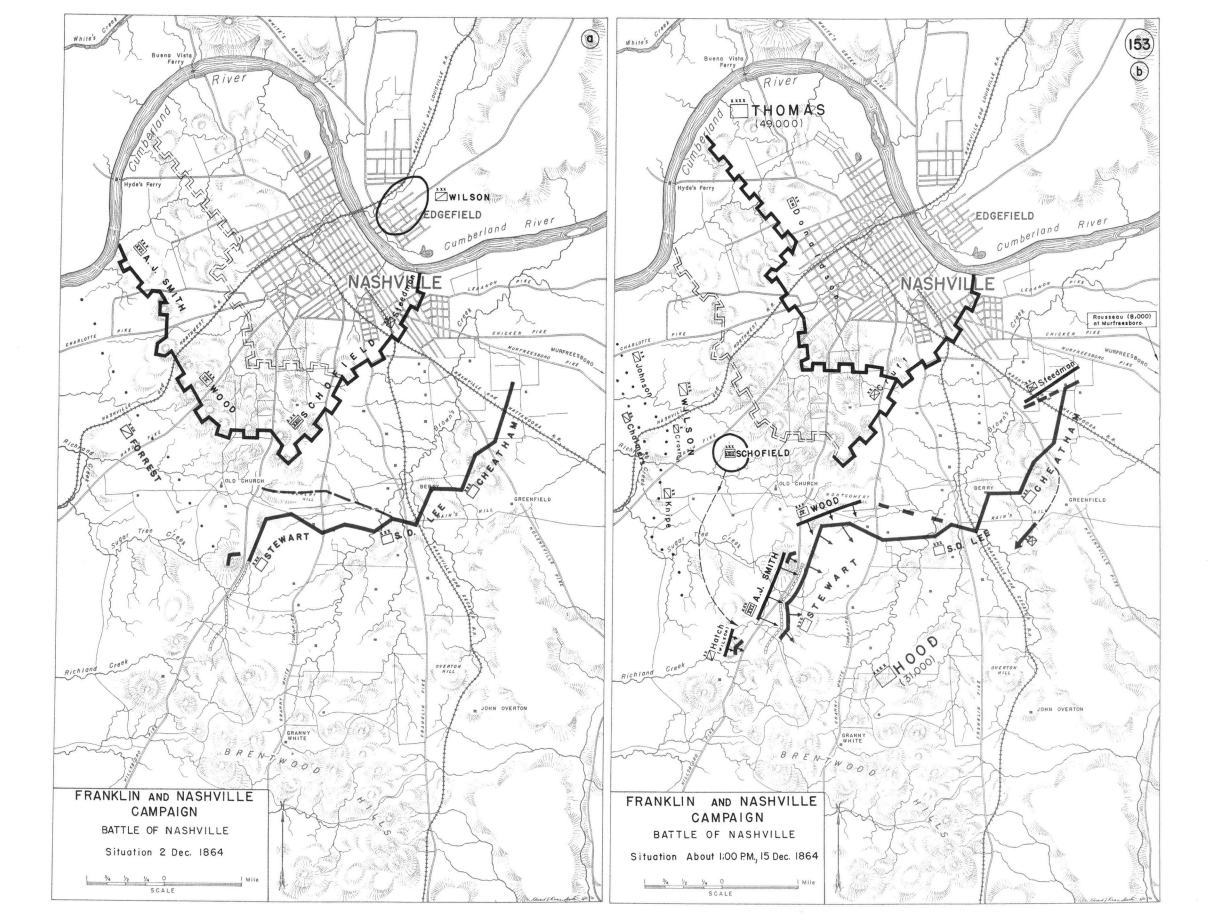

ⓐ

FRANKLIN AND NASHVILLE
CAMPAIGN

BATTLE OF NASHVILLE

Situation 2 Dec. 1864

¾ ½ ¼ 0 1 Mile
SCALE

ⓑ

THOMAS
(49,000)

Rousseau (8,000)
at Murfreesboro.

SCHOFIELD

HOOD
(31,000)

FRANKLIN AND NASHVILLE
CAMPAIGN

BATTLE OF NASHVILLE

Situation About 1:00 P.M., 15 Dec. 1864

¾ ½ ¼ 0 1 Mile
SCALE

FRANKLIN AND NASHVILLE CAMPAIGN: 4

After dark, Hood took up the entrenched positions shown on the left-hand side map below. He moved Cheatham's relatively fresh corps to the extreme left and slid Stewart's badly battered men over to the center. Though beaten that day, he was not about to give up.

That night, Thomas's troops remained in position where the battle had ended, and most of the next morning they were engaged in moving up to Hood's new line. Again, Thomas planned to concentrate on Hood's left. Schofield was to drive back Cheatham, while Wilson worked his way to the rear to block the Franklin Pike, Hood's only escape route.

Shortly after noon, Wood and Maj. Gen. James B. Steedman attacked S. D. Lee on Hood's right, but could not get any advantage. On the left, meanwhile, Wilson's dismounted troopers were putting pressure on Chalmers, way over on the Confederate left. Cheatham's corps broke and streamed back to the rear. Wood now renewed his attack in the center, and this time was successful. Stewart could not resist, and he, too, began to fall back. By now it was dark, and with the darkness came heavy rain. Under the cover of night and rainfall, Hood managed to collect his forces and retreat back to Franklin. The battle of Nashville was over. Definitive casualty figures are not known for Hood's army, but prisoners alone totaled 4,462. Thomas's casualties were 3,061.

The next day (17 December), Wilson continued the pursuit; but by now Hood had pulled himself together and, aided by Forrest, held off the Federals for the next week, as the remnants of his army trailed back to the Tennessee River, which they crossed on the 25–27th and moved to Tupelo, Mississippi. Here, Hood requested, and was granted, to be relieved of his command. The Army of the Tennessee was no longer an effective fighting force.

The right-hand map shows the route taken by Sherman in his March to the Sea. He had left Atlanta on 15 November 1864 with 62,000 men and rations for twenty days. Except for skirmishers with small Confederate cavalry forces, he was unopposed in his advance to Savannah. En route, he foraged freely, as well as destroyed the railroads and any industry he deemed to be of value to the South's war effort. Hardee, at Savannah, chose not to defend the city and withdrew to Charleston on 21 December, just as Sherman was about to assault the city. Hardee then went north, while Sherman set out for Columbia.

Johnston, meanwhile, had been recalled to duty and attempted to stop Sherman first at Averysboro and Bentonville on 19 March 1865. On 13 April 1865, Johnston, having learned of Lee's surrender, sought an armistice, and the next day surrendered, and except for some minor actions in Alabama and west of the Mississippi, the war was over.

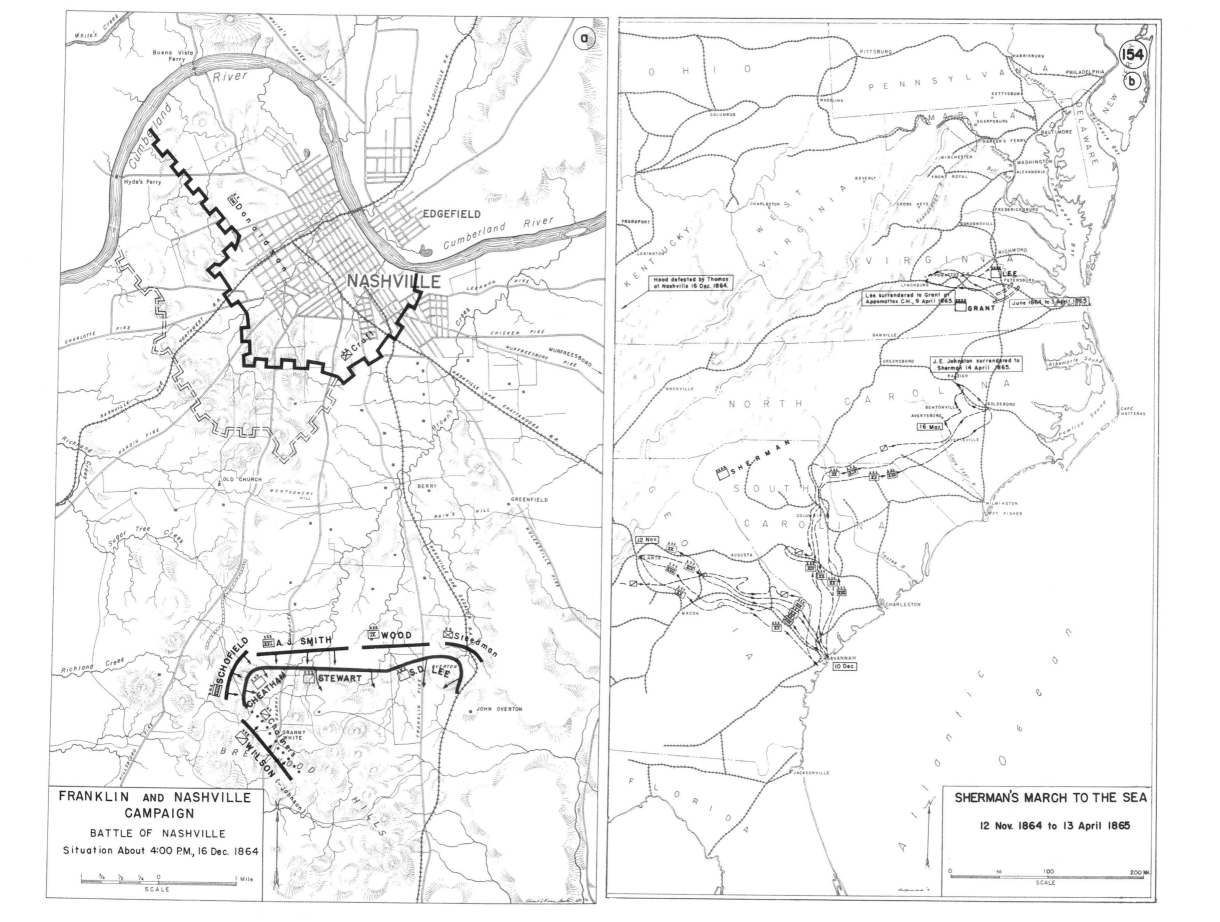

FRANKLIN AND NASHVILLE CAMPAIGN

BATTLE OF NASHVILLE

Situation About 4:00 P.M., 16 Dec. 1864

SCALE
¾ ½ ¼ 0   1 Mile

NASHVILLE

EDGEFIELD

Cumberland River

Buena Vista Ferry

White's Creek

Hyde's Ferry

Donaldson

Croft

Charlotte Pike

Old Church

Montgomery Hill

Berry

Greenfield

Chicken Pike

Murfreesboro Pike

Lebanon Pike

Nashville and Chattanooga R.R.

Nashville and Decatur R.R.

Rain's Hill

Brown's Creek

John Overton

Granny White

Sugar Tree Creek

Richland Creek

Hardin Pike

Hillsboro Pike

Franklin Pike

BRENTWOOD HILLS

Johnson

WILSON

HOOD

CHEATHAM

STEWART

S. D. LEE

Overton

A. J. SMITH

SCHOFIELD

WOOD

Steedman

SHERMAN'S MARCH TO THE SEA

12 Nov. 1864 to 13 April 1865

SCALE
0   10   100   200 Mi.

Hood defeated by Thomas at Nashville 16 Dec. 1864.

Lee surrendered to Grant at Appomattox C.H., 9 April 1865.

J. E. Johnston surrendered to Sherman 14 April 1865.

June 1864 to 3 April 1865

LEE

GRANT

SHERMAN

OHIO

PENNSYLVANIA

MARYLAND

DELAWARE

NEW JERSEY

WEST VIRGINIA

VIRGINIA

KENTUCKY

NORTH CAROLINA

SOUTH CAROLINA

GEORGIA

FLORIDA

ATLANTIC OCEAN

Columbus

Pittsburg

Harrisburg

Wheeling

Gettysburg

Philadelphia

Sharpsburg

Baltimore

Harper's Ferry

Washington

Alexandria

Winchester

Front Royal

Cross Keys

Beverly

Charleston

Frankfort

Lexington

Gordonsville

Fredericksburg

Richmond

Petersburg

Lynchburg

Danville

Greensboro

Knoxville

Raleigh

Goldsboro

Bentonville

Averysboro

Fayetteville

Wilmington

Fort Fisher

Columbia

Augusta

Atlanta

Macon

Savannah

Charleston

Jacksonville

Cape Hatteras

Albemarle Sound

Pamlico Sound

Cape Fear

16 Mar.

12 Nov.

10 Dec.

N

1862	EAST	WEST
JAN.		HENRY AND DONELSON CAMPAIGN
FEB.	PENINSULAR CAMPAIGN	Fort Henry / Fort Donelson — SHILOH CAMPAIGN
MAR.	Troops Embark	Battle of Pea Ridge
APR.	Siege of Yorktown — VALLEY CAMPAIGN	Shiloh — STONES RIVER CAMPAIGN — Capture of New Orleans
MAY	McDowell / Winchester / Seven Pines	Combined Fleet and Land Operations Against Vicksburg
JUNE	Port Republic / Jackson Leaves the Valley / Seven Days' Battles	Corinth Captured / Buell Starts
JULY	2D BULL RUN CAMPAIGN	Buell Halted
AUG.	Withdrawal — Cedar Mountain — ANTIETAM CAMPAIGN — 2d Bull Run	Kirby Smith Starts North / Bragg Starts North
SEPT.	Antietam	Buell at Louisville — GRANT'S FIRST ADVANCE ON VICKSBURG
OCT.	FREDERICKSBURG CAMPAIGN	Perryville / Corinth
NOV.	McClellan Relieved	Buell Relieved
DEC.	Fredericksburg	Rosecrans at Nashville / Stones River / Grant Reaches Oxford / Holly Springs / Chickashaw Bluffs

1863	EAST	WEST	
JAN.	Hooker Replaces Burnside	**VICKSBURG CAMPAIGN**	
FEB.			
MAR.		Period of Unsuccessful Attempts	**OPERATIONS AGAINST PORT HUDSON**
APR.	**CHANCELLORSVILLE CAMPAIGN**		Operations West of New Orleans
MAY	Chancellorsville **GETTYSBURG CAMPAIGN**	Grant Crosses the Mississippi Jackson Champion's Hill Siege Begins	Siege of Port Hudson Begins
JUNE	Lee Crosses the Potomac Meade Replaces Hooker	**TULLAHOMA CAMPAIGN**	
JULY	Gettysburg Lee Recrosses the Potomac	Surrender	Surrender
AUG.		**CHICKAMAUGA CAMPAIGN** Bragg Evacuates Chattanooga	**OPERATIONS IN EAST TENNESSEE**
SEPT.	**OPERATIONS ALONG ORANGE & ALEXANDRIA RY.**	Chickamauga Union Retreat to Chattanooga	Burnside Captures Knoxville
OCT.	Lee Crosses the Rapidan Confederates Retire	**CHATTANOOGA CAMPAIGN** Thomas Replaces Rosecrans Supply Line Cleared	
NOV.	Lee Recrosses the Rapidan Mine Run	Lookout Mountain and Missionary Ridge	Longstreet Sent to Knoxville Confederate Assault
DEC.			Siege Raised